168 HOURS

168 HOURS

YOU

HAVE MORE TIME

THAN YOU

THINK

LAURA VANDERKAM

PORTFOLIO

PORTFOLIO
Published by the Penguin Group
Penguin Group (USA) Inc., 375 Hudson Street,
New York, New York 10014, U.S.A.
Penguin Group (Canada), 90 Eglinton Avenue East, Suite 700,
Toronto, Ontario, Canada M4P 2Y3
(a division of Pearson Penguin Canada Inc.)
Penguin Books Ltd, 80 Strand, London WC2R 0RL, England
Penguin Ireland, 25 St. Stephen's Green, Dublin 2, Ireland
(a division of Penguin Books Ltd)
Penguin Books Australia Ltd, 250 Camberwell Road, Camberwell,
Victoria 3124, Australia
(a division of Pearson Australia Group Pty Ltd)
Penguin Books India Pvt Ltd, 11 Community Centre, Panchsheel Park,
New Delhi – 110 017, India
Penguin Group (NZ), 67 Apollo Drive, Rosedale, North Shore 0632,
New Zealand (a division of Pearson New Zealand Ltd)
Penguin Books (South Africa) (Pty) Ltd, 24 Sturdee Avenue,
Rosebank, Johannesburg 2196, South Africa

Penguin Books Ltd, Registered Offices:
80 Strand, London WC2R 0RL, England

First published in 2010 by Portfolio,
a member of Penguin Group (USA) Inc.

10 9 8 7 6 5 4 3 2 1

Library of Congress Cataloging-in-Publication Data
Vanderkam, Laura.
  168 hours : you have more time than you think / Laura Vanderkam.
    p. cm.
  Includes bibliographical references and index.
  ISBN 978-1-59184-331-3
  1. Time management.   I. Title.   II. Title: One hundred sixty-eight hours.
  HD69.T54V36 2010
  658.4'093—dc22   2009046867

Printed in the United States of America
Set in Minion
Designed by Neuwirth & Associates, Inc.

To Michael, Jasper, and Sam

Contents

168 HOURS

Introduction

Tuesday, July 14, 2009, was a good day.

I opened my apartment door around seven a.m. to find my *Wall Street Journal* delivered, with my byline in it. My two-year-old son, Jasper, woke up around the same time. We played with puzzles and had breakfast before I put him in the stroller at eight and walked in the easy sunshine to his preschool two blocks away. I spent the next 4 hours writing. Then I logged 45 minutes on the stationary bike, reading a book I needed to review to make the most of that time. After, I wrote for 3 more hours. I packed snacks for Jasper and picked him up shortly after four p.m., intending to take him to an exhibit I'd read about at the Museum of Modern Art. Alas, the museum was closed, as it is every Tuesday, so we had to regroup, buy a pretzel from a street vendor, and admire the more realist "art" of the Fifth Avenue bustle. At least during the expedition we found the new pair of sneakers he'd needed. We got home at 5:30 and played until the babysitter came an hour later. Then I zoomed out to Brooklyn to run a long-range planning meeting for the Young New Yorkers' Chorus, for which I serve as president. My board talked about how to commission new music, how to improve our musical craft, and how to make people feel at home in this grand city. I zipped home and spent 45 minutes talking with my husband, Michael, about our projects and potential names for the second son we were expecting in two months. It was roughly a 17-hour day by the time I went to sleep, with 8 spent working (0.75 of those also spent exercising), 4 spent interacting with family, 3 spent on my volunteer work, and a few transitions and other things in between.

It was a busy day, devoid of disasters, though devoid of spectacular triumphs, too. So why was it "good"?

Much has been written about the good life—what it means to be happy or successful, in our own minds at least, and how people become that way. I am as much a student of these books as anyone else, and I have always been drawn to the stories of people who love what they do, who live full lives and have grand aspirations. As a journalist, I have interviewed many such people, and I often daydream about what I'd like to get out of life as well.

Over the years, those daydreams have taken on some shape and substance. Since I was a child I've wanted to be a writer. I also wanted to be a mom. Growing up near the cornfields of Indiana, I wanted to live in a big city for at least a while when I was young enough not to mind the grit and noise. I love music, and I love to help create new things, be they songs or books. I love having health and energy.

But all these things are abstractions. All are ideas people think about in phrases such as "when I grow up" or "someday," or broadly as our identities and values.

A few years ago, though, I had a realization: while we think of our lives in grand abstractions, a life is actually lived in hours. If you want to be a writer, you must dedicate hours to putting words on a page. To be a mindful parent, you must spend time with your child, teaching him that even though he loves the new shoes he picked out, he has to take them off so mommy can pay for them. A solid marriage requires conversation and intimacy and a focus on family projects. If you want to sing well in a functioning chorus, you must show up to rehearsals and practice on your own in addition to setting goals and attending to any administrative duties. If you want to be healthy, you must exercise and get enough sleep. In short, if you want to do something or become something—and you want to do it well—it takes *time*.

What made that particular Tuesday a good day was the high proportion of hours I spent on things that relate to my life goals. For instance, I wanted to be a writer, and I am. That is what I spent big chunks of my time doing.

July 14 was, of course, a 24-hour day, and this is the way most of us are accustomed to thinking about our time: as 24-hour blocks. But as I've pondered the question of how I want to live my life, I've come to believe that it's more useful to think in terms of "24/7," a phrase people toss about but seldom multiply through. There are 168 hours in a week. My busy Tuesday was a good day, but so was my slower Sunday spent going to church, walking for 2 hours in Central Park, and—yes—working for 4 hours during Jasper's nap and after he went to bed. The way I see it, anything you do once a week happens often enough to be important to you, whether it's church, a strategic thinking session at work, your Sunday dinner with your parents, or your softball team practice. The weekly 168-hour cycle is big enough to give a true picture of our lives. Years and decades are made up of a mosaic of repeating patterns of 168 hours. Yes, there is room for randomness, and the mosaic will evolve over time, but whether you pay attention to the pattern is still a choice. Largely, the true picture of our lives will be a function of how we set the tiles.

This book is about how different people spend the 168 hours we all have per week. It is about where the time really goes, and how we can all use our time better. It is about using our hours to focus on what we do best in our careers and at home, and so take a life's work to the next level while investing in our personal lives as well.

I wanted to write this book for several reasons. For starters, despite the ongoing cultural narrative of a time crunch—a narrative often aimed at women like me, a working mom of small kids—I don't feel like I'm forever falling behind. I'd be the first to admit that my life is inordinately privileged, something I am sure some folks reading this book will delight in pointing out. But I know that I'm not the only one who feels this way. Some of the busiest, most successful people I've ever interviewed have told me that they could cram more into their lives if they wished. Looking at life in 168-hour blocks is a useful paradigm shift, because—unlike the occasionally crunched weekday—well-planned blocks of 168 hours are big enough to accommodate full-time work, intense involvement with your family, rejuvenating leisure time, adequate sleep, and everything else that actually matters.

Of course, there is also a political element in this portrait of time. I have written this book for men and women. It is for parents, nonparents, and people who never want to be parents. It is for people with all sorts of goals, careers, and interests. Still, I am particularly alarmed by how many of the brightest young women of my generation do not believe they can possibly weave together a Career with a capital C, motherhood, and a personal life in the hours the universe allots them without feeling frazzled, sleep-deprived, and pulled in ten directions at once. From time to time, pundits and bloggers set themselves howling over surveys that seem to show this. In September 2005, Louise Story announced on the front page of *The New York Times* that many female Yale undergrads planned to cut back on work or stop working entirely after becoming mothers. As she quoted one student, "My mother always told me that you can't be the best career woman and the best mother at the same time." The implication? You have to choose.

Likewise, the Princeton University student Amy Sennett polled fellow members of the class of 2006 for her senior thesis and found that women were still quite likely to believe that "being a successful career woman and being a good mother are mutually exclusive." Some 62 percent of women saw a potential conflict between career and childrearing; only 33 percent of men did. Of those women who saw a conflict, the majority planned to work part-time, and another high proportion planned to "sequence"—that is, take a few years off and then return to the workforce. A few young women did think combining a career and motherhood was possible, but they had stark ideas of other things that would have to go. As one history major told Sennett, "I plan never to sleep."

These dire predictions were certainly in the back of my mind when I decided to do something unusual for the Ivy League urban professional set and get pregnant for the first time at age twenty-seven. I won't pretend that becoming a mother has been entirely rosy, or that my household is a scene of domestic bliss. However, motherhood did not ruin my career, and my work has not detracted from how much I love being a mom, particularly the small moments of seeing another human being figure out the world—small moments the universe grants in abundance when you choose to pay attention. If anything, the combination of work and motherhood has given me more things to write about.

One of those things has been time use. Not long after I came back from whatever you call maternity leave when you're self-employed, I discovered the American Time Use Survey and fascinating research from the University of Maryland and elsewhere about how people— moms and dads in particular—actually spend their time. I began writing about these findings in my columns for *USA Today*, in a nine-part series for *The Huffington Post* about "Core Competency Moms," in features for *Doublethink* and the now-defunct *Culture 11*, in essays for the Taste page of *The Wall Street Journal*, and as a guest writer for Lisa Belkin's "Motherlode" blog at *The New York Times*. The more I studied time use and talked to people who do amazing things with their lives, the more I came to see that this bleak notion of mutual exclusivity between work and family is based on misleading ideas of how people spend their family time now, and how they spent it in the past.

On the flipside, I do want to demystify "work" a little, too. I put "work" in quotes here because, after studying how people spend their time, I believe that certain widespread (and self-important) assumptions about the way we work today are just as misplaced as our assumptions about how people lived in the 1950s: we assume we are all overworked, just as we assume everyone used to live like Ozzie and Harriet. In reality, neither of these perceptions is true. The majority of people who claim to be overworked work less than they think they do, and many of the ways people work are extraordinarily inefficient. Calling something "work" does not make it important or necessary. One of my missions in this book is to make people look at their time in all spheres of life and say "I hadn't thought of it that way before."

There are other ways in which *168 Hours* does not aim to be like many self-help or time-management books. I approach this not as a productivity guru, but as a journalist who is interested in how successful, happy people build their lives. I am particularly interested in how people who are not household names achieve the lives they want, and what we can learn from their best practices. There are plenty of books out there on Fortune 500 CEOs' or celebrities' tips for success. I'm more interested in the woman down the street who—without benefit of fame, outsized fortune, or a slew of personal assistants—is running a successful small business, marathons, and a large and happy household.

As a corollary to that, real life is often messy, but I don't believe there's much value in tales of composite characters that I made up just to show that my methods worked. Everyone in this book is real, with their real names and real stories. I find footnotes distracting, but the endnotes provide backup for the facts or studies cited. While I've put interactive material at the ends of most chapters, I can't promise 5-minute tweaks that will completely change your life. Certainly, everyone's life can benefit from quick tune-ups, but getting the most out of your 168 hours takes discipline in a distracted world. Reading fiction as you commute to a job you don't like will make you feel somewhat more fulfilled; being in the right job will make you feel incredible. Going for a 10-minute walk will lift your spirits; committing to run for 4 of every 168 hours for the next year will transform your health.

Finally, *168 Hours* is unlike many business- and life-management books in that—while I appear in the narrative—I can't claim to be writing from a position of authority as a great success story. I am not writing this book to impart a lifetime of learned wisdom. I wrote the bulk of this manuscript when I was thirty years old. My life is definitely a work in progress. I don't think I'm doing a bad job fitting the pieces together. Nonetheless, I have learned a lot during the process. I have tried to implement these findings in my own plans; *168 Hours* is, at least in part, about that journey of trying to have more good Tuesdays. And Mondays. And Saturdays. And all the other days that make up the 168-hour mosaic of our lives.

PART

1

YOUR
168 HOURS

· 1 ·
The Myth of the Time Crunch

Like many busy people, I live by my to-do list. Sometimes it's scratched on my church bulletin (the "silent confession" part of the service includes an apology for not paying attention). Sometimes it's scrawled in my must-not-lose black notebook that, alas, I once accidentally lost at LAX. Regardless, I obey its missives. I like nothing better than scratching off every entry. So, during one marathon late March day in 2009, when I saw a "to do" to follow up for this book with a woman named Theresa Daytner, who I'd interviewed a year before, I dutifully sent her a note.

But Daytner was not to be reached. I'm not sure what her to-do list said, but she was spending the day outside.

She told me later she had gone for a hike along a "babbling brook" near her Maryland home about 45 minutes west of Baltimore. It was a desolate area, so she'd borrowed her brother's dog to keep her company. The two of them spent hours tromping through the mud. An early spring rain had turned the landscape green, bringing out tiny shoots on the trees and making the wildflower buds sparkle against the gray sky. There was simply no way she was going to miss one of the first warm mornings that offered up the opportunity to, as she put it, enjoy the "peace and quiet" and "recharge."

As I talked to Daytner more, I soon realized that recharging was a normal feature of her life. This involved a reasonable amount of time in the dirt; she goes on trail rides on her hybrid bicycle in addition to her hikes. Until recently, she lifted weights with a trainer twice a week. She burrows into Jodi Picoult novels at night in addition to reading her book club's fare; she confesses a slight addiction to watching *24*. She gets massages. She gets her hair done. She recently planned an elaborate surprise party for her husband's fiftieth birthday, featuring guests she had arranged to fly in from all over the country.

In other words, Daytner seems to have a lot of time. Relaxed time. Time she can and does use in any way she pleases. That includes knocking off for some blissful solitude on a weekday morning when more *serious* people are at work.

Of course, this begs the question. How, exactly, does Daytner have so much time on her hands? Is she retired? Unemployed? A homemaker whose children have grown?

The answer may surprise you. Daytner is certainly busier than I am. She's busier than most people I know here in too-rushed-to-breathe Manhattan. Indeed, I would venture to guess that no matter who you are, you don't have as much on your plate as Daytner does. Barack Obama himself was floored when he met her. Not long before that muddy March morning hike, Daytner seized a chance opportunity to visit the White House with a group of small business owners to talk about economic issues. She introduced herself to the president by her two main identities.

The first: Theresa Daytner, owner of Daytner Construction Group, a seven-figure-revenue company whose twelve-person payroll she is personally responsible for meeting.

The second: Theresa Daytner, mom of six, including eight-year-old twins.

"When," Obama asked her, "do you sleep?"

But Daytner does sleep. Though a recent *Men's Health* article test-drove the "Uberman" sleep cycle—during which one naps 20 minutes every 4 hours as a way to free up time to "excel at your job, bond with the people you love, indulge in your dreams, or just chill"—Daytner does all these things while sleeping at least 7 hours a night. She coaches soccer and spends weekends cheering at her children's games. She is happily planning her twenty-one-year-old daughter's wedding while growing her business. She became interested in construction years ago as a college student when she learned that being honest and competent could actually make you stand out in this space. Now, despite the recent construction slump, DCG (which oversees $10–75 million projects) was, when we talked, reviewing résumés to bring on new project managers. She was also on track to post year-over-year gains and was negotiating to enter the general contracting space, a move that could expand her business by an order of magnitude.

She was certainly not immune to the pressures of meeting a payroll (which includes health benefits for her employees' families); she confesses to putting out fires at night, on weekends, and, if the earth would crash into the sun otherwise, by Blackberry while she hikes. She has not been immune from other entrepreneurial pressures, either. She launched DCG when her twins were still toddlers, and since she wanted her husband to work with her, she mortgaged the house to pay for child care. As her business has picked up, it's become at times quite "draining, mentally." That's why she watches *24*.

Nonetheless, when I spoke to her, she told me that her children had the next Thursday off from school and she planned to take the day off again. She was going to load as many of the kids in the car as would fit to go see Washington's cherry blossoms and just chill on the National Mall.

All in all, her life sounded pretty sweet. And so, as I've been writing this book, I've taken to recounting Daytner's biography at cocktail parties. Like Obama, people always ask, "How does she do it?"—or, if someone is feeling more peevish, "I don't know this woman but I already hate her." Our cultural narratives of overwork, sleep deprivation, and how hard it is to "have it all" suggest that a big career and big family like Daytner's should not be possible. Or if they are possible, we certainly don't expect daytime hikes and Jodi Picoult novels to wind up in there, too.

I won't claim it's easy. But as Daytner told me about her scheme to screen her e-mail (which takes "too much damn time"), and shift some of her employees' responsibilities to keep her workday at roughly 8:30–5:00, it soon became clear that she views her hours and minutes differently than most people.

For starters, she considers them all precious. She even takes advantage of the ten minutes between when her teens' school opens (8:00) and her twins' nearby school opens (8:10) to read Hardy Boys books to her sons in the car and nurture her relationship with them.

And second, "Here's what I think is the difference," she says. "I know I'm in charge of me. Everything that I do, every minute I spend is my choice." Daytner chooses to spend those minutes on the three things she does best: nurturing her business, nurturing her family, and nurturing herself. "If I'm not spending my time wisely, I fix it," she says. "Even if it's just quiet time."

But within these three priorities, she has found a little secret: when you focus on what you do best, on what brings you the most satisfaction, there is plenty of space for everything. You can build a big career. You can build a big family. And you can meander along a Maryland creek on a weekday morning because the day is too wild and beautiful to stay inside. Indeed, you can fill your life with more abundance than most people think is possible.

I thought about Daytner a lot as I was pulling this book together. Her life stands in such stark contrast to the way we twenty-first-century creatures have grown used to thinking about our time that she's hard *not* to think about. It is safe to say that time has become the primary obsession of modern life. Some people are having enough sex. Some people have enough money. But no one seems to have enough hours in the day.

The futurists didn't necessarily predict this. Back in 1959, amid the rise of labor-saving technology and massive productivity gains, the *Harvard Business Review* fretted that "boredom, which used to bother only aristocrats" had "become a common curse."

But with the rise of two-income families and then extreme jobs, the story goes, the trend toward boredom abruptly reversed. By 1991, the sociologist Juliet Schor asked in her bestselling book *The Overworked American,* "Why has leisure been such a conspicuous casualty of prosperity?" The image she created, of people looking at their watches to remind themselves what day it was, stuck. And this was years before we tethered ourselves to our Blackberries and cell phones. Now, *Harvard Business Review* runs anecdotes like those about "Sudhir," a financial analyst who works 90-hour weeks during summertime, his "light" season, and 120 the rest of the year. "Joe" actually rescheduled a family member's funeral so he wouldn't miss a meeting. "The 40-hour workweek," the December 2006 issue lamented in a story titled "Extreme Jobs: The Dangerous Allure of the 70-Hour Workweek," "is a thing of the past. Even the 60-hour workweek, once the path to the top, is now considered practically part-time."

Two decades into this narrative of the time crunch, most of us have fully accepted this worldview. And so, the parade of statistics supporting this argument marches on. We tell pollsters from the National Sleep Foundation that we sleep less than 7 hours per night; moms who work full-time and have school-aged children claim to spend less than 6 hours in bed on weeknights, with about 60 percent claiming there's just not enough time to sleep. About a third of Americans who work full-time say they work more than 50 hours per week. A recent Gallup poll found that 12 percent of employed Americans claimed to work more than 60 hours. We say that we don't have enough time to exercise; about a third of Americans tell the Centers for Disease Control and Prevention that we fail to do the mere recommended 2.5 hours of activity per week, and I suspect the only reason some people actually meet those guidelines is that the government counts vacuuming as a workout.

Being busy has become the explanation of choice for all sorts of things. The percentage of adults who vote in presidential elections hasn't changed drastically over the past 20 years, but the percentage of nonvoters who blamed their failure to get to the polls on their busy schedules nearly tripled between 1980 and 1996. We say we are too busy to read—only half of us, according to the National Endowment for the Arts, read a novel, short story, poem, or play in the last year. We're too busy to read to our kids. Moms and dads who are in the workforce clock a lousy 1–7 minutes of daily reading to or with children, but even stay-at-home moms of preschool-aged kids don't top 8 minutes per day. That's barely enough time to pull apart the sticky pages of *Goodnight Moon*. A full 92 percent of us say we believe in God, but only about 40 percent of us claim to attend religious services weekly—and some studies have shown that when it comes to confessing the frequency of our church attendance to pollsters, we put our souls in peril and lie. Actual attendance is probably less than half of that.

The narrative of busyness has so seized the culture that a group called the Simplicity Forum launched "Take Back Your Time Day" in 2003, publishing a companion handbook on "fighting overwork and time poverty in America." The handbook featured essays from Schor and others with more alarming stories and statistics. Dual-income couples, one author noted, could find only 12 minutes a day to talk to each other. Some 80 percent of children weren't getting enough sleep. A reported 20–40 percent of pets, primarily dogs, suffered from separation anxiety due to their absent, overworked owners. Medieval peasants, the cartoon illustrations screamed, worked less than we do!

Of course, medieval peasants also experienced a 25-percent-plus child mortality rate, which strikes *me* as stressful, so the idea that they somehow led more relaxed lives is odd.

Indeed, much of the time-poverty narrative takes on a rather absurdist tone if you think about it. For instance, the January 2007 issue of *Real Simple* magazine posed a question to its "time-starved" readers: If you had an extra 15 minutes in your day, how would you use it?

In wistful prose, the respondents daydreamed about all the leisurely, soul-restoring pursuits they'd indulge in if only their clocks would slow down for a while. Jenifer Thigpen of Orlando, Florida, wrote, "I'd play fetch with my dogs, who bring joy to my crazy, hectic life." Julie Lane-Gay of Vancouver pledged to "write thank-you letters. Not perfunctory notes, but real letters that thank people for things they've done that have made a difference . . . Someday I hope to do it." Sarah Nahmias wanted to "relearn how to play my flute. It's something I enjoyed immensely when I was younger but lost touch with as I got busy with children and family obligations." Andrea Wood of St. Augustine, Florida, lamented,

"I feel as if there's never enough time in the day to prepare the foods that are good and good for me, so I would spend some time chopping, prepping, and cooking large, healthy meals ahead of time." Others wanted to soak in the tub, read, relax on the couch, or, as one woman wrote, try the hammock she had assembled but had yet to touch. Katie Noah of Abilene, Texas, mused, "Fifteen minutes of uninterrupted writing time would be a priceless gift," though, presumably, she did find 15 minutes to read *Real Simple* and write a letter about her elusive dream.

Regardless, this message permeates the culture. An Amazon ad in my in-box highlights exercise DVDs that vie to offer the shortest workout, for example, "The 12 second sequence: Get fit in 20 minutes twice a week!" If we're scrambling over 20 minutes to exercise, no wonder achieving big things, like building a career while nurturing children, leading a nonprofit organization, and training for a marathon, seems downright impossible. Or perhaps they're possible, but only if you find a career you can do part-time, or downshift for a bit, which is the theme adopted by many work-life-balance speakers and authors.

Then there is Theresa Daytner with her six kids and her seven-figure business. While the rest of us lament our inability to find 15 minutes to read, she's in a book club. While we dream of 15 minutes to try out the hammock, she's out for a hike.

And here's the crazy thing. She—and the people who claim they're "too busy" to vote, or have only 12 minutes to talk with their spouses—all have *the exact same amount of time.* All of us. We all have 24 hours in our days, and 7 days in our weeks. If you do the math, that comes out to 168 hours each week to create the lives we want. We all have the same 168 hours, repeated until the span of our lives is through. And so, when we meet people like Daytner, we wonder: Why are they able to fill their time with so many meaningful things while others are dreaming of 15 minutes to take a bubble bath?

That is the central question of this book. *168 Hours* is the story of how some people manage to be fully engaged in their professional and personal lives. It is the story of how people take their careers to the next level while still nurturing their communities, families, and souls. As a journalist who writes frequently about career issues and social trends,

I've either interviewed or studied many such high-achievers—men and women—over the years for this and other projects. You know the kind—say, the mom of five and marathoner who happens to have governed the state of Alaska for a stint in her spare time. A man managing a nine-figure private equity fund who makes time to read *The Adventures of Huckleberry Finn* with his preteens. An entrepreneur working startup hours who tends a farm to nurture her connection to the earth. A father who finds time to train for a marathon by having his son bike along as he runs. A rising young biologist who earns her PhD while caring for one toddler and then interviews for, and lands, a tenure-track professorship while 8 months pregnant with her second child. When I hear these stories, I'm often tempted to ask, like Obama, "When do you sleep?" But I've learned that, like Daytner, many of these people do, and not in 20-minute spurts every 4 hours, either.

The point of these stories is not to make anyone feel bad or lazy. Rather, I view these stories as liberating, particularly as a young(ish) person trying to build my career and family—as well as nurture my personal passions for running, singing, and other things—in a world that continually laments how hard it is to do it all. Once you tackle the question of how some people do so much head on, you can start to ask others that the time-poverty narrative doesn't allow. For instance:

What if you don't have to choose between pushing your career to the next level and building forts in the backyard with your kids, because there is plenty of time for both?

What if you can have great health—because you're sleeping enough and exercising enough to be in the best shape of your life—and volunteer more often than 90 percent of the population?

What if you can have enough time to get reacquainted with your partner, both as lovers and friends, not just as co-parents hashing out the administrative details of your household? And what if you can do all of this—*and* play the flute, or write in your journal, or whatever else you secretly desire—without fantasizing about an extra 15 minutes per day?

The hard—but hopeful—truth is that you can. Yes, you have a lot going on in your life. You may be wondering if you have time to read this book. But before you put it down to go check your e-mail, I want to make sure you take away two thoughts: you can choose how to spend your 168 hours, and *you have more time than you think*.

In order to study how successful people spend their time, I first had to figure out how Americans in general clock theirs. It turns out that we know the answer to this question in rich detail. For several years, the federal Bureau of Labor Statistics has conducted a study called the American Time Use Survey (ATUS). Various universities and organizations have done similar "time diary" studies over the past 40 years. The ATUS and similar studies ask thousands of people to report what they did every few minutes over the previous 24 hours, more or less like a lawyer billing his time. Sometimes, this happens with a researcher on the phone, talking the respondent through the day and reminding anyone who tries to claim he did 28 hours of activities of the realities of time and physics. In other studies, researchers send participants diaries and ask them to record their activities on a certain day or, in some cases, for a week. Statisticians then break the answers down by category, and subject the data to various demographic cuts.

While such studies are more laborious than simply asking people how many hours they devote to work, sleep, and the like, audits find they are more accurate, and so they are considered the gold standard of sociological time research. The results, when combined with other studies, paint a fascinating picture of daily life. They show that many assumptions we have about how people spent their time in the past— and how they spend it now—are wrong.

To begin with, according to time-diary studies, Americans sleep about 8 hours a night, just as we did 40 years ago. This average isn't skewed by retirees and college students; even married moms and dads who work full-time and have kids under age six sleep 8.31 and 8.06 hours, respectively. Married, full-time working moms with school-aged kids still sleep 8.09 hours per night.

One of the reasons we have enough time to sleep is that we work a lot less than we think we do. Though the *Harvard Business Review* may have trumpeted the notion that 70-hour workweeks were becoming the new standard for professional workers, in reality the average parent who works full-time logs 35–43 hours per week. Indeed, the smaller print in a press release from the Center for Work-Life Policy about the *HBR* 70-hour-workweek study noted that about 1.7 million Americans had "extreme" jobs characterized by self-reported 60-plus-hour work-weeks and a few other things (like lots of responsibility or unpredictable workflow). That sounds like a high number, but 1.7 million people is just over 1 percent of the U.S. workforce. And since the 60-hour-plus workweek wasn't based on time logs, it's quite possible that 1 percent is too high an estimate (as we'll see below).

We keep our houses somewhat clean, but not as clean as we did in 1965, when stay-at-home moms spent, on average, 37.4 hours per week spiffing up their abodes (and married moms overall, including employed ones, spent 34.5 hours on such chores). But these days, even dads whose wives are not in the workforce spend more than an hour a day on household activities such as cleaning, food prep, and lawn work. That's on top of the nearly 4 hours per day their wives spend on these activities (about 26 hours per week). Married moms who work full-time manage to squeeze in a bit over 2 daily hours of mopping, chopping, and vacuum duty, or about 14.5 hours per week.

The situation is a bit dustier when it comes to kids, though. Many moms who work full-time worry that they're short-changing their children, and indeed, these women spend only about 11 minutes per day playing or doing hobbies with their kids (about 25 minutes if the kids are younger than age six). But moms who work part-time—cutting their workweek from 36 hours to 19 hours—only bump this up to 21 minutes per day. Moms who opt out of the workforce entirely barely top half an hour. Even if they've got preschool-aged kids, they play with them, on average, just 50 minutes per day, or about 6 hours per week, even though, by definition, such moms spend at least 35 fewer hours per week working for pay than the full-timers. Dads log only about 15–18 minutes per day playing with their children, which is approximately one sixth of the time employed fathers spend traveling to and from various places (that is, running around in the car).

Americans in general also watch a lot of television—more than 30 hours per week, according to Nielsen, though the time-diary studies put this number a lot lower (2.62 hours per day averaged overall, or 3.3 for people who watched TV, coming out to 18–23 hours per week).

That last stat, of course, begs the question: Why are the time-diary numbers wildly different than the answers people give in other surveys? With the TV numbers, the reason appears to be that for ratings, Nielsen wants to know whether the TV is on, whereas time diaries tend to record "primary activities." People mention the TV only if they are paying attention to the programming.

But other questions are more consequential. For instance, why would working moms claim to sleep only 6 hours per night when their diaries show they sleep 8? It is true that the 6-hour number is for weekdays, but in order for the weekly average to hit 8, this would mean that the average working mom sleeps 13 hours every weekend night (the equivalent of waking up at noon if you go to bed at eleven p.m.). I wish my family would let me do that! The more likely explanation is that women are drastically underestimating their sleep tallies. But why? Why create a false impression for young women that working moms are inevitably frazzled and sleep deprived? Why would Americans in general claim to work more hours than they do, dismissing 60 hours as "part-time"?

Sociologists have studied these questions as well. It turns out that there is a fundamental flaw in the data used to support the claim that we suffer from time poverty and overwork: we lie.

We may not do so on purpose, but we have trouble remembering or calculating things exactly when a pollster wants a quick answer, and in the absence of concrete memories, we are prone to over- or underestimate things based on socially desirable perceptions or current emotions.

For instance, few of us love the routine aspects of housework or household administration. Emptying the dishwasher or paying bills doesn't take much time, but we feel like we're always doing these chores. So if someone asks us how much time we spend on such things, we overestimate—by something on the order of 100 percent for both men and women—compared to the actual numbers recorded in time diaries.

We also feel pressure to work hard. In a world with lots of competition, many of us feel stressed about work, which makes our hours feel longer than they are. When our cell phones and Blackberries make us accessible most of the time, we may consider ourselves to be in work mode around the clock, even if we just popped in the DVD of *Talladega Nights* before quickly checking e-mail. And with little job security, we are keen to show that we are just as dedicated as our colleagues and competitors. Think about it. If publications such as *Fortune* and *Harvard Business Review* are claiming that 60-hour workweeks are the new "part-time," what manager wouldn't claim to be working 70?

And so we claim to work more hours than time diaries reveal we do. Indeed, back in the 1990s, when the University of Maryland sociologist John Robinson and his colleagues analyzed people's estimates of how much they worked, and compared those to the time diaries, they found that the more hours people claimed to work, the more inaccurate they were. You can guess in which direction. Almost no one who claimed a 70-hour workweek was *underestimating*. Indeed, the average person who claimed to work more than 75 hours per week generally logged about 55. When I contacted Robinson recently, he sent me a working paper he was drafting using more recent numbers, from 2006–2007. The time spent working had come up a little for people whose estimated hours showed workaholic tendencies, but even so, the average person who claimed to be working 60–69 hours per week was actually logging 52.6, and the average person claiming to work 70, 80, 90, or more hours was logging less than 60.

When you add up these overestimations of time engaged in work, housework, and other activities (like child care and exercise), you can see why some studies have found that people's accounts of an average week add up to 180 or even more than 200 hours—even though the mightiest among us is, alas, granted no more than 168. Time-diary studies are valuable in sociology because they force us to face the reality that a day has 24 hours and a week has 168, and all our activities must, in fact, fit within these limits.

While we overestimate work and housework, we do underestimate one major life component besides sleep: leisure time. One widely repeated statement from *The Overworked American* is that "Americans report that they have only sixteen and a half hours of leisure a week, after the obligations of job and household are taken care of." Yet they report that they watch more than 16.5 hours of TV weekly—an activity that is hard to classify as anything but leisure.

In other words, when it comes to daily life, the time-crunch narrative doesn't tell the whole story. The problem is not that we're all overworked or underrested, it's that most of us have absolutely no idea how we spend our 168 hours.

We don't think about how we want to spend our time, and so we spend massive amounts of time on things—television, Web surfing, housework, errands—that give a slight amount of pleasure or feeling of accomplishment, but do little for our careers, our families, or our personal lives. We spend very little time on things that require more thought or initiative, like nurturing our kids, exercising, or engaging in the limited hours we do work in deliberate practice of our professional crafts. We try to squeeze these high-impact activities around the edges of things that are easy, or that seem inevitable merely because we always do them or because we think others expect us to. And consequently, we *feel* overworked and underrested, and tend to believe stories that confirm this view.

But what if we approached time differently? What if we started with a blank slate? What if we viewed every minute, as Daytner says, as a choice?

Leave aside, for a while, the obligations and complications of the life you currently have. Picture a completely empty weekly calendar with its 168 hourly slots.

If you haven't thought about the concept before, I encourage you to spend a few minutes mulling it over. When I created a spreadsheet with 168 entries, the first thing that occurred to me is that, when you start with a blank slate and fill in the major components, 168 is a surprisingly vast number.

In 168 hours, there is easily time to sleep 8 hours a night (56 hours per week) and work 50 hours a week, if you desire. That adds up to 106 hours, leaving 62 hours per week for other things.

Recall that, according to the American Time Use Survey, the average stay-at-home mom spends less than 4 hours per *week* playing or doing hobbies with her kids (about 6 hours if she has preschool-aged children). In 62 hours, you can easily hit that. You can top the 17–18 hours the average stay-at-home mom spends weekly, total, on child care (in later chapters, we'll discuss why this number is as low as it is, and so different from the perception—obviously many full-time caregivers do much more, but the reality of an "average" is that some do less, too).

While many of us claim to have no time for exercise, when you add the numbers up, you can see that this isn't true. If you work 50 hours a week, sleep 8 hours a night, and spend 3 hours per day (21 total) tending to and interacting with your kids, this leaves 41 hours floating around. In that time, you can easily log the 2.5 hours of exercise our government's medical researchers have decided is associated with improved health. Indeed, you could double that figure to 5 hours, go on three 1-hour runs during the week and one 2-hour run on the weekend, and so train for a half marathon.

This still leaves time for other passions. People who give generously of their time to causes they care about tend to be happier and healthier than other people. Yet only about a quarter of Americans volunteer. Only about a third of these folks log more than 100 hours annually. One hundred hours per year comes out to 2 hours per week. In other words, even if you work a full-time-plus job and get adequate sleep, spend more time playing with your kids than the average stay-at-home mom while running upward of 25 miles weekly, you can still spend more time volunteering than 90 percent of your fellow citizens. You can even go on weekly dates with your partner.

If you add these hours up (figuring 4 hours for the date), you'll see that there are still 30 hours left. This is adequate time for eating and showering, cooking and cleaning if you try not to do much of it, and traveling around in the car (though again, you should try to minimize that, as we'll discuss in later chapters). If you spend 3 hours a day on these things (21 hours total), that still leaves more than an hour a day for experimenting with recipes, taking bubble baths, reading, zoning out on the couch in front of the television, or walking along a babbling brook with a borrowed dog, if that's your personal choice. And that's all while working 50 hours per week—far more than the average person works, even if he or she claims otherwise. If you work 40, like Theresa Daytner does, you get an additional 10 hours per week.

When you think about that, you begin to see the trouble inherent in the widespread belief that working part-time is the key to achieving work-life balance. If you're not living the life you want in 72 waking, nonjob hours (168 minus 56, and then minus 40), why would bumping that up to 92 hours change anything? You see the absurdity in even asking the question of what someone would do with an extra 15 minutes in her day. If you aren't practicing the flute in 72 hours per week, it's just silly to assume this would happen if you had 73.75 hours to work with instead. You already have a lot of time.

That's what Michael Schidlowsky, a Google software engineer in New York City, discovered when I asked him to keep track of his weeks. Schidlowsky doesn't have kids, but he's been in a committed relationship with his girlfriend for several years and spends a lot of time tutoring his much-younger sister. He teaches graduate-level computer science classes at New York University and, when we talked in spring 2009, was training for an Ironman Triathlon, which he completed that September. This competition involves a 2.4-mile swim, a 112-mile bike ride, and a 26.2-mile run. He'd already done several shorter triathlons.

Needless to say, this made for some busy weeks—but not quite as busy as you might think. His notes revealed that he spent a solid 40 hours per week coding for Google. He spent more time than that at the office, but he recognized that Google's free breakfasts, lunches, and dinners led to lingering and socializing. Regardless, 40 "real" hours was enough to get him promoted last year. He spent 3.5 hours per week commuting to and from his apartment, by bike, to work.

I might have been tempted to count those commuting hours as exercise, but Schidlowsky didn't, because he had a lot of "real" exercise built in, too. He spent 15 hours training each week, including at least two swims, several runs, and 6-hour, hundred-mile bike rides over the

George Washington Bridge and up through the Palisades on weekends. He spent 56 hours per week sleeping because hey, you try biking a hundred miles and see if you can sleep less.

He calculated that his teaching duties added up to 6 hours per week because he teaches three classes per year on open-source programming and the like, one per semester. He's taught them all before, so he doesn't have to spend much time planning lessons. He put in about 3 hours per week coaching other athletes, he spent about 2 hours a week grocery shopping, and 14 hours on chores.

When you add all these hours up—40 + 3.5 + 15 + 56 + 6 + 3 + 2 + 14—you get 139.5 hours per week. That leaves 28.5 hours per week for other things. "Despite everything I do, I still have more free time than I thought I do," Schidlowsky told me after he tallied everything up. He spends those hours watching about 7 hours of TV per week and hanging out with his girlfriend and the little sis and other family members and friends. "I feel pretty free," he says. "I always feel like I'm having a pretty good day." When I pondered his schedule, the only question I had was, why wouldn't he? Not only does he love and feel challenged by his job, he gets enough sleep and his nonwork hours are dominated by purposeful, rewarding activities such as teaching, training, and spending so much time puzzling through calculus problems with his little sister that not only does she no longer think she's bad in math, she wants to major in the subject.

This is what happens when you treat your 168 hours as a blank slate. This is what happens when you fill them up only with things that deserve to be there. You build a life where you really can have it all.

Of course, I should add the caveat that while your 168 hours may be a blank slate, fitting the pieces together will require some work. This is particularly true if children are involved. Much of the rest of this book deals with how to figure out this puzzle. You aren't going to read the Hardy Boys to your children at two a.m. If you take your twelve-year-old along on a hike at eleven a.m. on a weekday when he should be in school, the truancy officer will come looking for you—which is a shame, but that's a subject for a different book.

On a more fundamental level, you'll need to figure out what you want to do during your 168 hours. Many of us have no idea; one of the benefits of claiming to be overworked or starved for time is that it lets you off the hook for dealing with the burden of choice. From interviewing people who love their lives, I've found that these people focus, as much as possible, in the work and personal spheres, on what I call their core competencies. These are the things they do best, and that others cannot do nearly as well or can't do at all. For Daytner, these core competencies are the things she spends most of her time doing: nurturing her business, nurturing her family, and nurturing herself. Effective people outsource, ignore, or minimize everything else. The coming chapters will talk about how to identify these core competencies at home and at work. You'll need to change your life to spend more time on these things, and less on the things that are neither meaningful nor pleasurable for you or for people you care about.

I will not pretend this is easy. In order to get more out of their 168 hours, some people have had to change jobs, move, or otherwise create turmoil in the middle of already full lives. The chapters to come will talk about how to shake up your work time in order to achieve a career breakthrough, and how to change your focus at home to make a fuller family or personal life possible. Again, this won't be easy. While you can choose how to spend your own time, influencing others takes conscious effort. One of the reasons some parents devote lots of time to housework is that they believe that frequently doing their teens' laundry shows their love—and it's easier than investing the time to create the relationship capital that lets them interact with older children in more meaningful ways. A solid marriage can survive tragedies and give you great energy for achievements in the rest of your life, but this, too, requires an investment of time—time that's easily squashed in favor of television, errands, low-impact activities at work, other people's priorities, or guilt trips and other unquestioned assumptions of daily life. While 168 hours is a lot of time, time is still, in the broader sense, a nonrenewable resource. These hours still have to be carefully budgeted in order to turn the life you have into the life you want.

The best way to start on this project—and to get the most out of this book—is to do the equivalent of the American Time Use Survey on your own life. Like a lawyer billing time, record exactly what you're doing as frequently as you can. Ideally, you would do this every six minutes to make the math easy, or pay someone to follow you around like your very own Boswell, but more practically, this diagnosis will involve getting a small notebook and, every time you take a bathroom break, noting what you did since your last one. You can also use the worksheet at the end of this chapter, or download a spreadsheet from My168Hours. com. You might want to print up a few copies, since it may take a few weeks to get in the habit of recording your life.

Be as mindful as you can. What time did you get out of bed? How long did it take you to get ready? Did you spend time hunting for your cell phone and your daughter's math notebook? What do you do when you get to work? Be honest. Are you checking headlines that are remotely relevant to your job? How much time do you spend on e-mail? How many minutes do you clock on the phone or in meetings? What percentage of this time is actually relevant to your job description or life goals? When do you take breaks? When do you think? When do you exercise and for how long? When do you power down your home office computer or leave your workplace? How long does it take you to get home? What do you do on the way there? Are there errands or family activities? How much time do you spend playing with your kids or reading with them, or calling other family members and friends? When does the TV go on and when does it go off?

The next chapter will cover how to analyze this raw data, and at the end of this book you can find some more examples of real people's logs of their 168 hours, but the rationale for this exercise is to know where you are so you can see if this is where you want to be. Maybe you'll only need to make small changes, adding or subtracting things from the patchwork of spaces where many of us lose control of our time. We'll talk more about this later in the book, but as one example, while Katie Noah of Abilene, Texas, tells *Real Simple* that she dreams of an uninterrupted 15 minutes to write, Jill Starishevsky, a Bronx assistant district attorney and mom of two young children, finds the time to write poetry by using her subway commute between Manhattan and the Bronx to pen bits of verse. Net result? A creative outlet (and, since she set up a Web site called "The Poem Lady," where people can buy poems for Bar Mitzvahs and showers, a source of grocery money). Better yet: she didn't have to give up work, family, or sleep time, or dream of a 169.75-hour week to do it.

This was obviously a small discovery, though, frankly, in the time many of us waste watching TV we don't really like or frittering away hours on meaningless conference calls, we could make big changes. We could go back to school. We could write a novel each year. Seriously. It takes about 1,000 hours to write a book, and if you stop watching 20 hours of TV per week, you'll free up the time right there.

Again, the point of this arithmetic is not to make anyone feel bad. The fact that we can make such choices makes us incredibly blessed. This is not true in parts of the world where people spend 6 hours a day fetching water. But unless you're reading this book in a refugee camp, chances are you live in an abundant, educated, free society. The truth is, in such a society, there is already plenty of time for raising six kids while running a business, for working, teaching, and training for a triathlon, or whatever brings joy and meaning to your life.

Recognizing this requires changing the narrative. As Daytner explained to me, she doesn't tell herself *I don't have time to do X, Y, or Z.* She tells herself that she won't do X, Y, or Z because "it's not a priority."

Often that's a perfectly adequate explanation. I could tell you that I'm not going to sew my toddler's Halloween costume because I don't have time, but that's not true. I have time. In any given week, I have 168 hours. If someone offered to pay me $100,000 to hand-sew a Halloween costume, you can bet I'd find the time to do it. Since that's not going to happen, I can acknowledge that I don't think sewing is as good a use of my 168 hours as writing, or playing with my children, or, for that matter, sleeping.

But sewing Halloween costumes is one thing. Let's raise the stakes. It requires more courage to say "I don't read to my children because it's not a priority." If it's true that it's not a priority, then it's true—even if that's not politically correct to say. Be honest. Own that truth. Maybe you don't enjoy reading with children. Maybe they don't enjoy reading with you. Maybe you'd prefer to check your BlackBerry, or maybe you'd prefer to watch *America's Next Top Model*. Maybe your spouse is already doing a bang-up job in this department. Maybe you honestly do think that the income you provide, the service you do for society, or the joy you gain by working during the entirety of your children's waking hours is a bigger priority than interacting with them. There could be many good reasons for this. There are probably some bad ones, too. Nonetheless, it is a choice, and not a matter of lacking time. When you say "I don't have time," this puts the responsibility on someone else: a boss, a client, your family. Or else it puts the responsibility on some nebulous force: capitalism, society, the monster under the bed.

Regardless, the power slips out of your hands. "It's not a priority" turns those 168 hours back into a blank slate, to be filled as you choose with the things you decide matter.

This book is about how to do this, 24/7.

How to Keep a Time Log

If you want to get more out of your 168 hours in the future, it helps to know how you're spending them now. You can use the spreadsheet that follows, or download one from My168Hours.com, create your own, use a word-processing document, or record your activities in a little notebook.

Keep as complete a record as possible. "Work" and "call potential client" are both acceptable, but the latter will give you more information to analyze. Start whenever you want, but log your time for 168 consecutive hours. If you feel that the week you recorded was unusual, you can start over, but there are seldom "typical" weeks.

168 HOURS LOG

	MONDAY	TUESDAY	WEDNESDAY	THURSDAY	FRIDAY	SATURDAY	SUNDAY
5 a.m.							
6							
7							
8							
9							
10							
11							
12 p.m.							
1							
2							
3							
4							
5							
6							
7							
8							
9							
10							
11							
12 a.m.							
1							
2							
3							
4							

· 2 ·

Your Core
Competencies

I've been lucky to interview many fascinating people over the years. But few have been as fascinating as Roald Hoffmann.

Hoffmann, who is Jewish, was born in 1937 near the border of Poland and the former Soviet Union. Not long after World War II began, his family was shipped to a labor camp. His father perished there; he and his mother escaped and were hidden by a kind Ukrainian in a schoolhouse attic for more than a year. As a mom, I can't imagine the stress of trying to keep a little boy quiet and cooped up for that long. But you do what you have to in order to survive, and Hoffmann had one quality that helped pass the time: he was a keen observer. He would stare through a hole in the wall at the changing light and the changing seasons and watch other children play outside, recording these scenes deep in his memory. "I'm a watcher," he told me when I interviewed him in early 2008 for *Scientific American*'s website. "I look at how things interact. It interests me."

As the war was ending, Hoffmann and his mother fled to the Red Army lines and spent years in displaced persons' camps. His mother eventually remarried, and the new family settled in New York City in 1949. There, Hoffmann began to distinguish himself as a young prize-winning scientist at Stuyvesant High School, and then at Columbia University. But science was far from his only interest. At Columbia, the Great Books courses and poetry classes, in particular those taught by the Pulitzer Prize–winning poet Mark Van Doren, left him unsure about what he wanted to do with his life.

His parents had opinions. As a Jewish immigrant kid, "I was under a lot of pressure to become a doctor—a real doctor!" Hoffmann says. But he knew he didn't want to practice medicine, so he looked for something else that would be acceptable. "I had enough courage to tell my parents I wasn't going to be a doctor, but not enough courage to tell them I wanted to go into the history of art. So I went to graduate school in chemistry"—a subject that he also loved. He started putting his keen observing capacity to use, and soon chemistry returned the affection. He earned his PhD at Harvard while working under the future Nobel laureate William N. Lipscomb, Jr. He became a professor at Cornell, where his main advances in the field covered the structure and reactivity of both organic and inorganic molecules. Organic chemistry's Woodward-Hoffmann rules, which Hoffmann developed with Robert Burns Woodward, predict the positions of atoms within certain kinds of molecules. He and Kenichi Fukui shared the 1981 Nobel Prize in Chemistry for their work, done independently, on the course of chemical reactions.

A Nobel Prize is usually considered the culmination of a life, so normally, my profile would stop here. But the most interesting part of this story is that when I interviewed Hoffmann, he was actually calling from the lone pay phone at an artists' colony in California, where he'd just spent the morning writing a whimsical poem in which the narrator finds himself talking with a brain. It was far from his first literary effort. Shortly before he was awarded the Nobel Prize, he had begun to write poetry in earnest. He wrote about science and the beauty of the way things interact. He wrote poetry about his experiences as a child during the war, and often just about the things he's observed—moments of family life, or how his two children interacted with the world when they were young. "Maybe there's something of the scientist in that watching," he says. "But then you have to endow it with some emotional currency so it means something to a reader." While aware that people might initially read his poetry for the novelty factor, Hoffmann has made a conscious effort to get better at his craft. He studies other poets, edits himself, and attends retreats like the one in California. This is not easy. When it comes to poetry, "some of my scientific colleagues say 'If I only had the time I could do it.' They don't know how difficult it is," he says. "My poems go through many more drafts than my science articles."

But he loves the process. "I love that point of putting pen to paper," he says, and this labor—as he continued to teach chemistry at Cornell—has borne fruit. In his second career, Hoffmann has published several books of his work (including *The Metamict State* and *Gaps and Verges*, both from the University Press of Florida), and individual poems in *The Paris Review* and *The Kenyon Review*. He has also written plays and nonfiction books about his observations on science and life and hosts a monthly show called "Entertaining Science" at the Cornelia Street Café in New York City.

He's the kind of person who brings to mind the term "Renaissance Man," but Hoffmann is not, in fact, good at everything. As he told me, there are some fields, such as math and music, that require blinding flashes of talent and to which he has never felt particularly drawn. "These often manifest themselves through there being child prodigies," he says. "But I don't know any great child chemists, or politicians, or poets. Children write beautiful poetry. They have an innocence and power of observation not stunted by too many things. Children are also repositories of our romantic notions about innocence. They write interesting poetry. They don't write great poetry." He paused on the phone. "I think I like things where there are no prodigies. I think I like them because I think I can do them. They are accessible to you and me."

We should interpret the "you" in that sentence as a poetic turn of phrase—in order to write my profile of Hoffmann, I had to spend half an hour on the phone with my chemist sister-in-law getting her to explain the Woodward-Hoffmann rules very slowly. But this is what I took from Hoffmann's musings. At this point in his life, this brilliant man knows what he is good at, and what he can do better than almost anyone else. He is a watcher, an extremely patient observer, able to see connections over time and with persistence draw larger inferences from them. He has been able to leverage this ability in multiple spheres—from filling the time as a frightened child hiding from the Nazis, to chemistry, to poetry. I think the rest of us can learn a lot from his decisions as we, too, try to use our 168 hours to build the lives we want.

"A job is, in essence, a bundle of tasks that have been clumped together and assigned to an individual," Troy Smith and Jan Rivkin of Harvard Business School once wrote. A life is likewise a bundle of tasks and activities an individual takes on. Some, like sleeping and eating, are required, but the rest are simply combinations of choices each of us makes, bundled together for one reason or another, and as Smith and Rivkin wrote, "there is no reason to assume . . . that tasks must continue to be bundled together in the future in the same pattern they have been bundled in the past." The bundle of Nobel Prize–winning chemist and poet is not necessarily an intuitive one, but there's no reason it can't exist.

Though Hoffmann might cringe at this unpoetic explanation of his time use, I would argue that he has figured out a key principle of modern economics. In order to build his full life, he has leveraged what are known in the business world as "core competencies."

Here's what this means. Once upon a time—in the prehistoric days of 30 years ago—corporations generally viewed themselves as behemoths of strategic business units. These were not necessarily related businesses, but they wound up banded together as a result of mergers, acquisitions, and product launches. If a business area was profitable, the thinking went, a large corporation would do best if it either acquired another business in this area or launched its own business unit and let it grow. For instance, over the years U.S. Steel bought railroad operations and—even as late as 1982—Marathon Oil, because energy seemed like the field of the future. GE has, over the years, looped in everything from investment banks to television networks because these were all profitable properties. Profit is good, and hence anything that can add to the bottom line looks like a winner.

But in 1990, the management gurus Gary Hamel and C. K. Prahalad floated a different idea in a *Harvard Business Review* article. A business could do all right for a while running profitable but unrelated units, they noted, but we were entering a far more competitive, global era. As markets became more efficient, and the labor market became more flexible, top talent would become a scarcer resource than the raw materials or capital companies were used to allocating. There is an opportunity cost in "clarity of strategic intent" when you devote this scarce resource to things that you might be good at, but that other people can do as well or better. It takes energy and focus away from what a company does best. In the globalized era, Hamel and Prahalad wrote, a company would do best by focusing on what they called "core competencies."

They defined these competencies in three ways. "First, a core competence provides potential access to a wide variety of markets. Competence in display systems, for example, enables a company to participate in such diverse businesses as calculators, miniature TV sets, monitors for laptop computers, and automotive dashboards." Second, "a core competence should make a significant contribution to the perceived customer benefits of the end product." And finally, "a core competence should be difficult for competitors to imitate. And it *will* be difficult if it is a complex harmonization of individual technologies and production skills." Few companies, Hamel and Prahalad wrote, could achieve world leadership in more than five or six competencies.

Over the years, this idea has been honed a bit more. What the phrase "core competencies" usually means are things that a company does best and others cannot do nearly as well. In our efficient, global marketplace, companies succeed by focusing on their core competencies and minimizing, outsourcing, or ignoring everything else.

And so, over the past two decades, this honing has become a business obsession. The world, to quote Thomas Friedman, is flat. Bean counters have found ways to outsource just about every task from drafting to dentistry. U.S. Steel—that quintessential conglomerate—separated from Marathon Oil in 2002. While GE started focusing on its core competencies under its previous CEO, Jack Welch, getting out of every business where it couldn't be number one or number two, these days it's floated ideas of spinning off everything from its capital to appliance divisions.

Corporate fortunes rise and fall, but businesses that succeed in modern times tend to be very focused on what they do better than anybody else. For instance, Wal-Mart offers low prices. Target sells cheap chic. When Wal-Mart has tried to offer cheap chic lines, it has generally failed and gone flailing back to the low-price concept, which has proved to be a big winner in the current recession. In 2008, while much of retail was in free fall, Wal-Mart's same-store sales rose by 3.3 percent. As Harry Snyder, cofounder of the In-N-Out burger chain, often said, "Do one thing, and do it the best you can."

We usually read about these concepts in the business pages. But it turns out that we can learn something about achieving greatness in our own lives, too, from the labor modern companies have undergone to become focused and lean. We don't need to do just one thing. Even In-N-Out sells fries and drinks. There's little point, though, in being too scattered to master something, or in spending much time on activities in which you can't excel. What I want to argue in this chapter is that people, like companies, can have core competencies too. The same Hamel-Prahalad three-part definition can still apply. An individual's core competencies are best thought of as abilities that can be leveraged across multiple spheres. They should be important and meaningful. And they should be the things we do best and that others cannot do nearly as well.

Roald Hoffmann, for instance, leveraged his core competency of patient observation across chemistry and poetry. He devoted enough time to these competencies to make them important and meaningful in his life. And rather than try to use his gifts in fields where he didn't think he could be world-class (for example, child prodigy fields such as math and music, or those he didn't like as much, such as medicine), he threw his efforts into areas where he could shine.

Broadly, those who get the most out of life try to figure out and focus on their core competencies. They know that at least one key difference between happy, successful people, and those just muddling along is that the happy ones spend as many of their 168 hours as possible on their core competencies—honing their focus to get somewhere—and, like modern corporations, chucking everything else.

So what are these core competencies? Or in other words, what *should* you be doing during your 168 hours?

Some people are blessed to know this from a very early age. Most don't. Hoffmann didn't start writing poetry until he'd been a chemist for decades. Even if you have a good idea, you might not see all the possibilities, so it helps to spend time finding your own "clarity of strategic intent."

In order to figure this out, though, you first have to look at how you actually spend your 168 hours.

To do this, go back to the time logs from Chapter 1. This was the equivalent of the American Time Use Survey that you did on your own life, recording what you were doing as frequently as you could for at least 168 hours. Once you have the raw data from one week or a few weeks, classify it into categories. Though the categories shift from year to year, in 2008, the ATUS used these (each category includes related travel time):

Personal care (with a subcategory of "sleep")

Eating and drinking

Household activities (housework, food prep and cleanup, lawn and garden care, household management)

Purchasing goods and services (grocery shopping, purchasing consumer goods)

Caring for and helping household members (with a broad subcategory of "children," which is then broken down to physical care, education-related activities, reading to/with children, and playing/doing hobbies with children)

Caring for and helping nonhousehold members

Working and work-related activities, including commuting

Educational activities

Organizational, civic, and religious activities

Leisure and sports (socializing and communicating, watching TV, participating in sports, exercise, and recreation)

Telephone calls, mail and e-mail

Other activities

These are reasonable ones, and there is space to tally up your totals in some of these categories at the end of this chapter, though I'd also recommend breaking some of the bigger categories down into subcategories.

"Working" is a key one. Some of us have multiple jobs. But even if you have one job, your workday probably looks more like the "bundle of tasks assigned to one person" that Smith and Rivkin described than a uniform block of time. I call myself a writer. But I also function as a detective, a bill collector and invoice sender, a meeting planner, and, I must admit, an Internet surfing fiend. Break your work down into its main tasks, and calculate the time you bill to each. "Socializing and communicating" also benefits from analysis. How much time are you spending socializing and communicating with your spouse or children? Is the lion's share of this category spent on something you enjoy, like dinner parties with friends, or something you don't? "Other" may mean many things; don't sweat the seconds, and don't worry if your tally doesn't add up to exactly 168 hours. Almost everyone loses an hour or two in recording, and some activities are really hard to categorize.

I invite you to share your results on the My168Hours.com Web site, or with your family and friends. Ask them to keep the same logs. I'm guessing that you'll make some surprising discoveries, and develop some easy tune-ups before you even get to the bigger question of whether you're in the right job (which I'll discuss more in Chapter 3).

Here's what I learned from doing this exercise multiple times over the months when I was writing this book. First, though I feel like I work a lot, I actually work about 50 hours per week. My experience is common; many people doing this exercise learn that they're not working as much as they think they are.

Some of this is due to gray definitions of white-collar work. If you're watching *Wedding Crashers* while on a flight to a conference, is this work? Is drinking your coffee and reading the *Wall Street Journal* work? If you're doing it in your office, you'd say yes. If you're doing it in your easy chair at home you'd probably say no—but there's no logical reason to count the former if you wouldn't count the latter.

Aside from gray definitions, there is also the human tendency to discount exceptions that don't fit the mental pictures we create of our harried lives. For instance, if you work four 12-hour days, then cut out after 8 hours on Fridays, you'd think a "usual" day was 12 hours. So you might say you work 60 hours per week. But you don't. You work

56—maybe. Odds are, at least one of those 12-hour days featured a late arrival, or you cut out early to beat traffic or for a doctor's appointment, or you took a break for lunch. Pretty soon we're down in the low 50s. Several of the people who volunteered to keep time logs for me as part of this project asked to start over with a different week because (for example) they took a half day on Thursday, so it wasn't a "typical" 168 hours. But unless you will never take another half day in your life, exceptions add up.

While we underestimate exceptions, we overestimate other things— for instance, time devoted to repetitive small tasks. If you pulled out your Blackberry ten times over the weekend, you might give yourself credit for several hours of work, even though each incidence took 5 minutes. In other words, this totaled less than 1 hour, even though ten Blackberry checks will make you feel like you're in work mode 24/7.

Add these tendencies up in a culture where busyness is a sign of worth, and you see how easy it is to miscalculate. The vast majority of people who work full-time come out somewhere, as I do, within the 30–60 hour range.

The breakdown of my time within my 50 working hours gave me as much insight as the total. I spent about 25 hours writing or editing my own work. I spent 5–10 hours doing research, 3–5 hours on phone calls, about 1 hour on marketing and prospecting, 1–2 hours on administration, 5 hours on e-mail, and the balance on stuff that might be research or might not be (reading magazines for story ideas, surfing the Web). Since I write fiction and want to do more of this, I was willing to count time spent reading fiction as work if I took notes while I did it. Unfortunately, at least the first few times I kept logs, I discovered that I was spending almost no time on this at all. I was also spending almost all my 50 hours at my home office, which is not wise—I needed to be doing more in-person interviews or attending events that might generate ideas or contacts.

I was doing well in the exercise department. I have a target to run twenty to twenty-five miles per week, and since I don't run fast, this seldom takes me less than 4 hours. On better weeks, I did 6–7 hours including cross-training (the split between running and cross-training shifted over the course of writing this book as my pregnancy progressed, though I tried to keep my total exercise volume steady at 5 hours or so).

I was spending about 3–4 hours interacting with Jasper, my toddler, most weekdays, and about twice that on weekends. (Sam was born right before I turned in this manuscript, so he isn't included in these logs.) Quite a few of these hours were spent on physical care: dressing, changing, bathing, pouring milk, eating breakfast together. However, we were also spending a fair amount of time playing with puzzles, building with blocks, and crawling in and out of "forts" made from empty boxes. We read stories together most nights, though I wasn't doing as much of this as I thought I should, partially because I was bored with his books. Since this would increase my reading of at least one form of fiction (that core competency thing!), I decided to order as many Caldecott Medal winners from Amazon as our bookshelves could tolerate. As the quality of literature on his bookshelf crept up, so did our reading time, hitting 20–25 minutes on the 4–5 days per week I put him to bed.

I was sleeping about 8 hours per night—a little less on weekdays, a little more on weekends. I wasn't spending much time on hair and clothing, because my home office has a casual dress code. I did look for ways to cut down the routine when I needed to look nice, such as showering the night before so my hair would dry while I slept.

While I usually ate lunch at my desk (frozen meals or leftovers), I was cooking dinner several times per week. This never took me more than 30 minutes of hands-on time, and usually took 15. I didn't devote much time to cleaning the house or doing laundry. There are tips for reducing housework in Chapter 7.

There were definitely categories where I needed improvement. My husband and I weren't spending much grown-up time together—an issue many dual-income couples encounter. Time spent socializing was low too. I spent about 5 hours each week during the school year practicing with my choir, going out to bars after rehearsal, going through the music, and doing administrative work in my presidential role, but getting together with friends outside of choir was challenging.

I was watching about 7 hours of television a week—not much compared with the average American, but still more than I was exercising.

That's probably not the way the ratio should go. I also had many hours I simply couldn't account for, which means it's unlikely I was spending them in an optimal fashion.

On the other hand, I was happy to see that I was spending a reasonable proportion of my time on the big categories that I considered important. The trickier question was how to improve within these categories. Could I be doing more enjoyable things with my son? What else should I be doing at work, or what shouldn't I be doing? I know that writing is a core competency—if I'm not sure what topics I cover best—but research isn't, nor is marketing, which is why I wasn't doing this rather necessary activity.

And I'm starting from a good spot. I know I am in the right job (there's more on this in the next chapter). I work for myself, so I can choose where I focus my time, and hence I can spend a lot of time nurturing my family, which is also a core competency. Many people are starting from different places. To build a more focused and lean life, you have to figure out what you want to be doing during your 168 hours. Once you know what you *are* doing, you can turn your attention to this more profound question.

For years, Caroline Ceniza-Levine led University Relations for Time Inc. This, along with her previous consulting experience at Oliver Wyman & Company, and some recruiting jobs, gave her a lot of exposure to young people trying to plan their careers. Ceniza-Levine is also a Julliard-trained pianist and an improv actress, appearing regularly at the Magnet Theater near Penn Station in New York City. She recently leveraged these various competencies—largely, an ability to shine in front of youthful groups and make a coherent narrative out of whatever random idea you throw at her—to cofound a company called Six-FigureStart. This firm coaches young people as they try to figure out "What do you want to be when you grow up?"

Many people have no idea what the answer is, personally or professionally. So in her workshops, Ceniza-Levine tells me that she often pulls out a signature exercise she calls the "List of 100 Dreams."

Here's how it works. At the end of this chapter, after the section where you can record your weekly hour tallies, I've provided a space to start writing down a list of one hundred things you'd like to do during your lifetime. "This could be something as simple as ten places you want to visit, ten books you want to read, ten restaurants you want to try, skills you want to learn, or ten financial goals you have for yourself," Ceniza-Levine says. Go ahead and include ones that you've already accomplished, like graduating from college, getting married, or having kids. You'll probably be stumped by the time you get to one hundred, but if you find brainstorming easy, then call it the "List of 1000 Dreams" and keep going in the margins or on another sheet of paper. The point is to shoot for such a big number that you're not editing yourself, or debating how improbable some of these dreams might be. Winning a Nobel Prize in chemistry and maintaining a nice stash of Trader Joe's dark-chocolate-covered caramels can all go on the list.

Come back to this list several times over the next week or two as you think of more items. Here are some of mine, as of April 2009 when I started writing this chapter:

Attend a performance of Bach's B-Minor Mass

Sing in the Bach B-Minor Mass with a really good chorus and orchestra

Commission a major choral work

See a live performance of Wagner's Ring Cycle

Have fresh flowers in my office regularly

Have nice stationery and notepads with my name on them

Write a regular series of columns/articles for a major magazine or newspaper on an important issue that involves traveling to exotic places around the globe

Do a wine tour of Argentina

Do an African safari with my kids when they're teenagers

Get a novel published

Hit the bestseller list for fiction and nonfiction

Write a fiction series so compelling it makes Harry Potter look like a small phenomenon

Teach journalism and creative writing at a top-tier college

Have a clothing wardrobe I love that makes me excited to get
dressed

Spend time doing a writing retreat near a beach

Fit into my 26-inch-waist skinny jeans one month after birthing
baby number two

Maintain a nice stash of Trader Joe's dark-chocolate-covered
caramels

Run long races in gorgeous locations

Read more fiction

There were several things on the "List of 100 Dreams" that I've already done. For instance, I wanted an office with a great view, and right now I'm writing this while looking at the Manhattan skyline. I've published nonfiction books and articles. I've lived in New York City. When I was a young, poor intern living in Washington, D.C., I saw a fabulous painting of a strawberry hanging in the Torpedo Factory in Alexandria, Virginia. It was so bright red and vivid that I actually mentioned it in some fiction I was writing (that "get a novel published" item has been in the works for a while). When I began earning better money a few years later, I tracked down the artist and the painting and bought it. When you think of these things that you dreamed of doing and have now done, congratulate yourself.

Then it's time to look at the dreams you haven't turned into reality. Go through the list and start knocking off items that require just a few bucks or a few hours. After writing down my "List of 100 Dreams," for instance, I got a nosebleed section twenty-dollar ticket to a performance of the Bach B-Minor Mass at Carnegie Hall. I bought a nice orchid for my office.

Ceniza-Levine calls this exercising the "passion muscle." The experience helps people figure out "what it's like to like what they're doing." You will learn a few things by grabbing this low-hanging fruit.

For starters, you will learn that some of your hundred dreams have no business being on the official List. Ceniza-Levine used to tell herself that she would love to sew—if only she had time! She spent hours reading craft magazines, and imagining the gorgeous hand-crafted pieces she'd make. So, when she was in a life transition herself, she plucked this item off her "List of 100 Dreams" and made it happen. She signed up for a sewing class. "It was an absolute nightmare," she says. It turns out that when the needle hit the fabric, she really didn't want to take this on as a hobby. "I have never looked at a craft magazine again." That's now mental energy that can be devoted to other things. Likewise, if "win an Academy Award" is on your list, and also "act in a play," and you knock off the latter with a community production of *Evita* and discover that the experience wasn't life changing, you can stop writing your Oscar acceptance speech.

But more important, by trying lots of things you think you might enjoy, you will learn more about yourself, and what you are actually good at, what might be your core competencies, and which of the biggies are worth going for. You may be shocked by what you discover. This is why you just have to keep an open mind and try things.

That's what happened for Jackie Camborde of New Mexico. Back in the early 1990s, she had a fairly normal item on her list of dreams. She had just stopped smoking, packed on weight, and tipped the scale at over two hundred pounds on her five-foot-four frame. Since she was getting married soon, she wanted to lose weight and look good in her wedding dress. So she took a standard next step to tackle this dream: she joined a gym. Her first experiences there as an overweight former smoker would have sent many of us packing.

An initial fitness assessment required her to step on a scale in front of various people (an experience she calls "mortifying"). She was told not to attempt anything interesting until she lost weight, and so, day after day, she did her requisite 30–60 minutes on the cardio machines. When she finally got to take a class, a "mirror queen" aerobics instructor acted as though she were sullying the room's aesthetics by hauling her body in there.

But here's the thing. She didn't leave. It wasn't just a matter of persistence. Plenty of people trying to lose weight continue exercising despite a general lack of affinity for it. Camborde discovered that she *loved* working out, and in particular, she loved group classes. She found a more accepting instructor, and kept coming back, soaking up the gym atmosphere and losing forty pounds quite quickly. Her instructor suggested that she sign up for a weekend certification course so she could teach classes herself. Camborde was hesitant but decided to give it a shot. She got certified and discovered that she excelled at teaching. She loved learning new techniques and she loved choreographing combinations. Her own experience of being an overweight former smoker made her quite accepting of different body types, and her classes became big draws (even as she stopped being in the overweight category herself. She ultimately lost more than seventy pounds).

Meanwhile, she was still holding on to her day job as a nonprofit fundraiser. But after working all day, she'd still teach aerobics at night, and come home and tell her husband only about the classes. Clearly, she was stumbling into a core competency. So she made a list of dreams in the fitness world. Chief on this list? Opening her own studio. A few years later, she cut the ribbon for Santé Fitness Studio in Santa Fe.

Even having accomplished this goal, though, she made a point of focusing on her core competencies within this sphere: group fitness, and encouraging people of all body shapes to participate. Santé doesn't have expensive cardio equipment. It's not big—just one classroom that's packed with "funky little props," and rather than expand to include more of a gym, Camborde is opening a second location with a similar model. Her six teachers cover yoga, dance, classes for children, and classes for seniors. Camborde herself teaches about 15 hours per week. She released her first exercise DVD not long ago called *Real World Yoga: Real People with Real Bodies,* featuring shapes and sizes you will not see in fashion magazines. But she doesn't do personal training. It pays well, but it is not a core competency. "Every time I wavered from that, and did a little personal training, I've hated it," she says. "It's pulling me from other things I want to do in life."

Some of those things include volunteer work. Here, too, she has focused on her core competencies. For a while, "I was kind of known as the warm-up queen of Santa Fe," she says, rallying the troops before charity walks. Since her daughter's elementary school doesn't offer physical education unless parents raise funds for it, she hosts an annual community dance. She teaches schoolkids a dance combination (to, say, a *Hairspray* number), teaches the same combination at her studio, and then teaches it to community members who show up on the designated evening. Then everyone gets to perform it. This has raised three thousand dollars in a night, and also has the benefit of getting Santé Fitness Studio before hundreds of potential customers—for which Camborde makes no apologies. "If your community service can benefit your business, it should," she says.

She also tries to focus on her core competencies in her family life, and she and her husband and two daughters do their own version of "group fitness" (everyone hiking together, for instance). Of course, simply nurturing her daughters is a core competency in itself, and she tries not to foist her own interests on them. But she maintains lists of things she likes and things she hates to do and, as much as possible, tries to "make the hate-to-do ones go away." This is particularly hard for people who are caregivers, she notes, because "it's not nice to say I hate to sit and watch my daughter's softball game," but if you acknowledge that as being true for you, then you can deal with it. Maybe you go to a few games and invest more time in some other activity that is a core competency.

I think Camborde's story is instructive because while Camborde had done a lot of musical theater earlier in life, it would still take considerable imagination to look at an overweight former smoker who's working as a nonprofit fundraiser and identify "group fitness" as a core competency. Indeed, it's as much of a leap as figuring a Nobel Prize–winning chemist might be a really good poet. This is why you just have to keep trying things, noting your reaction, noting what you learn from any experience, noting what you can scratch off your list and what makes you "almost insatiable," as Camborde puts it, to learn more.

Like a successful modern corporation, you probably don't have more than half a dozen core competencies. Broadly, most people's core competencies fit into certain categories. If you're in the right job or jobs, which the next chapter covers, then the substance of your paid work will be a core competency. Nurturing your family members and close friends is also a core competency. No one else can do it quite as you can, though there are probably activities within this larger competency that you do better than others. As a confirmed, lifelong free agent, I stink at teaching my son to follow directions and behave well in a group setting. His nursery school teachers, who do this professionally, excel at it. On the other hand, I tell pretty good stories. Ideally, your leisure activities are also based around your core competencies—things you do best, and that you are willing to devote enough time and effort toward to make them meaningful. People who get the most out of life spend as much of their time as possible on these core competency activities, and as little as possible on other things.

Unfortunately, if you're like most people, looking at how you allocate your time with this thought in mind is going to be a sobering experience. Many of us spend vast hours at work on non-core-competency activities. At home, we also devote far more time to errands and housework—generally not core competencies—than to nurturing our family members. In our leisure time, we devote vast hours to watching television or shopping. Few people classify these activities as meaningful or important.

The next few chapters discuss how to change this, first in your work life, and then in your home life. It won't be easy. But the important thing to remember is that you do have a choice in how you spend your 168 hours, and you have more time than you think you do. There is extraordinary power in knowing what you want to be doing with your time. When companies execute with this clarity of strategic intent, they thrive. When people do, they thrive too.

Classifying Your Time into Categories

After you complete the time log at the end of Chapter 1, go through and put the entries into categories. Some of the most common ones include personal care (including sleep), household activities, purchasing goods and services, caring for or helping household members, working and work-related activities, leisure (including TV), exercise, and "other," though you are free to use your own. Record your daily and weekly totals, filling in the major categories that are relevant to you.

Daily Totals:

Your Categories	Monday	Tuesday	Wednesday	Thursday	Friday	Saturday	Sunday

Weekly Totals:

Subcategories

You can use the space below to break the major categories into subcategories. For instance, child care can be separated into physical care, playing, education, and reading. Housework can be divided into laundry, food prep, house cleaning, lawn work, and so on. Work can also be divided into different activities (phone calls, meetings, presentations, e-mail, research, fighting fires, or whatever you happen to do).

The List of 100 Dreams

What would you like to be doing in your 168 hours? Use the space below to list as many activities as possible that you'd like to try or accomplish during your life. Cross off the ones you've done, and note how they made you feel. Don't let the size of the page restrict you. Make the list as long as you want.

_____

_____

_____

_____

_____

_____

_____

_____

_____

_____

_____

_____

_____

_____

_____

_____

_____

_____

_____

_____

Your Core Competencies

After trying enough different activities, and looking back through your life, you may start to discover certain themes. Use the space below to answer these two questions:

What do I do best, that other people cannot do nearly as well?

_____

_____

_____

_____

What things do I spend time on that other people could do, or could do better?

_____

_____

_____

_____

_____

PART
2

@ WORK

· 3 ·

The Right Job

The first time I interviewed the marine biologist Sylvia Earle, in 1998, she was five miles off the coast of Florida and sixty feet underwater. I, thank goodness, was not. There was a phone line installed into the *Aquarius,* an 860-square-foot underwater base with bunk beds and an Internet connection, from which Earle, explorer-in-residence at the National Geographic Society, could study the health of the coral reefs off Key Largo—and their inhabitants.

"There's a barracuda looking at me right now," she said as she stared out the window. "We did a little inventory, and there are fifty species within a thousand feet." She described silver tarpons, bar jacks, and "just clouds, curtains of small fish. They look like silver coins." Sixty feet down, she and her colleagues were thrilled to learn that they could see the full moon the way the fish see the moon, with the dim light bewitching the coral until the reefs spawn and "all heaven breaks loose underwater."

It was a dazzling image. But what was more dazzling to me, then nineteen years old, was the joy in Earle's brusque voice. She was sixty-two. That's currently the average retirement age in the United States. But even after 40 years of studying the oceans—40 years of more than full-time hours, hunting for projects, finding funding, grueling travel, battling often blatant sexism in the scientific community, and building a career while raising three children—Earle could not talk about her work without smiling. That affection comes through in *Sea Change*, the memoir she had written a few years before our conversation. When she was three, she wrote, a great wave on the New Jersey shore knocked her over. Ever after, she had been "irresistibly drawn, first to the cool, green Atlantic Ocean; later, to the Gulf of Mexico, warm and blue, serving as my backyard and playground through years of discovery; and thereafter to other oceans . . . The 'urge to submerge' came on early and continues, seasoned and made more alluring by thousands of underwater hours"—more than 7,000, not counting the shower, she told me when I tracked her down in 2009 to interview her for this book—"each one heightening the excitement of the last."

I found that affection intriguing as I pondered what to do with my life. Though Earle's primary message in that 1998 interview was about ocean conservation, there was a second missive hidden in her words like a barnacle clinging to a ship: if you choose your life's work well, something bewitching can happen through your labors. Each hour you log can be a source of joy.

That message is the reason I am including a chapter about "The Right Job" in this book, and as the first chapter in the @Work section. I realize that the connection to time management and productivity may not be obvious. As the folks at Portfolio noted when we hashed out chapter ideas, this is not a career guide. I'm not going to ask you a series of questions and then tell you that, based on your personality type, you'd be a great accountant or, as one online quiz told me, either a novelist or veterinarian.

I also can't tell you how to find and land the right job, though, frankly, neither can some coaches who will charge you dearly for such wisdom. I attended one conference recently where a headhunter informed us that even in a down market, companies hired people in sales, and a career consultant advised my breakout session that people often find their jobs through networking. There you go—that advice cost you nothing more than the sticker price on this book.

Instead, I can say this: I'm including a chapter on being in the right job because, in the context of overall life management, it matters that much.

We spend a lot of our waking hours working. Generally not the bulk, but a lot nonetheless. Like choosing the right spouse, being in the right job can give you amazing energy for the entirety of your 168 hours.

You'll certainly have more zeal for your work if you love what you do. When I spoke with her again in 2009, not only was Sylvia Earle, at age seventy-three, heading off for trips to the Yucatán Peninsula in Mexico to study whale sharks, and to Australia to study the reefs, she was finishing up a book called *The World Is Blue*, had recently worked with Google to add oceans to the Google Earth database, was flying around the world to campaign for marine sanctuaries as part of winning the $100,000 TED Prize, and was involved in the operations of Deep Ocean Exploration and Research, a submarine consulting company she founded.

But here's the fascinating part: if you love what you do, *you'll have more energy for the rest of your life, too.* If you're trying to build a career while raising a young family, you will have more energy for your children if you work 50 hours a week in a job you love than if you work 30 in a job you hate. Or at least you'll come up with better art projects; Earle recalls that she often had her three kids make slides out of seaweed specimens.

I also say that being in the right job matters knowing that, as I write this book, Tim Ferriss's *The 4-Hour Workweek* has been sitting on the business bestseller list for two years. Ferriss downplays the idea of dream jobs. As he writes, "For most people . . . the perfect job is the one that takes the least time. The vast majority of people will never find a job that can be an unending source of fulfillment, so that is not the goal here; to free time and automate income is."

Clearly, he struck a chord, probably because many people aren't thrilled by their work. According to one late 2006 survey of 6,169 fulltime workers conducted by Harris Interactive on behalf of CareerBuilder.com, 84 percent of respondents said they weren't in their dream jobs (though there's plenty of evidence that most people aren't miserable, either).

Perhaps some people are better off following the *4-Hour Workweek* prescription of setting up automated online businesses and using their free time to pursue adventures.

But, on the whole, I think that all play and no work makes Jack as dull a boy as the other way around. There's evidence that most people agree with me. Despite the popularity of TV shows about the leisure class such as *The Real Housewives of New Jersey*, the 2002 General Social Survey (GSS) found that most people would continue to work in some fashion even if they didn't need to. There is much happiness to be gained by throwing yourself into a meaningful professional pursuit, be it building a company whose products make people's lives easier, making scientific discoveries no one else has thought of before, or composing symphonies. Indeed, if you are in the right job—like Earle—then getting to study the oceans for only 4 hours a week would seem downright torturous.

I can't tell you what your dream job is, but I can tell you—within our evolving labor market—what the research on happiness and creativity says its characteristics would be. I can tell you that beyond sheer satisfaction, there is a business case for being in the right job that has implications for the rest of your 168 hours. I can tell you that the chances are minimal that someone else will create the perfect job for you. You'll have to invest the hours to design it in an entrepreneurial fashion, whether you're working for someone else or for yourself. I can also give you some questions to ask about your work that might help you figure out how close or how far you are from the right job, because if you're far, then there's an even clearer link to the issue of time. Harsh as this sounds, if you're not in the right job—a job that is moving you toward where you want to be in life—then you're wasting almost all the time you're spending at work. You can have efficient meetings. You can negotiate a great flex-time schedule, but what's the point? You'll spend 40 hours a week doing something you don't like instead of 50. You may be doing good things with those 40 hours, such as supporting your family or improving society, but there are other socially beneficial, remunerative jobs out there. There is no bonus virtue gained by choosing one that doesn't make you happy. Better to build a life where you don't need to write off *any* time as an inevitable obligation.

Creating the right job is the first step to using the hours you do work in the most effective way possible.

What Does the Right Job Look Like?

For all the angst that work can inspire, the fact that we even get to ask what we'd like to do with our lives—with the working chunk of our 168 hours—is an incredible luxury. Even a few generations ago, such questions weren't really part of the cultural conversation. I recently reviewed another book in which the author recounted his grandfather's 40 years of labor in a quarry. That wasn't a penal sentence. It was simply the job that was available to him at his level of skill and education that paid enough to support his children. So he reported to his shift for decades.

Now, "we live in a country that has latitude to follow your dreams," Earle says. Not only does the Census Bureau report that 85 percent of Americans have high school diplomas, but nearly three in ten Americans over age twenty-five have finished college. The economy is more varied. And so the abundance of choice facing young men and women can be paralyzing. Looking out my window at the skyscrapers of midtown Manhattan this morning, I see the headquarters of Pfizer, Citigroup, and the United Nations, all suggesting hundreds of professions, as well as the street-level delis and dry cleaners, the police officers directing traffic around the Midtown Tunnel, maintenance guys checking the roof of the condo across the street, and the barge operator directing a giant vessel north on the East River.

With so many lines of work, perhaps the surprising figure isn't that 84 percent of full-time workers say they aren't in their dream jobs, or that we change jobs relatively often. I serve on the Princeton University Alumni Council's Committee on Careers, and a recent informal survey of alumni approaching their twenty-fifth reunion found that about 72 percent had changed jobs three or more times since graduation, and 41 percent had changed jobs five or more times. Only 6.6 percent of people were in the same job they got after college or graduate school. Instead, the surprising figure is that the 2002 GSS (according to writings from the American Enterprise Institute president, Arthur C. Brooks) found that 89 percent of adults who work more than 10 hours per week are either very satisfied or somewhat satisfied with their jobs. In other words, while most people aren't in their dream jobs, they have managed to squeeze enough peaches at this economic farmers market to come up with something that's not wildly off the mark.

So this chapter is mostly about optimization—about using what social science research says inspires the best performance to make the leap from a good job to the right job.

The right job turns out to have a specific definition, according to a 1997 *California Management Review* article called "Motivating Creativity in Organizations," by Teresa Amabile, a Harvard Business School professor who's studied this topic for decades. As she wrote: "You should do what you love, and you should love what you do."

A graduation speech cliché? Perhaps. But Amabile meant two related and research-based ideas by this statement. First, "you should do what you love" means finding work that "matches well with your expertise, your creative thinking skills, and your strongest intrinsic motivations." Intrinsic motivation means liking the substance of the work for its own sake. The second part, "you should love what you do," means "finding a work environment that will allow you to retain that intrinsic motivational focus, while supporting your exploration of new ideas."

In other words, the right job leverages your core competencies—things you do best and enjoy—and meets certain working conditions, including autonomy and being challenged to the extent of your abilities.

The first part—the importance of being intrinsically motivated—is backed up with several studies. For one of them, Amabile and her colleagues asked a group of aspiring scribes to write poems, which would then be judged by writing experts. Before they could compose the poems, though, the writers answered questions about their motivations for entering the profession. Amabile found that those who were asked about the pleasure they experienced in writing something they could be proud of (that is, who were intrinsically motivated) scored higher marks than those who were asked about wanting to be rich and famous (which are external motivations). That doesn't mean that there is anything wrong with wanting to be rich and famous, just as there is nothing wrong with bosses coaxing better work from their employees with pizza, bonuses, and other adult equivalents of grade-school gold stars. On some level, external rewards like paychecks are necessary in our capitalist society. It's just that the best work—the most meaningful work—comes from some other well of motivation. Or as the poet Anne Sexton once told her agent, "I am in love with money, so don't be mistaken, but first I want to write good poems."

Chances are, you've seen that well of motivation somewhere in your life. Often, as with Sylvia Earle speaking of oceans as her "playground" and "backyard," it has to do with the activities you felt great affection for as a child. While fewer than one in six Americans told Career-Builder.com that they were in their dream jobs, a full 35 percent of firefighters said they were, the highest among any profession. I'm sure this has something to do with the fact that 41 percent of firefighters grew up wanting to be firefighters.

As you look over your "List of 100 Dreams," consider whether any involve ways you played as a kid, ways that consumed blissful hours when you didn't have to worry about making a living or impressing anyone with your job title. Writing has always been this activity for me. I wrote and illustrated my own books in kindergarten. When I was bored in high school, I wrote dozens of short stories at night. They weren't very good, which confused the issue, because from an objective standpoint, I seemed better at other subjects such as math. But I never doodled differential equations in my notebooks for fun. Fortunately, I realized that before I became a middling and unhappy math professor.

I do, however, enjoy writing about math and science. For about a year, I wrote a weekly column for *Scientific American*'s Web site called "Where Are They Now?" that profiled former finalists in the Westinghouse Science Talent Search. This competition, started in 1942 and now called the Intel Science Talent Search, identified forty top high school scientists each year based on their independent research projects. As I studied these scientists' lives and careers, I found that, inevitably, those who spoke with the most awe of their jobs had indications of their intrinsic motivations when they were kids, too.

Ilan Kroo, for instance, now an aeronautics professor at Stanford, grew up in rural Oregon in the 1960s. He spent his childhood dreaming of flying machines. Once, he constructed a hang glider from bamboo poles, duct tape, and plastic. He and some friends took the contraption to a nearby dairy farm, ran down a hill, and got a few feet off the ground before crashing. "Any landing that we could walk away from was a good landing," Kroo told me.

Fortunately, he survived that experiment and, in high school, with assistance from a research program at the Oregon Museum of Science and Industry in Portland, he decided to build a better wind tunnel to help him understand the aerodynamics of flight. One problem he saw with wind tunnels is that the object being tested requires a support structure to stay in place as air blasts around it. But these supports affect airflow, and skew the data.

To solve this problem, Kroo built a wind tunnel lined with magnets. A photo sensor monitored the test object and sent signals to change the strength of the magnets' field so they, rather than a support structure, could hold the object in place. This design won him a finalist spot in the 1974 Westinghouse competition, and with such an honor under his belt, he never looked back. He earned his PhD in aeronautics, and over the years has created many innovations used at Boeing and elsewhere, always with an eye to the practicalities of flying, and often, trying to do more with less. One particularly fascinating creation is a vehicle known as a "foot-launched sailplane," now licensed to the Belgian company Aériane as the SWIFT. It is, in some ways, a more elegant solution to the problem he tried to solve at that old dairy farm, of how humans can fly without the bothersome hum of an engine. No one was paying him to ponder that question as a kid. He threw himself into the work simply because he wanted to. He loved the substance of the work for its own sake. And so, like Earle talking about her ocean playgrounds, when I asked Kroo to describe flying the SWIFT, he spoke with joy in his voice. "I probably can't do justice to that," he said. But, "flying at the speed of birds . . . totally quiet, looking down, seeing the mountains and desert floor eight thousand feet below you is unlike any other kind of flying . . . It's absolutely amazing."

Of course, just because the stuff of your job—in Kroo's case, planes and flying—leverages your core competencies, doesn't mean that the second part of Amabile's test will be met. Not only do you have to do what you love, you have to love what you do. That is, the job conditions need to be optimal to coax out your best work. Kroo's job as a professor gives him autonomy and the constant challenge of trying to break new ground with his research. While there are other jobs that could involve his core competencies—such as flying planes for the military—they might not necessarily fit the way he works best, though they might be great for someone who relishes the challenges of combat.

To study the effect of job conditions on work quality, Amabile and her colleagues conducted several other studies, such as one that examined the practices of a thirty-thousand-employee corporation they called "High Tech Electronics International." They identified several High Tech Electronics projects where innovation was the desired outcome, and asked managers and workers to rate the projects in terms of whether the results actually had been creative or not. Then they asked about the presence or absence of several work conditions for all of these projects. They found that the best results required three things:

- that people be given a great deal of freedom in figuring out how to carry out the work—that is, the opportunity to make day-to-day decisions in the project
- that team members felt challenged in a positive fashion by the work
- that people felt they had sufficient organizational support (resources, a supportive work group, a supportive supervisor who communicated well, and an organizational environment where creativity was encouraged)

The first condition, autonomy, is straightforward. No one wants to be micromanaged, and if you're being paid for your ideas, as at least some of us are these days, there's no reason for someone else to dictate how to do the work—or even when and where you work. Indeed, there are good business reasons not to. According to a meta-analysis of forty-six studies, published in the November 2007 *Journal of Applied Psychology,* telecommuting—usually meaning working from home on your own schedule, though it can mean working from anywhere you choose—is associated with higher supervisor performance ratings, increased job satisfaction, and a reduction in the intent to leave one's company. The growing proportion of self-employed Americans naturally works this way much of the time, which may be why self-employed people tend to have more job satisfaction than other workers.

Of course some work does need to be done at a certain time and place. Most second-grade teachers still report to a classroom. Policemen report to their precincts. Even so, there is a big difference between having every action dictated and being held accountable for a result (for example, high test scores) and having reasonable freedom to choose the means.

There is not necessarily a right way to work, but there is a right way for you. Think about the times when you felt most creative and productive, and try to identify the "who, what, when, where, and why" answers we reporters learn to cram into the first paragraph of a story. Were you working closely with other people, or by yourself? What kind of work were you doing—looking at the big picture and zeroing in, or starting from the details and moving out? What time of day does your best work happen? Some people are useless after or before a certain hour, but some people have waves of concentration that come and go. Where were you? Were you in a Zen-like office space, a coffee shop, or surrounded by plants, paint tubes, or puppies? It makes sense that if there's a way that you work best then the right job should allow you to work in that way more often than not.

The second part of the "love what you do" equation—that the right job needs to be challenging—is more intriguing. At first blush, people often seem to prefer easy tasks. But as Amabile tells me, "Most people get bored with 'easy' jobs." Ultimately, you want work that's optimally challenging, where "the work calls on your best skills, and helps you develop new skills—but is not completely beyond your skill level."

This is because such work puts you in a state that the psychologist Mihály Csíkszentmihályi terms "flow." Decades ago, in a now famous and widely chronicled experiment, Csíkszentmihályi and his colleagues decided to figure out exactly when people were happiest. They gave thousands of people pagers that would go off randomly throughout the day, and asked them to record what they were doing and how they felt (aside from being annoyed at the incessant buzzing). They found that people were happiest when they were completely absorbed in activities that were difficult but doable, to the point where their brains no longer had space to ruminate about the troubles of daily life. Time seemed to warp, as Csíkszentmihályi wrote in his 1990 book *Flow: The Psychology of Optimal Experience*. "Hours pass by in minutes, and minutes can stretch out to seem like hours." When researchers interviewed people with considerable skills in certain areas—for instance, composers seated at the piano, figure skaters in the middle of intense practice—such people spoke of feeling as though they were carried along by water. They were almost floating. Hence, "flow."

Such a state doesn't have to occur at work, but the structures and goals of work do provide ample opportunities for losing yourself in difficult but doable tasks. Do you ever feel this way with your job? What are you working on when you do? When I have the skeleton of a chapter written, and I'm going in and fleshing it out, I can start typing at 7:30 a.m. and not look up until 1:30 p.m., when I realize I'm starving for lunch.

Pay attention to when you feel most absorbed at work. If you want to be blissful, your job should involve spending as much time as possible in that space where you are leveraging your core competencies, and working in the way you choose on something demanding enough that, as Earle puts it in *Sea Change*, "one discovery leads to another, each new scrap of information triggering awareness of dozens of new unknowns."

If you're spending some time in this state, then you are probably at least close to the right line of work. The key question becomes how you can improve your ratio. What existing project could you scale up, or what new project would make you excited to come to work in the morning? If you're not sure, schedule 30 minutes two to three times a week to think about this, and to have conversations with your colleagues, your mentors, or anyone in your network who's thoughtful enough to get you unstuck.

Of course, if you rarely or never experience this bliss and absorption at work, or if you're in an organization that actively or passively thwarts your attempts to focus on the substance of your work (the third aspect of Amabile's three job conditions), then you have some hard thinking to do. If you never feel absorbed at work, are there other points in your life when you feel this way? What are you doing then? If you can't recall, start working your way through that "List of 100 Dreams." Do any of these activities challenge you and absorb you to the point where you don't notice the time? Does the "stuff" of these activities make you happy?

Write these down. Over the next 6 months, start thinking about ways that you can incorporate them into your life's work, ways you can change your life's work, or ways you can find a more supportive work team or organization. I can't tell you what the answers to these questions are, but I can tell you not to dismiss this exercise as impractical. In the next section of this chapter, I want to convince you that it's far more practical to love your work than to be in the wrong job.

The Business Case for Being in the Right Job

I am writing this book in—to put it charitably—uncertain economic times. Over the course of 2009, the U.S. unemployment rate bumped rapidly into double digits. In recessions, we tend to focus on people who are out of work, but one of the more insidious consequences of a slack labor market is the mismatch between jobs and skills that high unemployment rates cause among people who have jobs.

The morning I began writing this chapter, *The Wall Street Journal* ran a piece called "From Ordering Steak and Lobster, to Serving It" about Carlos Araya, a former crude-oil trader on the New York Mercantile Exchange who, following a layoff, was working as a host at the Palm Restaurant in Tribeca. At least he'd been able to stay in New York. By the time I was revising this chapter, the situation had deteriorated; the *Journal* began a story called "Unemployed Hit the Road to Find Jobs" with this sentence: "After seven months without a paycheck, Tim

Ryan turned into a werewolf." Not literally of course, but Ryan, a laid-off construction worker, had finally found work hours away from home playing the wolfman at Clark's Trading Post, a tourist attraction in the White Mountains of New Hampshire. "For $12 an hour, about half what he made before, he dons furry rags, a coonskin cap and an eye patch and jumps out of the woods when the Trading Post's steam train chugs by, snarling and growling at passengers," the *Journal* reported. Araya had also taken a steep pay cut, but with both men in trouble on their mortgages and needing to support their families, they were grateful for the work.

When you are drowning, any job that pays the bills is a good job. But in the long term, when we all come up for air in this transformed economy, getting as close as possible to the right job is not just a sentiment for graduation speakers. There is a two-part business case for doing work you love if you can.

First, happy people are more productive and successful than unhappy people.

Though this would seem obvious, researchers have been trying to study the exact mechanism and direction of that statement for years. The logical explanation would be that career success (and the associated income) makes people happy, but this may not be the case. In a 2008 review of the literature in the *Journal of Career Assessment*, the University of California, Riverside, professors Julia K. Boehm and Sonja Lyubomirsky suggested that, in fact, the equation goes the other way. "Happiness," they wrote, "is an important precursor and determinant of career success."

Some of this is sheer temperament (possibly about 50 percent, Lyubomirsky postulates in her 2007 book, *The How of Happiness*). One longitudinal study found that the most cheerful first-year college students were earning more, 16 years later, than their more morose peers, even though few eighteen-year-olds have any clue what they want to do with their lives.

But other elements of happiness are more situational, or are at least within the realm of one's personal control. Boehm and Lyubomirsky highlighted studies finding that people induced to experience positive emotions set higher goals for themselves, persisted at difficult tasks longer, thought they were doing a better job and, in many cases, really were. People in a good mood are more likely to try new things. Amabile and her colleagues once asked various corporate employees working on creative projects to keep diaries; they found that the workers were more creative and productive on days when they were happier. Interestingly, there was also a carry-over effect. People who were in a good mood one day were more creative the next day as well, even if their moods had returned to earth since.

While it's hard to tease out the chicken-and-egg problem with these questions—are you happy because you're in the right job, or does being happy make any job seem better?—we do know this: if you are blissful at work at least a few times per week, the carry-over creativity boost, compared with someone who isn't happy, can soon cover the full 40–50 hours.

In other words, being in the right job isn't just about whistling while you work. If you are in the right job, you will be more productive and creative than you otherwise would be, and in our increasingly competitive world, productivity and creativity matter. The barriers to entry for many knowledge jobs are low. We've become used to stories about factory jobs going overseas, but with technology and mobile capital and labor, almost any knowledge job can be outsourced, too. A book publisher can contract with an Indian cover designer just as easily as she can with an American one. To thrive in a world where someone else is always cheaper, you have to be distinctive at what you do. In some cases, just to survive, you have to be world class.

You do not get to be world class at anything without devoting long hours to the deliberate practice of your craft. In recent years, a number of books including Geoff Colvin's *Talent Is Overrated* and Malcolm Gladwell's *Outliers* have popularized the findings of studies by K. Anders Ericsson (now of Florida State University) and his colleagues claiming that you need at least 10,000 hours of focused practice in order to achieve expert performance. Researchers found this, most famously, for violin students in Berlin, though these findings have been extended to other areas such as sports. Ten thousand hours is a lot of time. To put that in perspective, back when I was playing the piano seriously as a teenager, I practiced about 5 hours a week. That comes out to 250 hours per year. Over ten years, this comes out to a measly 2,500 hours.

Parents can obviously force their children to practice musical instruments for some amount of time whether they want to or not, but it's hard to force 10,000 hours unless you're standing over the kid with a whip. And, indeed, since deliberate practice requires a focused concentration on getting better, you'd have to use that whip to enforce results, not just hours. Long term, it doesn't work. Eventually, you have to *want* to practice. You do not do that unless you *love* the stuff of the job. Only if you love the stuff of the job will you relish thinking about problems and brainstorming solutions in the grocery store line. When Joe Kennedy, CEO of the Internet radio company Pandora, was deciding whether to take his current job, he realized (as he said in a speech I attended recently), "I'm thinking about it in the shower. I'm having *fun* thinking about it in the shower." This is a man who spent his college years writing Gregorian chants. Clearly he has a thing for obscure music.

This obsession is the only way to stay on top, because you can trust that your competitors are thinking about *their* jobs in the shower. Advantages do not stay static. These days, best practices are quickly dispersed. In 1896, the world record time for male marathoners was just under 3 hours, a time that amateurs post regularly now. Indeed, Paula Radcliffe's world record women's marathon time (2:15:25, set in 2003), would have been the world record men's time up until 1958. Think about that and what it says about how much more intense and focused marathon training has gotten in 50 years. Half a century ago, if elite women runners were privy to modern marathon training methods, and men were not, we would have thought that women were faster than men.

So it goes in other fields. Once, people who took entry-level jobs at blue-chip companies might have expected to retire from the same place 40 years later, and so they didn't need to keep their skills sharp enough to impress people at other companies. This is not an option now. The original premise behind consulting firms was that MBAs were rare and managers rarely moved between corporations, so these lords of strategy could show companies how to be more efficient. Now you may as well stick a revolving door on some C-level suites.

Plenty of people are willing to work hard and will do a reasonable job on the tasks in their job descriptions whether they love what they do or not. But it's hard to go beyond that if you don't love what you do. You'll put in the hours you have to put in and do the things that are explicitly and immediately rewarded. Then you'll come home and think of other things, like what's on TV. Indeed, you'll watch a lot of TV. One recent University of Maryland study found that unhappy people watched 20 percent more television than happy ones. Unhappy people like to escape. They don't spend their time solving problems or thinking their way around personal obstacles.

People who are in the right jobs will. This is what happened to Lise Menn, a pioneering linguist. Like Kroo, she was a finalist in the Westinghouse Science Talent Search, in her case back in 1958 (as with Kroo, I interviewed her for my ScientificAmerican.com "Where Are They Now?" column). She was inspired as a teenager by a book called *The Story of Language*, in which the author, M. Pei, claimed that by comparing the structures of different languages related to English, you could reconstruct the one that must have been spoken as an ancestor of our current Indo-European tongues. "The idea that you could peer that far back in time—when the actual words and speakers were dead but the patterns still survived without speakers, like the grin on the Cheshire cat—that made the hair on my arms stand up," she told me. "It was the most romantic, ghostly thing I'd ever read in science."

But in the post-Sputnik era, the hard sciences seemed like a better bet to her parents. She majored in math as an undergrad, and went to Brandeis University in Massachusetts for graduate school in the subject. There, "I discovered what real mathematicians were and I wasn't one of them," she says. So, because she had married another graduate student and become a mom shortly thereafter (eventually having her hands full with two small boys by age twenty-four), she decided to pause her education and figure out what she wanted to do.

It didn't take her long to come back to linguistics. Earning her degree in the field, however, was slow work. "There wasn't any money for babysitters," she says. She would trade babysitting duties with other mothers. But in the larger sense, because she was so drawn to linguistics, she turned the hours she spent caring for her sons and other children from an impediment to her linguistic career into a boon.

Supportive graduate student girlfriends volunteered to loan her books on children's language development from the Harvard University library. What Menn read was "not like what I was seeing in my own kitchen with my second kid," she says. Textbooks said that children learning to speak would say the first consonant of a word and the vowel ("mih" for milk, "doh" for dog). "That is the majority pattern, but in fact lots of kids don't do that," she says. "Instead, if a word ends in a consonant, they'll change the first consonant to match it." Little Danny Menn was—contrary to expert opinion—calling dogs "gogs."

So Menn called up the famed child language researcher Roger Brown in the Harvard psychology department and asked if he'd heard anything like that. He told her to write up her observations. She did and, using her home address because she had no institutional affiliation, sent the paper to the journal *Lingua*, where it was published in 1971.

Cheered by this success, Menn decided to earn a PhD in linguistics from the University of Illinois at Urbana-Champaign, where her husband had landed a job (although she soon moved back to Boston after the marriage ended—and started building an academic career with help from a new partner). For her dissertation, she did a case study of how one child named Jacob learned to speak. She transcribed about 100 hours of his babbling and early words as she babysat him from twelve to twenty-one months old and saw that he, like Danny, would experiment with saying the same word in different ways. She discovered that before a child would come up with regular patterns to simplify words, he would go through a period where similar words influenced each other.

What's fascinating about this story is that you'd think people in the field of children's language development might have done such case studies before, but much of the theory of children's language development, Menn notes, had been proposed by people who weren't moms and "if they were dads, I don't think they listened to kids a lot when they were babies." Instead, they took a more standard approach to building their academic careers by writing papers in quiet, child-free offices.

Menn loved her work so much, though, that she turned personal obstacles into an opportunity to change the field. Her work "served as inspiration for much of the fieldwork and diary studies of children that followed," says Andrea Feldman, a former student of Menn's who has also taught at the University of Colorado at Boulder, where Menn took a job in 1986. Her notes on Jacob "are still being studied by child language researchers," she told me.

Many times, this sheer motivation translates into earning more, and some studies have found a link between happiness and income—proof of the adage to "do what you love and the money will follow"—though it doesn't always hold true.

But even in the absence of income guarantees, there's a second part to the business case for being in the right job. If you take a job you don't like just to make money, there is a good chance you won't do it very well, and it will suck the life out of the rest of your 168 hours.

That's what Danny Kofke discovered. A few years ago, he was teaching first-graders to read and write in Sebastian, Florida. He loved seeing their eyes light up when they figured out the connections between letters and the concepts they represented. Unfortunately, as a teacher, he was earning only $35,000 a year, so when his first daughter was born, he decided to try something more lucrative that he felt would better support a family. A friend who managed a company that sold high-end floor coverings offered him a job. Some of the salesmen were making six figures.

Now, there is nothing wrong with selling flooring. In the case of high-end, hand-crafted rugs, it's like selling art. Plenty of people become obsessed with the intricacies of Oriental rugs, and would consider expertise in this art form to be a core competency.

Danny Kofke was not one of those people. He started out enthusiastic, but "I slowly realized I wasn't passionate about it. I made a pretty bad salesman," he says. When people came in wanting a four-thousasnd-dollar rug, he'd find himself thinking, "I don't care if you like it." There was no way he was going to hit the top end of his potential income range, and looking forward, he realized that if he hated his job, he was going to be spending a lot of the additional salary he earned above his teaching income trying to make himself happy.

But he figured the opposite was true, too. "If you do have a job you like, if you're happy in life, you don't need those materialistic things to make you happy," he says.

So when a job working with autistic children opened up, he quit and went back to teaching. Now he's supporting his family on about $40,000 a year and has written a book called *How to Survive (and Perhaps Thrive) on a Teacher's Salary*. The Kofkes live frugally, but when you love what you do, it's a lot easier to come home and sit on a second-hand sofa than if you're miserable for 8 hours a day.

Creating the Right Job

While I believe that there is some truth in the statement "do what you love and the money will follow," or at least you'll feel better about the money you have, I do want to clear up one misconception many people have about landing the right job. You are highly unlikely to find your dream job by hunting through online job postings. It's not a problem with the medium. You are also highly unlikely to find your dream job by reading flyers on telephone polls, by sending your résumé to recruiters or working with headhunters, or even by networking until you've passed out all five thousand of those snazzy business cards you ordered. It's like the scene in *Being John Malkovich*, when Craig diligently scans the classifieds, looking for "puppeteer." The audience titters. We know he's not going to find it, just as Sylvia Earle did not find the job of ocean explorer/author/conservationist/submarine entrepreneur in *The New York Times*.

And yet how many of us think our perfect job would be listed in a similar fashion? The truth is that any existing job description has been conceived of by someone else. Expecting someone else to have conceived of your perfect job is roughly similar to expecting someone else to read your mind. It's better to build your career with the idea that you will always be responsible for creating the right job for each stage of your life, whether you work for someone else or on your own.

While a growing number of people are choosing the latter, either permanently or at some stage in their careers, the former is more possible than many people think. Yes, you can change your job description and working conditions in a million ways that will get you closer to the right job. It doesn't necessarily matter what you were hired for. Fundamentally, most employers want you to make more money for them (or bring more attention to your enterprise, or post better results than your stakeholders anticipate, or whatever the currency of your profession happens to be—but don't fool yourself. It often comes back to money somehow). If you're an administrator in HR and start staging puppet shows that make all the employees in the regional offices weep with delight, pledge eternal loyalty to your corporation, and hence attrition falls by 25 percent, what manager with half a brain wouldn't let you keep doing that? An entrepreneurial mind-set can get you a long way toward creating the right job in a way that makes everyone happy. If you think hard enough, there is bound to be some way you can spend the working chunk of your 168 hours solving your organization's problems in a way that aligns, neatly, with what you want out of the job.

For instance, another of those Westinghouse finalists, Kraig Derstler, is currently a paleontology professor at the University of New Orleans. He studies dinosaur fossils, which isn't what the University of New Orleans hired him to do. He came in as an expert in echinoderms, which are a class of creatures that includes starfish. Then he realized that dinosaur fossils were where the fun was, and had to figure out how to become a dinosaur expert in the roughly 5–7 years most universities give you to make tenure. This is difficult in the sciences, because most universities expect you to obtain outside funding for your research, and the usual grant-making bodies tend to require a track record in a subject, which he didn't have.

So Derstler decided to finance his own dinosaur research and expeditions by starting a program that had laypeople pay to tag along and do the grunt work of digging for dinosaur bones. Many found this to be an exciting way to spend their vacations; he compares this to Tom Sawyer getting people to whitewash his fence. He also notes that he's not sure he could get the university to approve such a program these days, given the unclear flow of liability, among other things. But it worked at the time, and the net result was that Derstler got his specimens, financed his research and the training of his students, and was able to publish enough papers on his findings to attract grants and attention. He got tenure—as a dinosaur expert—in due time.

If you like something enough, you will find a job in an organization that you think will be flexible and open to your talents, and then you will figure out a way to concoct your dream job within it, remembering that it is often easier to ask for forgiveness than permission.

Or you'll design such an organization yourself—which is my approach, and one that is increasingly common in the American economy. Here in New York City, according to numbers that the comptroller's office shared with me, there were 807,750 self-employed workers in 2006. That was about a fifth of the roughly 4 million nongovernmental jobs in the city at the time. Of the 773,000 jobs that Gotham added from 1981 to 2006, a stunning 491,000 were people working for themselves. That made self-employment the biggest source of job creation in the city during those generally fat years.

The same trend seems to be playing out across the country, though the numbers can be slippery, thanks to varying definitions of self-employment, people who hold multiple jobs, off-the-books work, and other factors. The Bureau of Labor Statistics says that the national self-employment rate—the proportion of total employment made up of the self-employed—has hovered between 7 and 9 percent since the 1970s, but according to the Census Bureau, the number of "non-employer businesses" (that is, one-person shops) rose from 15.4 million in 1997 to 21.7 million in 2007. The U.S. Small Business Administration (SBA) reports that the country had 4.5 million businesses with fewer than four employees in 2005; the owners of these businesses have much in common with true solo workers. That's a lot of people calling themselves boss—around 25 million in the 125-million-strong U.S. private workforce. And that was a few years ago. More recent queries on whether people consider themselves "free agents" produce a slightly higher rate.

According to Kelly Services (the temp agency and staffing company), a full 26 percent of the workforce called themselves "free agents" in 2009, compared with 19 percent in 2006.

There are many reasons—good and bad—for this rise. Corporations focused on their core competencies outsource almost everything else these days, which creates space for small PR firms, conference planners, freelance report writers, and the like. Part of this is to avoid the payroll expenses of taxes and benefits, and part is because smaller firms and individuals can be more nimble. Contracting with them gives firms a flexibility that they can't have when they maintain a high head count.

Of course, many people wind up self-employed not entirely by choice—one of the reasons the Kelly Services figure jumped seven percentage points in 3 years is that the U.S. unemployment rate also spiked during this time, even if, broadly, economists report that self-employment is not particularly countercyclical. That is, people don't choose to work for themselves just because they can't get other jobs. For many people, going solo is about push *and* pull factors.

Marc Matsumoto, for instance, always loved to cook. As a kid, he baked his own birthday cakes. In early 2008, this New York City resident started a blog at NoRecipes.com to celebrate freestyle culinary arts. But he didn't have much energy to cook or blog because, as the head of marketing at a finance-related startup, he was having trouble planning his schedule to give himself concentrated blocks of free time. He could shop for groceries and experiment in the kitchen only on weekends. Until December 2008, that is. Shortly before Christmas, his employer failed to secure another round of venture capital, and Matsumoto joined the millions of Americans who lost their jobs since the recession's onset.

It could have been a crisis, but instead, Matsumoto chose to view it as an opportunity for a career change. He drummed up enough consulting gigs to pay the bills. Then he threw himself into building his "dream job" as a food personality. Now, he spends his weekdays perusing farmers' markets, cooking dishes such as *karaage* (Japanese fried chicken) and using his marketing skills to lure 100,000 unique visitors to his site each month. Becoming a free agent was a bit of a "forced move," he says, "but now that I'm doing it, I actually kind of like it. I wonder why I didn't do it sooner."

If this isn't a career book, then it definitely isn't a guide to starting a business. One thing to keep in mind is that entrepreneurship need not mean borrowing huge sums of money to start a high-tech giant. Many business owners are lifestyle entrepreneurs, meaning they work solo or "try to invent the company that they would like to work for," says Susan Sobbott, president of American Express OPEN, the division devoted to business owners. In my previous book, *Grindhopping*, I told young entrepreneurs to ask three questions:

> What do I love so much I'd do it for free?
>
> How can I get someone to pay me to do that?
>
> If there's no obvious job title in an organization doing what I love (and often there isn't), what's a low-cost way I could start a business doing that, and get the cash register ringing quickly?

None of this is easy, of course. As Sobbott notes, while many people start businesses to escape the corporate grind, "none of them spend less time working. Zero." It's not about changing how many of your 168 hours you work, it's about changing how much control you have over them. With self-employment, you may invent your dream gig doing what you love, as Matsumoto is doing, or you may simply change the "love what you do" part of the equation, but if this ups the autonomy and challenge factor, this may be OK, too.

Julie Pickens and Mindee Doney, Oregon-based creators of Boogie Wipes, a line of saline-infused kids' tissues, are examples of the latter. A few years ago, Doney was having a beastly time cleaning up the caked-on mess of snot caused by one of her children's colds. She threw some of the saline from a nose spray on a tissue and had an epiphany. She knew Pickens—also a mom of young kids—professionally, and since both were between businesses, they decided to launch Little Busy Bodies Inc. to sell Boogie Wipes in 2007. While they love the stuff of consumer goods marketing, and like making a product that's helpful to parents, I didn't get the impression from talking to them that they dreamed of tissues as kids like Sylvia Earle had dreamed of waves.

Nonetheless, the second half of the equation—love what you do—is clear for both women. Running their own business has given them incredible autonomy. Before they launched, they hashed out the details of the Boogie Wipes product lines during epic play dates. Now, Pickens helps her daughters get ready for school in the mornings, then works in the office from 8:30 to 2:45, Monday through Friday. Her four-year-old often joins her around noon, after preschool, and plays in the office playroom. Yes, they have an office playroom. Why not? Pickens leaves to pick up the other kids around 3:00, and does some work from home while they do homework. After dinner and bedtime, she fires the laptop back up around nine o'clock and puts in a few more hours. She occasionally comes in on Saturday mornings, but manages to leave at least one weekend day e-mail-free. Doney, who has an infant, works from home slightly more often. After running in the mornings on the treadmill while her kids watch cartoons, she comes in to the office roughly three days a week from 9:00 to 3:00. In the afternoons, she works at home while her older kids play outside. The computer goes off during dinner, then after baths and books and prayers, she puts in another work shift during the evenings, which she does on weekends, too.

Both women work full-time hours, but since they have complete freedom to choose those hours, they also pack in a lot of family time. They give their dozen employees the same flexibility. "We hold employees to the same expectations as ourselves," Doney says. "What I mean by that is that if they need to work at home occasionally, they work at home . . . We have faith and trust in their ability to get the work done when it needs to be done."

They also appreciate being challenged at close to the extent of their abilities. They describe their first two years running Little Busy Bodies as the equivalent of earning their MBAs. For instance, here's a problem Doney and Pickens had to solve recently: How do you get a product into Wal-Mart? The answer: you find the right person who knows the inside scoop. You play up the fact that you are a women-owned business. You show up in Bentonville, Arkansas, with a pitch that is not just about the product's efficacy, but about its story as the creation of mompreneurs who are just like the target-market moms, and who give the products an authenticity modern consumers crave. Most important, you show them how your product will make them money and that you know how to manage your enterprise. Then when the buyer says yes, you watch your company's sales go north of $5 million in less than 2 years in business. You set a goal to sell the company to a major consumer goods brand in the next 5 years, and use the cash to start something else fun, flexible, and as satisfyingly tough as getting dried snot off a wriggling toddler's face.

Gut-Check Time

In the busyness of daily life, it's easy to forget to reflect on a life's work, and how satisfied you are with the way you're spending the working chunk of your 168 hours. Small frustrations loom large. Doney and Pickens speak ruefully of the time a retailer imposed an eight-hundred-dollar fine because they filled out a form incorrectly. If you get a call like that, the first thing that pops into your head is unlikely to be that this is a minor detail in the reality of running a $5 million business that affords you so much autonomy that you can put an air hockey table in the warehouse for your kids. Likewise, while Sylvia Earle says that her work "was never a job," I'm sure that at least once or twice in her career, her equipment broke down, she got sick while traveling, or journalists asked her stupid questions.

This is why it's a good idea to take a few minutes at the end of the day—perhaps during your spouse conference (see Chapter 6) or instead of watching TV—to reflect on what you want your career and life to look like. Then you can reflect on whether what you're doing is close enough to the right job that you can start making small tune-ups to be more efficient, and then launch your career to the next level.

How do you know for sure that you're in the right job, or at least close? I was recently talking about this with Laura Wellington-Gerry, creator of the Wumblers, a children's cartoon about sustainable living.

She had drawn the Wumblers characters in her notebooks as a teenager and kept them in her head all through the years. She ran two other businesses with her husband, but about a decade ago, he was diagnosed with cancer, and passed away shortly after September 11, 2001—leaving her as a single mother of four children under age ten.

As she attempted to process her grief, her children's grief, and that of everyone around her in New Jersey who'd lost neighbors in the terrorist attack, she started drawing those cartoon characters again. Feeling she had nothing to lose, she decided to develop them a bit more. She contracted with various people in the entertainment field to turn her vision into reality, and now, many years later, you can purchase Wumbler DVDs, find them on TV and as spokespeople for the National Watermelon Association (Wumblers, conveniently enough, hatch from watermelons—something they did before the National Watermelon Association got involved, but which turned out to be a nice marketing tie-in nonetheless). Wellington-Gerry is blissfully happy spending her days living in her cartoon characters' world. When we talked on the phone she gushed that if someone offered her $400 million to stop developing their stories, she didn't think she'd take it.

I laughed. I mean, she has investors, and they would probably force her to take a $400 million buyout. But I do think she's on to something with this idea. If you want to get the most out of your 168 hours, instead of looking for a 4-hour workweek, look for work where the $400 million question would give you pause. If someone offered you $400 million to walk away and never do the "stuff" of your job again, would you take it?

I imagine most people would, even if they love their work. We have families to consider, debts that need to be paid, and many other interests we wouldn't mind pursuing. But perhaps the question is more "would you have to think about it?" and "would you be grieving despite your ability to buy the San Diego Padres?"

If you would, then you're on the right track. The next few chapters are about using your work time more effectively, so you can ramp up your career even as you're ramping up your family or personal life as well.

Creating the Right Job

We spend a lot of our 168 hours working, so being in the right job matters. To find out if you're in the right job, ask yourself these questions:

Does my job tap into my intrinsic motivations (things I loved as a kid or would do for free)?

Does my job give me a reasonable amount of autonomy?

Am I challenged regularly to the extent of my abilities?

Do my work environment, organization, and coworkers encourage my best work?

If the answer is "no" to any of these four questions, what can I change? In the next week? In the next year?

Can I create the right job within my organization? Another organization? Or will I need to go out on my own?

If you're pretty sure you are in the right job, then try asking this question:

If someone offered me a windfall to never do the "stuff" of my work again, how would I feel about that?

· 4 ·

Controlling
Your Calendar

What does it mean to use the working part of your 168 hours effectively?

When I started writing this book, I asked everyone I knew for examples of people who did a lot with their time—building Careers with a capital C, maintaining full personal lives, and so forth. A colleague in California told me to look up John Anner, a father and motorcycle racer who'd started an organization called the Independent Press Association in 1996 with a budget of a few thousand dollars. By the time he left the organization in 2002, the IPA had a multimillion-dollar budget and was providing business services to hundreds of independent magazines, including *Mother Jones, The Nation,* and the *Utne Reader.*

Intrigued, I learned that Anner had since been tapped to head an organization called the East Meets West Foundation, which works primarily in Vietnam (he moved to Hanoi in 2007, but is now back in the United States working at the Oakland, California, headquarters). Upon taking over this nonprofit in 2003, he decided to focus on the three core competency areas where he thought EMW could have the most impact: clean water, medical treatment, and education.

In the second category, Anner and his colleagues surveyed the space and found an opportunity to make a big impact on the Vietnamese health system. While anyone who's given birth can appreciate that entering the world is not *easy* for babies (or their mothers), it is a particularly perilous journey for those who are born prematurely in developing countries such as Vietnam. While American neonatal intensive care units can save the vast majority of babies born too early to fully regulate their own lung function, until recently, Vietnamese hospitals would lose about 30 percent of premature babies during the first 24 hours of life due to respiratory distress.

So EMW decided to pioneer the deployment of infant continuous positive air pressure (CPAP) machines in the National Hospital of Pediatrics in Hanoi. A year later, National Hospital's 24-hour death rate for its most fragile babies had dropped from the 30 percent range to about 10 percent. East Meets West decided to scale up what came to be known as its Breath of Life (BOL) program, and by 2009, BOL had equipped 95 percent of Vietnam's provinces with seven hundred CPAP and complementary machines—which collectively treat about fifteen thousand babies per year—and trained two thousand doctors and nurses in their use.

Net result? Vietnam's infant mortality rate began dropping like a rock. In 2003, the country suffered 30.83 deaths per 1,000 births. By 2008, this figure had fallen to 23.61 per 1,000. The BOL program is not the sole reason for this decline, but it is certainly a big one.

Some might call it a miracle, but it's not the only thing that makes the organization remarkable: EMW's 125 employees get home at a reasonable time, and ordinary meetings rarely last longer than an hour.

"The most useful thing I've ever done in any organization is to train the staff on how to have an efficient meeting," says Anner. There's a simple formula in Anner's organizations for getting the most out of work time: no one goes to a meeting who does not need to be there. Every meeting has an agenda, with a clearly defined, *short* time frame next to each item. The limited minutes impose discipline; things that are not supposed to happen during the appointed times do not happen. At the beginning of the meeting, the meeting leader spells out the goals. At the end, the participants go back through the agenda and review assignments to be clear on what needs to happen. At the next meeting, they'll need to confirm that they've done what was assigned. After all, there's no point in having the same meeting four times in a row, simply because it is Friday again, to learn that everyone is still working on their projects. By increasing meeting efficiency, "that alone probably gives me ten hours per week," Anner says.

Not only is there a simple formula, there's a simple reason behind it: Time wasted in meetings that either do not need to happen or do not require a particular person's presence is time not spent putting CPAP machines in hospitals to save sick babies (or any of EMW's other projects). The 10 hours saved in meetings each week also give Anner and his colleagues space for the personal lives that keep them energized enough to deal with issues of extreme poverty. Anner, for instance, now leaves the office around 5:30 p.m. Doing the substantive work of EMW's mission and nurturing their own lives are the EMW employees' core competencies. Listening to two coworkers debate the same point they debated last week is not.

Simple as it seems, though, this is far from a universal philosophy. One of EMW's partners on a venture recently brought Anner to one of their meetings. "I walk into the meeting, and there are sixteen people—ten of whom don't need to be there," he says. The meeting went on for more than 3 hours, covering the same ground repeatedly as people hashed out their feelings on issues that didn't concern the majority of people in attendance. Listening to the back and forth, Anner decided, "I might as well be asleep."

Confession: I actually did spend the 90 minutes before I wrote the opening paragraphs of this chapter asleep. Thanks to my very energetic toddler, my day got off to an earlier start than intended, and by 11:30 a.m., I knew I was going to need more coffee to be functional. So I took a nap instead. When I woke up, some previously elusive ideas on chapter organization for this book popped into my brain. I wrote them down and have now spent the afternoon executing against them.

In other words, during that 90-minute nap, I made significant progress on my top-priority project for the year. Granted, I did not send a single e-mail, attend any meetings, edit any PowerPoint slides, read any headlines related to my job, call any clients, sit through any conference calls with my colleagues, travel anywhere, manage the papers on my desk, or do anything that most knowledge workers have come to think of as "work." Still, I'd say it was an incredibly productive morning, though if you'd seen me during those 90 minutes, I doubt that "productive" is the first word that would have popped into your head.

So who's right? Productivity, like religion, is a concept prone to much interpretation. All of us bring our own biases to the table. As with religion, many of us spend vast amounts of time trying to understand wise men's teachings on the topic, and so we lap up books on "Getting Things Done." We learn to "Never Check Email in the Morning," to "Leave the Office Earlier," and other methods of creating more efficiency in our lives. There's now a *Productive!* magazine, which features one guru per issue on the cover. The blogosphere boils like a tent revival with writers evangelizing about their "lifehacks," their reliance on forty-three folders, and their tech systems for pursuing that ideal of In-box Zero.

Some of these lifehacks are laughable. Case in point: a new iPhone app that lets you walk while e-mailing—safely—by changing the screen to be a view of what's in front of you, courtesy of the iPhone's camera.

On the other hand, some are good, and if you find yourself with extra minutes, you might read a few. I invite you to share the ones you find most useful at My168Hours.com. I always carry a notebook to record tasks and thoughts. Life seems a lot less overwhelming—moving from intention to results—when you ask "what's the next action?" as David Allen, author of *Getting Things Done,* suggests. Bloggers offer great ideas from the big (regularly review your daily and weekly goals)—to the small (do not take conference swag. Ever).

The commandments all have their place. But as I've been interviewing people for this project, and thinking about how to make my work hours more "productive," I've realized that many of these bits of wisdom don't have a lot to do with my life. For starters, most assume a corporate office culture. One key premise of many productivity tomes is that there's all this "stuff" coming at you—a constant bombardment of paper and people—that you need a system to process.

As Allen writes, "More and more people's jobs are made up of dozens or even hundreds of e-mails a day, with no latitude left to ignore a single request, complaint, or order. There are few people who can (or even should) expect to code everything an 'A,' a 'B,' or a 'C' priority, or who can maintain some predetermined list of to-dos that the first telephone call or interruption from their boss won't totally undo."

Maybe it's the sole-proprietor life, but you can call me one of those few people. I don't feel bombarded enough to turn my desk into an F shape (as one blogger suggests) in order to battle the incoming fire. No one comes into my home office unannounced, and I mute the phone unless I'm expecting a call. As for e-mail, I don't file anything. It takes time, and I have a search function. As I'm writing this, I have more than thirty thousand e-mails in my in-box, including hundreds of unread ones. Zen-like? Not really, but I've found it doesn't matter, either during my magazine and newspaper jobs, or now.

As we saw in Chapter 3, a growing proportion of people work as I do—on my own, doing creative work, often at home or in coffee shops, or occasionally while visiting a client. If one in four workers doesn't even have a boss, then it's hard to be interrupted by one. Another thing to keep in mind with productivity systems is that a big chunk of the non-free-agent labor force doesn't have jobs that involve sitting at a desk processing e-mails. I was recently speaking with two young consultants who'd done a project with the Philadelphia police department. With much amazement, they noted that most of the officers didn't have e-mail addresses that could be used for force communications. The proportion of the labor force toiling in a cubicle farm is not as large as we think it is.

So I think it's most helpful to start from a principle for managing your work life and then see how to put it into practice broadly, whether you're working in a nonprofit like EMW, as a soloist like myself, in a hands-on job like managing a floral shop, or in a more traditional corporate environment. This is the *168 Hours* principle for work: Ideally, there should be almost nothing during your work hours—whatever you choose those to be—that is not advancing you toward your goals for the career and life you want.

Indeed, given the esteem in which we hold the idea of "work" in our culture, I'd like to propose a new personal definition that you should keep in mind when you make decisions about your work hours. Any "work" that is not advancing you toward the professional life you want should not count as work. It is wasted time.

I know this seems stark—"I can't just not do what my boss says!" you may be saying—but there are a few reasons to think this way.

First, "my boss said I had to" (or "my client said I had to") is no more a reason to do something than "I don't have time" is an excuse not to do something else. Everything in life is a choice of whether to accept certain consequences. The consequences may be untenable, or you may trust that your supervisor has more wisdom and experience than you do, and so you may choose to do absolutely everything she asks, but recognizing that this is a choice gives you as much control as possible of your life and your 168 hours.

Second, a lot of the busyness that goes on during workdays gives us a false sense of productivity that's dishonest to indulge. Doing a lot does not mean you're doing anything important with your 168 hours. If your job involves lots of meetings and you saw that Anner's schedule for the day featured 2 hours of meetings and yours had 6, you might think you were being more productive. If you work until 8:00 p.m., and he works until 5:30, you might think you're doing more. But remember, this is a man whose work is saving thousands of fragile babies a year. Just as there is nothing noble about sitting in a meeting when there are respirators to be deployed, there is no more nobility in being on a conference call at 7:00 a.m. with the same people you talked with at 10:00 p.m. than there is in watching TV. Or, for that matter, going to sleep, perchance to dream up better ideas than you ever would have had checking e-mail.

This chapter is about clearing your work calendar of things that shouldn't be there so you can focus on your core competencies. Obviously, the first, most important step is to be in the right job. Recall the question from the last chapter—if you were offered $400 million to never do the stuff of your work again, would you be bummed about it, despite your riches? If you would, then it's time to ask a follow-up question. If you did land a windfall, and could still do the stuff of your job, what parts of your job would you change? Given that you'd never have to work a day in your life, what would you do more of and what would you shove off your plate?

Spend some time thinking about this question, and write these tasks and changes down. I'm guessing that you'd keep the parts of your job that you do best, where you have the biggest impact, and that make you excited and energized. You'd probably pitch in on the grunt work that needed to get done, too, as long as you could see the point. You might still go to meetings. Bill Gates goes to meetings—but only to meetings in which he plays a critical part. Other people plan ahead for these meetings so as not to waste his time. His meetings do not wander aimlessly to someone's gripe about office fridge policies, just because she has the entire department captive in a conference room.

A windfall may never come to you, but the point of this exercise is to figure out what the ideal situation looks like—what you'd spend your work hours doing and not doing if you had complete freedom. When you know what the ideal situation looks like, you can start changing the working component of your 168 hours into something that looks closer to the ideal than it currently does. There is a four-part process for doing this:

1. Seize control of your schedule.
2. Do not mistake things that look like work for actual work.
3. Get rid of non-core-competency tasks by ignoring, minimizing, or outsourcing them.
4. Boost efficiency by getting better at what you do.

Seize Control of Your Schedule

Here's a question you may not have asked yourself recently: What do you *want* to do during your workday? Part of being effective during the hours you choose to work is developing the discipline to spend real time on what's important even if other things—including, frequently, your own bad habits—try to shove you off course.

So the first step is to be as clear as possible on your priorities. What do you want to accomplish as your life's work? This will be informed by your "List of 100 Dreams." Go through and highlight the ones that are most important to you professionally. Then you can start figuring out what actionable steps it will take to get there.

For instance, Harris Brooks of Texas decided in his twenties that he wanted to lead a hospital. So, as the next step, he earned a joint MHA/MBA from the University of Houston–Clear Lake. In order to gain management experience as soon as possible, he did his administrative residency at the smallish Palo Pinto General Hospital in Mineral Wells, about an hour outside Dallas–Fort Worth, rather than at one of Texas's larger institutions. He made a point of learning about all operational aspects of running a hospital, including the political part (he spent a chunk of his time there working to defeat a local proposal that would have cut the hospital's tax revenue). He took a job at Palo Pinto as a project administrator after his graduation in 2000, and a year later, since he was already familiar with the hospital's operations, became the chief operations officer. Having achieved that position, he started taking on projects that would give him the leadership track record he'd need to be considered for CEO jobs in the next 5–10 years, such as obtaining seven figures in grants for the hospital, and overseeing an $8 million construction project that was finished on time and just 0.5 percent over budget. With that kind of track record, when the previous CEO left in early 2007, the hospital board decided not to do a broad search. Brooks could step in as CEO around age thirty-five. There was obviously still some element of chance and timing in all this—we'll talk more about the anatomy of career breakthroughs in Chapter 5—but his next steps led pretty clearly to his goal.

Like Brooks, as you work toward your "List of 100 Dreams," try to figure out what actions you can do to achieve your priorities in the next 10 years, 5 years, and in the next year (devotees of David Allen's *Getting Things Done* system use an airplane image, as in 50,000-feet or 30,000-feet priorities, to think about this same concept). Yes, your organization or boss's priorities matter, and if you're in the right job, these priorities will be similar to yours. But remember, there is a good chance you won't be working for the same person or company in a decade. We have projects now, not jobs. So make sure you're clear on what *you* want to get out of every job you do.

The "1 year" list starts to be workable from a scheduling perspective. What would need to happen in the next year for you to know, concretely, that you are closer to your career goals than you are now? I sometimes think of this in terms of what I'd say in that family résumé known as the Christmas letter. If you work 30–50 hours per week for 50 weeks, a yearlong time frame gives you 1,500–2,500 hours to allocate to your professional goals. If you work 60-hour weeks, this gives you 3,000 hours.

Unless you're a lawyer with a billable-hour quota, I'm guessing you've never thought of your years on the job in this way, but it's a useful mental model. Two thousand hours—or even 3,000 hours—is a lot of time. It is not, however, an infinite amount of time. There is only so much you can do in 2,000 hours. That realization has certainly had a focusing effect on me (and helps keep me from checking Facebook every 15 minutes—but we'll get to that).

Once you know what you'd like to do in the next year, you can break this down into what you'd like to do in the next month (120–240 hours) or week (30–60 hours). On Sunday nights, or before the start of your workweek, sit down and list the actionable tasks you need to do to advance you toward these goals. Then, this is the key part: schedule them in, *knowing exactly how long they will take.*

This time component is not a difficult bit of information to come by. You probably know the answer for many tasks if you do them often enough. If you don't know, ask around. Be observant. As Stephanie Wickouski, managing partner of Drinker, Biddle & Reath LLP's New York office told me, many people "don't know how long the subway takes from downtown to midtown, and they're riding it every day."

Wickouski, a bankruptcy lawyer, has this down to a science. She figures out "when I have to start to get done, not just today, but the whole week." For instance, if a filing is due at 3:00 p.m., and she cannot start until the day it is due, and she knows it will take 4 hours, she will count back and start by 9:00 a.m. Why not 11:00? "I always build a buffer into things," she says. Another client might call, in which case she can offer 5 minutes right then, or much more time after 3:00. If she gets done before 3:00, she can start returning calls or relax a bit ("I spend way, way, way too much time on the Internet," she confesses).

This discipline came in handy when Wickouski embarked on a big project back in the late 1990s. She couldn't find any good books on bankruptcy crimes, so she decided to write one. Her employer at the time said she could write the book if she wished, but she had to do it outside of her usual billable hours. The prospective publisher wanted the manuscript in 6–9 months. She had to figure out how to make this all work.

Wickouski calculated that the book would run about three hundred pages, with thirty chapters. She thought about how long it usually took her to research and write papers and briefs. Using that figure, she decided that writing the manuscript would take her 1,000–1,200 hours. If she planned to do that in the next 9 months—about 38 weeks—that would come out to roughly 30 hours per week. So then she had to look at her weekly calendar and figure out where she could schedule in 30 hours. She decided to do 4 hours most weeknights, and 12 hours or so on weekends. She blocked those times out. It was a grueling schedule, but "it came to pass just like I had visualized," she says, with the finished book, *Bankruptcy Crimes*, raising her profile within the space and leading to bigger career opportunities later on.

Now, I'm sure that—passionate as Wickouski is about her work—at least a few Thursday nights during those months, she came home feeling like kicking up her feet rather than cranking out another five hundred words. But here's the true secret of seizing control of your schedule. *It just doesn't matter.*

If you want to use your 168 hours effectively, once you make a commitment to yourself to spend a certain number of hours on a task, keep it. Never miss a deadline. Follow through on anything you say you'll do as a matter of personal integrity. If you lose 4 hours because of a blackout, make it up somewhere else as soon as possible. If someone else doesn't turn in their part of a project, proceed without them and find an alternative solution. It doesn't matter if the party on the other side of the deadline doesn't care, and it doesn't matter if you have a good excuse. Many excuses and emergencies are, in the broad sense, foreseeable. Yes, you and your children are going to get sick for a certain number of days per winter, and their schools will be closed for snow, too. There will always be traffic jams on Friday afternoons and when it rains. Build it in. Make backup plans for working at home, for getting to the airport if your first method falls through, and for people you can call on to help.

If you adopt this philosophy, look objectively at your schedule, and are honest about how much time projects will take, I'm betting you can find space for almost anything that matters to you within your 168 hours. That includes big projects like going back to school or starting a business. While 30 hours per week (Wickouski's time commitment) sounds like a lot, the average American could find it by cutting out all television, cutting down on housework, and holding sleep to 8 hours per night (Saturday and Sunday mornings are often a great time for getting things done). If you can use saved hours during your work time—like the 10 hours Anner doesn't have to spend in meetings— even better.

If you don't have the space for something, then be honest about it and either don't make the commitment or agree to a more reasonable time frame. I'm always grateful when my research assistants tell me no, I cannot complete that by Monday but I can by Wednesday. It beats when someone tries to garner points for heroism by saying she'll do a project by Saturday and then blows through that commitment. It's not that 2 days matters much. But once you start breaking commitments to your-self and the people around you, the whole system of discipline—the trust you build up in yourself to be in control of things—breaks down. Again, the world is not going to make it easy for you to stick to your priorities. Don't let your own weakness contribute to the problem.

Do Not Mistake Things That Look Like Work
for Actual Work

This may be the workplace woe that is responsible for more wasted time, and perhaps lives, than anything else. You can have a great system for organizing e-mail, or scheduling daily conference calls on various projects, but I'm guessing at your retirement dinner, people won't talk about your pristine in-box or packed schedule. They'll want to talk about what you've *done*. If you're not getting anything that matters done—like, say, lowering Vietnam's infant mortality rate—then you're not really working. This holds true in nonoffice jobs, too. A cop can run herself ragged responding to three hundred 911 calls a year about a certain street corner. Better to figure out what the problem is at that street corner and solve it.

Of course, some people grasp the distinction intuitively. I am quite sure that the speakers toasting a biologist named Carol Fassbinder-Orth at her retirement dinner 50 years from now will not struggle to figure out what she's done. For the past few years, I've been following the career of this rising young scientist who's now, as a twenty-something mom of two, a professor at Creighton University in Omaha, Nebraska. Fassbinder-Orth grew up in Elgin, Iowa, on an apiary featuring 100 million bees. This involved about as many bee stings as you'd imagine. She got stung as she played in the yard. She got stung as she helped her dad tend the hives, and she got stung as a teenager as she started doing experiments on natural ways to treat honeybee parasites. As she says of the constant stinging, "you get used to it." I'm not sure that's true, but I do believe this developed unflappability has given her a refreshing perspective on what it actually takes to build a career as an academic scientist, as opposed to what some people—and here I would be thinking of the former Harvard president Larry Summers—think it takes.

A few years ago, Summers, now director of the White House's National Economic Council, famously claimed that a big reason women weren't making it as mathematicians and scientists is that they weren't willing to put in the 80-hour weeks necessary to build such careers. Leave aside that, as we learned in Chapter 1, almost no one—including people who think they work 80-hour weeks—actually works 80-hour weeks. Fassbinder-Orth did not put in 80-hour weeks as a graduate student earning her PhD in avian immunology at the University of Wisconsin; as the mom of a baby daughter, born during her first year of graduate school, she didn't have time for that.

Fortunately, somewhere along the way she had a realization: scientists are not ultimately judged on the hours they put in at the lab, or on the number of slides they can prepare, tests they can run, or meetings they can attend. They are judged on the quality of the results they obtain and publish in peer-reviewed journals. So that was what she needed to focus on. She didn't chase experiments with a limited chance of success, and she didn't delve much into academic politics. But she did such a good job on the metrics that did matter that, despite all the horror stories of 8-year PhD programs and people forced to do multiple postdocs before a tenure-track job opens up, Fassbinder-Orth finished her PhD in 5 years, and landed her professorship over people who'd done postdocs, even though she interviewed when she was 8 months pregnant with her second child.

In other words, Fassbinder-Orth succeeded by making sure she knew exactly what constituted "work" versus "not work."

This is a powerful time-saver. For an avian immunologist, analyzing the effect of age on birds' susceptibility to the West Nile virus (as Fassbinder-Orth did at the University of Wisconsin) probably is work. On the other hand, for an avian immunologist, playing Tetris online is not work. I don't need to write a whole chapter on how to clear your calendar of activities like that. If your time diaries show that you're often surfing Zappos or checking Twitter during work—and the average office worker admits to wasting 1.7 hours per day on these kinds of things, according to a 2007 survey by Salary.com—then you need to get a grip and cut it out. Schedule a few short "time waster" breaks per day or, when you find yourself wandering, make a hash mark in a notebook and force yourself to return to the task at hand. Make a game of it. If you can cut your number of hash marks in half, you can reward yourself with a 30-minute Facebook session.

The real question is what to do about all the stuff in the middle.

Sometimes an extra specimen analysis is important and sometimes it is not. Sometimes e-mail is important and sometimes it is not. Sometimes calls or meetings result in multiyear lucrative relationships and sometimes they result in everyone being bitter that they wasted 2 hours of their lives. Sometimes the first 15 minutes matter and the next 45 do not. Sometimes documentation is critical and sometimes it's paper-pushing nonsense. We tend to define all these things as "work," but the big breakthroughs in efficiency come with learning to see the difference between real work and not really work.

I define "work" as activities that are advancing you toward the career and life you want. If they aren't, then they are not work. This is true even if they appear on your work calendar or you've always done them, and they should not have more esteem in your mind than playing Tetris. That doesn't mean you won't do them—again, remember the average office worker wastes 1.7 hours per day on personal e-mail, phone calls, gossip, and so on—but you shouldn't harbor any illusions that your unnecessarily long conference call is anything but disguised and ineffective leisure time.

This is the approach Fassbinder-Orth is now taking to the next hoop of her academic career: earning tenure. While whole treatises have been written on how women and minority academics sometimes miss the bar because the old boy professorial network doesn't share the metrics, when I asked Fassbinder-Orth what it would take to make tenure at Creighton, she rattled it off without missing a beat. In the next 5 years, she would need three to five publications in major journals—not necessarily *Science* or *Nature*, but in the tier close to that. She needed to attract outside grants of a certain magnitude and prestige. And she needed to do a reasonably good job teaching and advising undergraduate students (thus carrying a certain departmental workload).

So those are exactly the things she executes her time against. She spends time readying lectures, working in her lab, and directing her undergraduate students toward the most promising experiments—the ones that are going to lead to papers. She works on grant proposals. And she tries to minimize time devoted to other things, even if they might look like "work."

"If it's a waste of time, I don't do it," she says. "I do what things I am interested in and that I feel can have the most benefit." While she is always happy to meet with students who need her help, she has also been known to politely extract herself from meetings if she finds that they are not relevant to her. While some people might worry about ruffling feathers, Fassbinder-Orth has endured enough bee stings in her life not to fret about these things, especially since she learned at her recent annual review that she was right on track. She works an 8- or 9-hour day, and then "I usually get burned out at four thirty." She goes home and plays with her kids and then does some more work after they go to bed. She plans her experiments as carefully as possible so she rarely has to show up at her lab at night.

Still, sometimes it happens. On one recent Friday evening, when the biology labs were deserted, Fassbinder-Orth took her five-year-old and one-year-old in to finish something up. Normally, "I always take the stairs—I can't wait for elevators," she says. But her daughter wanted to push the buttons, so in they went. Then, in every mother's nightmare, the elevator shook violently and broke down, leaving them stuck and stranded between floors. Fortunately, campus security was able to pry open the doors wide enough that they could all crawl out. Not exactly the way the evening was supposed to go, but when you grow up getting stung by bees a dozen times a day, you learn not to let things like that faze you.

Get Rid of Non-Core-Competency Work

Look over your calendar with this new definition of "work" in mind. In order to spend as much time as possible focusing on your core competencies, you're going to need to get rid of things that you don't do best, and that other people can do as well or better. I want to stress that just because something is not among your core competencies doesn't mean it's not important to the broader universe. The seminars and meetings that Fassbinder-Orth skips matter to someone. I also want to make it clear that if you're working in an organization, particularly a small one, sometimes there are going to be all-hands-on-deck moments when you may choose to pitch in on things that aren't related to your career goals (though, again, this definition is fuzzy—maybe getting a good recommendation from your current supervisor *is* critical). The point is to minimize the amount of time spent on these things so you can focus more of your time on your long-term priorities. Remember, there's a reasonable chance your company won't be around in 10 years, or if it is, that you won't be working for it, no matter how indispensable you are.

You can compress time spent on non-core-competency activities with a three-part strategy:

- Ignore it
- Minimize it, or
- Outsource it

Let's look at each in turn.

IGNORE IT. A great way to clear your professional calendar is to quit projects or give up responsibilities that are leeching time that you could devote to core-competency activities. You can also decline to take these projects on in the first place.

These tactics free up an incredible amount of time. They are also scary as hell, whether you're working for somebody else or for yourself. On one of the freelance writing sites I visit, every few weeks someone starts a thread about how he or she has turned down an assignment. The pay may be lousy, the conditions awful, but inevitably the poster is looking for moral support. "Did I do the right thing?" You worry about burning bridges. You worry that no one will ever hire you again. You worry that your income will plummet.

There may be something to these worries. A few years ago, I decided that I wanted to spend the bulk of my time writing books and longer "serious" articles. I was also starting a family, so I knew that I had to be strategic with my time.

However, more than half my income was coming from writing short pieces, with a big chunk of that coming from one gig writing the non-bylined "Only in America" section of *Reader's Digest* each month. Any work-life-balance book would tell you this was the perfect job for a new mom. It took me 20 hours a week, I could do it from home, and it paid what many people would consider a full-time income. But it also took a lot of mental energy to conceive of, research, and write seven or eight extremely short articles per month. It was hard to find the mental space to think through feature pitches when I was trying to schedule twenty to thirty interviews on eight different topics. So, ultimately, I thanked *Reader's Digest* for giving me the opportunity to write the section for two years, and moved on.

Sure enough, my income fell by half the next year. But in time it came back, mostly from books and longer bylined pieces. Given that the Reader's Digest Association filed for bankruptcy in 2009—and pricey contractors are an easy budget line to cut—it's probably wise that I took the pain when I could do it on my own terms.

While I work for myself, it is also possible to quit projects or refuse work if you're working for someone else. Any job description is an ongoing negotiation, and you'll do best if you're negotiating from a position of strength. Ideally your position of strength is that you are really, really good at what you do. Then, all you have to do is appeal to your supervisor or your team's reason, or else simply do what you wish and figure that no one will demand apologies if things go much better than planned. If you are a rock star at a few tasks, certainly it would be best for all involved if you spent most of your time doing those activities instead of things that are less helpful, overall, to your team's performance. Why not ask or try it?

If you don't work in such a reasonable situation, then you'll need another position of strength, which ultimately comes down to the ability to walk away if you don't get what you want. Perhaps you have another job offer, or you have a financial cushion built up. Hopefully it won't come to that, of course, but I believe people perform better when they don't desperately need their jobs. You're more willing to take risks. You're more willing to stretch yourself and push back. You don't try to ingratiate yourself with the boss under the misguided notion that in an era in which whole departments can be laid off at a moment's notice, this will do anything more than undermine your dignity.

How do you get to that position of confidence? While this isn't a money book, there are two ways that can work for people.

First, if possible, don't be the only person in your family earning an income. While two-income families have their own issues, they give the person who would be the sole breadwinner more flexibility. When you are your family's sole means of support, it's hard to quit a project or take a big career risk that might allow you to focus more on your core competencies. Some partners are supportive of such moves, but others are not.

Second, if you really want to feel less clingy about a job, build up an emergency fund that will cover at least 8–12 months of expenses. You do this by living within your means or, if your base income just matches your needs, moonlighting and banking the rest. This isn't easy, but like anything else, it's a matter of discipline, or in my case, sheer terror of going broke, and it helps if you start young. You don't need much to live on then anyway. When I moved to New York at age twenty-three to embark on my freelance career, I lived so frugally and saved so obsessively that at one point before I got married, I'd built up a cash cushion that was equivalent to two years of my rent, health insurance, groceries, and other bills. While I was being stupid in other ways (such as keeping the cash in a non-interest-bearing checking account), it's liberating to go into any negotiation knowing you can say "no."

MINIMIZE IT. Some things won't come off your plate. Sometimes this is because they have to get done in order to enable your real core-competency work, and sometimes it's because you really should do them. They might not be your purest core competencies, but they have value, and so you want to devote some time to them. How can you make sure they don't eat up too many of your work hours?

That's the question Trista Harris asked herself as she started her new job as executive director of the Headwaters Foundation for Justice in Minneapolis, Minnesota, about a year ago. She wanted to come up with strategies for minimizing important but non-core-competency work as she managed her seven-person staff and tried to leverage her $1.5 million budget for addressing poverty and supporting progressive causes. She decided to do two things.

First, she is as proactive as possible about nipping crises in the bud. Since long, drawn-out multiperson meetings are inefficient, Harris schedules regular, short, one-on-one conversations with the people reporting directly to her. These conversations all have an agenda, but because her staff members know they will happen frequently, "most of them can hold big, pressing questions until that meeting," she says. This does not require a huge investment of time. Two 15-minute meetings per week with each of seven direct reports would come out to only 210 minutes, or less than 4 hours, but this has a big impact on minimizing interruptions. Headwaters is also transitioning to a Results-Only Work Environment, a program pioneered at Best Buy a few years ago that lets people work wherever, whenever, and for however long, as long as their work gets done. Such a model requires setting very specific goals, deadlines, and responsibilities, which turns out to be a good management technique anyway, even if everyone just sits in her cubicle. Untold work time is wasted due to muddled directives that then need to be clarified.

The second strategy is to minimize the time available for lower-value activities. To do this, you need to set a reasonable limit on the total number of hours you intend to work. Trista Harris aims for 40. Harris Brooks, the Palo Pinto General Hospital CEO, aims to leave by 5:00 p.m. each day, as does Carol Fassbinder-Orth. John Anner, the head of the East Meets West Foundation, shoots for 5:30. A 30- to 50-hour week (or at most 60) is perfectly reasonable, no matter what your job title.

Then, after limiting your hours, you commit to filling big portions of your limited time frame with higher-value work. Trista Harris blocks off chunks of Monday, Wednesday, and Friday mornings for strategic thinking time. Before the scheduled strategic thinking time, she chooses the issue she'll think about, and gathers all her research. During these few hours, her door is closed, she doesn't check her e-mail, and she ponders new fund-raising strategies, what philanthropic trends will be in 10 years, or areas Headwaters should enter or exit. If you work in one of those offices with shared electronic calendars where people can stick meetings at any time that appears to be free, you should code your higher-value work times as unavailable. If it's important enough, people will find you. It usually isn't.

You can go a step further and schedule specific times for work housekeeping that needs to get done. Harris deals with e-mail mostly between 2:30 and 3:30 p.m. She'll check it at other times to see if anything urgent has shown up, but she won't respond until later. A woman I met at a retreat not long ago told me that she schedules a block of time to deal with nice-but-not-critical calls on Friday mornings. When someone requests time, she copies her assistant and says, "We should definitely work this out, how about on a Friday?" This is code to her assistant that the matter is not her top priority, and she can stack these calls quickly, one on top of another, in the Friday block.

There are all sorts of other ways to minimize non-core-competency work. Don't travel unless you have to. I'm sure you're fun, but your clients probably don't want to see you nearly as often as you think they do, particularly if they're footing the travel bills. Perhaps they even suspect that you're watching movies on the flight to their headquarters rather than working on the project they've given you. Try teleconferencing software. People who've sampled the highest-end versions say it's uncannily like being in the same room with the people across the table. Work from home whenever you can, and nix the temptation to go to a tangential meeting just because your boss is there and they have doughnuts. Indeed, as John Anner and the East Meets West Foundation have done, try to establish a culture in which every meeting has a point, an agenda, an extremely limited time frame, an outcome, and a bias toward involving fewer people rather than more. Change your mind-set. You weren't invited to the meeting because you're important—you were invited because people don't think you have anything better to do!

All that said, you should try to strike the right balance so you don't underinvest in things that do matter. Sometimes in my attempts to be uber-efficient, I don't spend as much time as I should reading in order to find ideas I could pitch, or trying to find new and bigger markets. I skip industry events because I'm shy in cocktail party situations and bat around 0.050 in finding conference panels that impart enough useful information to justify the time they take. I put off sending "how are you" e-mails to other writers and editors I haven't talked with in a while. Then I schedule 2 hours to do things like this, or show up at a lunch and wind up with some amazing and unforeseen opportunity for a new project or other endeavor. So I try to be smart about it, choosing a few events that seem most promising, and setting goals for myself to, say, meet five new people (there is more about this in Chapter 5).

Harris, likewise, tries to find time for a few things that aren't terribly efficient, but do matter. Long-term, she wants to diversify the field of philanthropy, and so she makes time to mentor young women or people of color who approach her about getting their feet in the door. Nonetheless, since she found herself answering the same questions over and over again at these informational interviews, she created a handout listing resources that people could peruse first, and asks her mentees to send her questions beforehand or a list of people with whom she can facilitate introductions. That keeps these meetings focused on ways she can add value, and minimizes the number of times she needs to say what kinds of résumés foundations are looking for.

OUTSOURCE IT. If you have a dedicated assistant, or one you share with one or two other people, great. Find one who isn't just able to handle administrative tasks, but excels at the problem-solving part of the job and sees it as his mission to advance you.

However, in today's lean, high-tech economy, such situations are rarer than they used to be. Harris used to have an assistant. Then the woman moved to India, and she decided to use the freed-up funds for programming rather than support staff. When people are OK with leaving voice mail, having someone answer your phone becomes less important. We all type our own letters now. Anyway, the reality is that the best outsourcing is not about getting rid of work you don't want to do. If it's truly dumb work, maybe it doesn't have to be done at all. Maybe processes can be automated. As one example, that once laborious assistant task of calling around for a last-minute dinner reservation is much easier in the era of OpenTable.com, when you can type in your time and the number of people in your party and figure out who has available seats.

Smart outsourcing means remembering that "Just because I can do something doesn't mean I should be doing something," as Harris puts it. "It's really important to invest in people's professional development." If you run a foundation devoted to achieving justice, you'll soon notice that there's a lot of injustice out there, and relatively easy ways to correct it, which leads to "death by a thousand opportunities." You simply cannot take them all on. It's not just a matter of protecting your personal life, it's a matter of realizing that you won't invest adequately in the professional activities that matter most if you're busy doing other things.

Consequently, if you want to get the most out of your 168 hours, you need a work team and a home team, all focused on their core competencies, so you can focus on yours. On the work side, some of these people may work for your organization, and some may not. As part of her mission to diversify the foundation world, Harris created a blog called "New Voices of Philanthropy" that is separate from Headwaters. She personally hired someone from eLance to design the site. Then she hired a virtual assistant to do research for the posts. This outsourcing broadens her reach while saving her time. When she's invited to speak at conferences or on panels that she doesn't think she'd be best for, she also sometimes reaches outside her organization and suggests people who would relish the opportunity. "I have a really broad professional network," she says, and creating opportunities for these people leads to more goodwill for Headwaters and her.

She obviously outsources things to her staff, too, here with an eye toward building up people's skills and expertise. She gets invited to numerous external meetings and community events—which could lead to great projects—simply because she is the head of the foundation. But some of the meetings deal with topics that are closer to other people's portfolios, and she wants her staff to feel fully responsible for their work. So she asks, "Is there somebody else that might be more appropriate," sends a staff member, solo, and tries to resist the temptation to attend just because a big name might be in attendance or, for that matter, because she might do a good job. In economics, the law of comparative advantage states that even if one party in a transaction is better at everything than the other party, it can sometimes still make sense for both to specialize, since time and resources are always going to be limited.

Interestingly, she's been implementing some of the same lessons at home with her two children. On the day we talked, her ten-year-old daughter forgot her homework, a crisis that came to light long after they'd gotten in the car and were cruising toward school. In the past, Harris might have turned around and driven the extra 45 minutes, total, to retrieve the assignment. "I don't want to see my kids disappointed," she says, but she decided that instead this could be a good opportunity to teach her daughter that she needs to be responsible for dealing with her own work, rather than relying on Mom. Harris started a discussion with her daughter on how the girl could approach the teacher and work out a solution. This counseling utilized her core-competency skills as a mom, rather than the lower-value skill of playing fetch.

Boost Efficiency by Getting Better at What You Do

Though you will save many hours by seizing control of your calendar, and clearing away non-core-competency activities, in the long run, the best way to create more time is to actually get better at your professional craft.

I don't like the idea of compensating people for "years of experience," since many people labor in the trenches for years without improving. But all the same, it's quite exciting to realize that it is possible to get better at your work over time. Sometimes you get better at little things that make a big difference in productivity, even if you wouldn't have thought of them. A chef frying eggs never cracks them in anything but a perfect circle. When I was first writing professionally, I'd be assigned a story at 1,000 words. I'd crank out a draft, hit "word count," and find the tally to be 1,600—very difficult to hack down without changing the focus of the piece. After eight years, this never happens. If I'm assigned a 1,000-word piece, my first draft word count will be between 900 and 1,100 words. I'm not counting as I write, I just have a sense of how long any given word count is. I know what kind of thesis will fill that length when I'm writing tightly, and how much research to do.

Some people are naturally better at things than others, and you should choose work that is aligned with the things you do best. But just because you do things best doesn't means you can't get better. The only way this happens is through focused "deliberate practice," as Geoff Colvin's book *Talent Is Overrated*, makes clear.

You do this, Colvin says, by delving deeply into your craft, and studying other examples of it critically to learn what you can. You analyze your own work and have others do so too, focusing on your weak spots and laboring again and again to make these better. You have to do a lot of whatever it is you do. If you mean to maintain a personal life, which you should, then the bulk of your work hours should be focused on the meat of your professional craft, with every assignment viewed as a chance to improve.

In the past year, as I've been writing this book, I've tried to implement these lessons in my own life. I now aim to read one novel a month, along with longer narrative nonfiction pieces, to see what works. It is comforting to see that even the great writers in the English language have their awkward moments; I have realized that the important thing is not to be flawless, but to be compelling enough to make up for the flaws. I have hired coaches to analyze my writing. I analyze my own writing. Do I use the word "actually" too much? I learn to go through and strike it half the time. I write as much as I can, aiming for more than half of my working hours. If I don't have an assignment, I blog or write in my journal, or sketch scenes for my next bout of fiction. All of these are better uses of my time than checking Facebook or writing short pieces on topics I don't care about.

As you focus on improving your craft, make a list of the signs that you are getting better. Maybe more of your proposals are being accepted, freeing up hours in the day to focus on delivery or landing bigger fish. Potential clients cold-call you. Planning lessons or menus or landscapes takes less time. You seem to be getting lucky more often because you are making your own luck. When these things happen often enough, you have the power to say no to distractions. And when they seem to be happening all the time—when you are a smooth-running machine— then you can launch your career to the next level.

Controlling Your Calendar

Your "List of 100 Dreams" covers what you want, personally and professionally, out of life. This chapter looked at achieving your professional goals within the working part of your 168 hours. Some big goals may require decades, but even those can be broken down to the level of life as we live it—that is, 1 hour at a time. Ask yourself these questions:

- What do I want to accomplish, professionally, in the next year? That is, what could I say in a year-end review or in the family Christmas letter?
- What actionable steps will these goals require? How many hours will these steps take?
- How many hours do I want to work per week? Multiply this by 50 to get a rough total for the year (1,500 to 3,000 hours if you're working 30–60 hours per week).
- Are my goals reasonable within this time frame?
- Where can I block these tasks in to my work schedule?
- What do I want off my plate at work?
- Of these things, what can I ignore? Minimize? Outsource?
- How can I get better at my professional craft?

THESE ARE SOME SIGNS THAT I HAVE GOTTEN BETTER
AT MY PROFESSIONAL CRAFT OVER THE YEARS:

1. _____

2. _____

3. _____

· 5 ·
Anatomy of a Breakthrough

The story of Leah Ingram's career breakthrough comes in two versions.

Here's the first, the kind of dumb-luck tale you might hear at a cocktail party. A few years ago, Ingram, her husband, and two daughters moved to her dream house: a white Colonial on a shady street in New Hope, Pennsylvania. Unfortunately, due to maintenance costs and some hangover from a blown home-equity loan on their last place, living in this dream house turned out to be more expensive than Ingram's family imagined. As the economy tightened, she hunted for ways to be thrifty. She started blogging about her family's adventures doing laundry in cold water, using their library cards, and shopping in thrift stores. When *BusinessWeek* decided to do a cover story titled "The New Age of Frugality" in the fall of 2008, a reporter found Ingram's blog and featured her rather attractive family in a photo spread. Before long, she had landed a book deal to write a tome called *Suddenly Frugal*. It was a big career break for this long-time freelance writer.

Here's the second version of the story. Nothing about the *BusinessWeek* article or the book deal was random.

A few years ago, Ingram, who had carved a niche writing about etiquette and nuptials, decided, "If I have to write about another wedding,

I'm going to put my head through the wall." She'd been raised in a frugal family, and finding herself in more debt than she liked as she entered her forties, she decided that she wanted to make low-budget living her new area of expertise. "Having seen so many people who did a blog that launched into a book, I sort of threw caution to the wind and just said I'm giving it up to faith and fate that this will actually work." She committed to posting on her new frugality blog roughly 5 days a week as she tried to raise her profile in this area. She knew blogging could easily take 5–10 of her 168 hours, and they would be uncompensated, but as she explained later, "The topic is important to me, I think it is timely, and will lead to a book, so what the hell."

Things went swimmingly at first. She met a "big shot agent" at a journalism conference in early 2007. She later sent him a query about her book idea, which at the time was styled as saving green (money) while being green (environmentally friendly). He liked the concept and agreed to take her on. But when her agent shopped the proposal around for the rest of 2007, he got "nothing, nothing, nothing . . . We missed the green boat. The green boat had already sailed. He went from the A list to the B list to the C list" of publishers, getting rejected every time. So Ingram just kept carving out time to blog about frugality amid the other assignments that were paying the bills.

At times she wondered if the investment was worth it. But after a year of diligent 5-days-a-week posting and advertising her blog through various social media, people started to notice her. The economy cratered. News media outlets wanted examples of frugal families. Some found her, and she found others by responding to queries on the "Help a Reporter Out" service (an e-mail list that I've also used to find "real people"—including for this book). She started doing interviews. Colgate-Palmolive, the consumer goods company, contacted her about doing an Earth Day satellite media tour as the "Lean Green Mom," which netted her five figures for, in essence, one day of work. "I was starting to get a sense that this blogging thing might actually lead to something," she says.

In September 2008, the *BusinessWeek* reporter Steve Hamm posted a query on "Help a Reporter Out" stating that he was seeking newly frugal people to profile. Ingram sent him her story and a link to her blog, which, by that point, was fleshed out enough for Hamm to know that Ingram could speak coherently to reporters and on camera, that she was near enough to New York City to visit, but not in New York City (reporters for national media outlets never want to write about New York people), that she looked acceptable enough to feature in a magazine, and that she had made progress on getting out of debt (she paid off a $20,000 car loan early). He called, then came out to interview the family in person. His coworkers descended on the house in New Hope to take photos and video clips for the *BusinessWeek* Web site. When I opened my October 8 issue, on "The New Age of Frugality," there was Ingram, her husband, her kids, and her dog staring back at me.

I wasn't the only one who read the story. So did an editor at Workman Publishing, who loved the concept and asked if Ingram had a book proposal. Well, she said, funny you should ask. She revamped her prior proposal to lean more toward the frugal side and less toward the "green" side. Unfortunately, the Workman editor couldn't sell it to the editorial board. But Ingram's agent convinced her to shop her book again with a new name and a new slant. In November 2008, he sent it around to publishers. To take her mind off what she figured was going to be yet another round of rejections, Ingram wrote a draft of a 58,000-word young adult novel in January 2009. Just in January. Seriously. But finally everything clicked. By the end of the month, she had an offer from Adams Media. "Not a huge offer, but it was an offer," she says. After nearly two years of daily labor, she could start writing her book in this new area of expertise, and take her career to the next level.

Maybe, like Ingram, you feel like your career and your life are at a turning point. You know you're in the right job, or at least you're close. You've seized control of your schedule and have cleared as much of your non-core-competency work from your calendar as possible. You've engaged in "deliberate practice" of your professional craft for a while, maybe even the 10,000 hours necessary to compete for world-class status. Now what? How do you achieve a breakthrough?

Ingram's story—the second version, at least—is typical of these tales, in the sense that it involves massive amounts of undernoticed or undercompensated prep work, and making the most of chances when they come. On the other hand, I think her story gives plenty of reason for optimism, too, in the context of figuring out how to allocate our 168 hours to get the most out of life. While Ingram certainly worked hard, she did not have to turn into a hermit to turn her vision into a reality. She did it while billing six figures on other projects—something I can attest, as a fellow freelancer, is hard to do. She achieved it while finding time to write a novel, walk her dog for an hour each morning, serve as the statistician for her daughter's basketball team, and cook dinner for her family most days.

I find this encouraging because her story does not fit the dominant cultural narrative that achieving big new things in a career is necessarily going to conflict with a full personal life. While that may not be the intended message of all the work-life-balance literature out there, it's a message all the same. In 2009's *Womenomics,* Claire Shipman and Katty Kay write that they'd "offer each other private advice on turning down plum jobs and avoiding tantalizing promotions that might upend the hard-won balance of our daily lives." You can't open business publications these days without reading glowing stories about companies that allow people to "downshift" or make lateral career moves, or universities that postpone tenure decisions after people have children and the like, all in the name of work-life balance. There is nothing wrong with these ideas. In many cases, they're quite good ones. They're certainly better for the economy and people in general than the idea that work needs to be 100 percent of your time or 0 percent of your time. But as we saw in the earlier chapters, work rarely consumes 100 percent of anyone's time, even if people think it does. A full personal life—as we'll see in the later chapters—doesn't require 100 percent of anyone's time, either.

So while I think work-life-balance programs are great, I disagree with the assumption inherent in some of them, which is that it is not possible to build a Career while maintaining an intense personal life that involves raising multiple children and/or engaging in intense fitness pursuits and volunteer activities or other passions. It is possible to ratchet up your career while investing in other parts of your life as well.

It isn't *easy*, certainly not as easy in the short run as outsourcing 100 percent of your personal life to your spouse or destroying your health and relationships out of some misguided notion that this is what is required for your "art." But since these actions have their own long-term consequences, people who want to get the most out of their 168 hours follow a slightly different formula for achieving career breakthroughs than the dominant cultural narrative, that of the recluse, deems necessary.

This is the anatomy of a breakthrough for busy, balanced people:

Know what the next level looks like
Understand the metrics and gatekeepers
Work up to the point of diminishing returns
Spin a good story
Be open to possibilities and plan for opportunities
Be ready to ride the wave

Know What the Next Level Looks Like

Before she started blogging, Ingram figured out what the next level of her career would look like. She would be considered a frugality expert with a subspecialty in reducing waste, and she would write a book on that topic. Having landed that, she's now set her sights on hosting a reality TV show devoted to frugal living or frugal makeovers.

What would the next level look like for you? You probably already thought about this question while reading the section on seizing control of your schedule in Chapter 4, but if you haven't, carve out at least half an hour to daydream about it several times over the next few weeks. Think about the question during your commute, or while you're jogging. Try to picture the next level as specifically as possible. Maybe you work in an organization where the next level is clear: you make partner, get promoted to vice president, or become a full professor. Maybe you lead a small organization, but you'd like to lead a bigger one. Maybe you're a small business owner, and you want to take your revenue up a notch. Put a dollar figure on that notch. I recently attended an American Express competition for women business owners where these entrepreneurs had to announce their receipts to a panel of judges, and publicly commit to boosting their revenue, be it to $250,000, $500,000, or $1 million. American Express had a very specific reason for asking business owners to do this. Once you picture an outcome, it becomes easier to focus your efforts on meeting it (and, of course, businesses that rake in $1 million charge more on their AmEx cards than ones that pull in $100,000).

Feel free to aim big. Few calculated risks end in disaster, and any investment made in a project you care deeply about is likely to generate some return. Even if a $100,000 business owner aims for $1 million and doesn't hit it, as long as she hasn't bet the whole farm, reaching $200,000 would be a nice consolation prize.

Another tip for making a breakthrough more likely: start behaving, the best you can, as if achieving the next level is a done deal. Interact with your clients in the collegial way a partner would. Think of yourself as a frugality expert; think of your time as being worth the billable rate you'd like to achieve. Much of life is how you frame it. If you want others to believe you are successful, it helps to believe this yourself.

Understand the Metrics and Gatekeepers

To land her book deal, Ingram knew she needed an agent, a book proposal, and a business case for someone to publish her. By the time Adams Media bought *Suddenly Frugal,* she could point to blog traffic that hit five thousand visitors some days, a promised promotional tie-in with RecycleBank—a company that distributes smart recycling bins nationally and rewards recyclers with points at various businesses— plus her proven ability, as evidenced by the *Business Week* article, to garner publicity.

In other words, she could show a publisher that giving her a chance wouldn't be a big risk.

Once you know what the next level looks like for your career, you, likewise, need to figure out the metrics and gatekeepers. Sometimes organizations publicize these standards, or else are fairly consistent in their decision-making. Carol Fassbinder-Orth, the Creighton University professor profiled in Chapter 4, knows that she needs three to five publications in major journals plus a certain volume of grants to get tenure. If she aims for the high end of this range, or just over it, she will know her chances are good.

If these standards aren't publicized or obvious, you can still figure them out. Interview several people who have attained the level you want. What do they think mattered? Who actually made the decision? What do these gatekeepers care about? The answer may surprise you. Many people think that if they quietly and diligently do the tasks outlined in their job description, coming early and staying late, they will be rewarded. This is not necessarily true. Often, you need a powerful champion (or two or three) who gets it in her head that the organization will not function without you, and consequently, she will bang on the conference table during the decision meeting if she doesn't get her way. If you're serious about your career, it should not be hard to find two or three senior people in your organization or industry who honestly like you. But it is your responsibility to seek these people out. Figure out who might share your general attitude toward life, and set up opportunities to work with them. It is also your responsibility to give these people a track record of results they can point to while pounding on the conference table.

What should that track record look like? This differs between fields. In creative or knowledge-based careers, you often need a portfolio showing what you can do. Unfortunately, many people—and particularly young people recently sprung from school, where you'd never do a project that wasn't assigned—believe they need to wait for someone to give them an opportunity to create this. In highly regulated fields, this may be true, but often it isn't. At a conference recently, a young woman who wanted to get into public relations asked me how she could show results even though she'd never worked in the field before. Since she had a good sense of what PR entailed, I suggested finding someone who needed help—a starving artist or a small nonprofit—and volunteering to create a publicity campaign. You don't need a license to do PR; if her press releases or events garnered coverage, she would have a portfolio every bit as impressive as someone with more experience.

One thing to keep in mind as you build your track record is that people in almost all fields love numbers. They love numbers because impressions are fuzzy. Numbers, even when abused, appear to provide objective evidence of your argument. They convince people where words do not. You should use this to your advantage.

While some people work in industries or jobs that make finding numbers easy—for instance, a fund-raiser who clearly boosted an organization's budget by $1 million—the fact that your job doesn't involve many numbers doesn't matter. Find them. Track them down. Create situations where they'll occur. Make them look good. The choir I sing in, the Young New Yorkers' Chorus, had a sense that we were reaching a young audience consisting of people who were not typical classical music patrons. But in order to make sure, we created a survey and pestered everyone at one particular concert to fill it out. We learned that 80 percent of our audience was between the ages of twenty-five and thirty-five, and the majority did not regularly attend other classical music concerts. Being able to cite that statistic has helped with donor outreach and grant applications.

To flesh out the numbers, it also helps to have a certain number of testimonials to go with your track record. Imagine your career as a movie. Who would write the blurbs on the poster? What would you like them to say? If you work in a public manner, such as serving in an elected office, you might get spontaneous fan mail. But in most lines of work, you'll need to get in the habit of asking the people you work with to write short blurbs for your personal use about exactly why you are so wonderful.

As a side note, these testimonials are great to haul out and read when you go through rough patches in your life and career.

Work to the Point of Diminishing Returns

I don't think it should come as a surprise that achieving a career breakthrough will require you to work hard. Ingram spent two years putting in time, every day, to lay the groundwork for becoming a frugality expert. There is much to be said for working efficiently. But there is something to be said for sheer volume of hours, too. Though I know this is heretical for a time-management book, for some people, working more—at least to the point where additional hours don't help much—may be the key to career advancement, and to making all parts of your life work better.

Here's what I mean. Much of the literature in the work-life-balance or time-management genre—including from experts I admire—approaches this issue from the perspective that this thing called "work" is keeping you from having a personal life. Leave aside that, as I'm writing this in summer 2009, the average American workweek is down to 33 hours and that, as I've noted many times already, most people claiming to work 80-hour weeks are mistaken. Nonetheless, we feel overworked and so, to make the pieces fit, the work-life-balance literature tells us, we must negotiate a way to change our work schedules. I'm a big fan of flexibility and telecommuting, but a growing number of women in particular think that a bigger accommodation—working part-time—is the key to "having it all." (Very few men work part-time by choice). A Pew Research Center survey found that between 1997 and 2007, the percentage of working moms of kids under age eighteen who say full-time work is the best solution for them fell from 32 to 21, and the percentage who said part-time work was ideal rose from 48 to 60. (Interestingly, some 16 percent of stay-at-home moms said full-time work would be ideal and 33 percent said part-time work would be, meaning that while more than 80 percent of working moms want to be in the workforce, only half of at-home moms prefer their status).

I am not surprised by these numbers. But I worry that this widespread—and I'd say inaccurate—perception that full-time work and a personal life are invariably at odds leads to some unnecessary and often career-limiting trade-offs. If you are serious about advancing your career, there really is a limit to how low your work hours should go, but not because you need to impress the boss or keep him from assigning you to the "mommy track." Many of us don't have bosses to blame these days. There are certain economic principles that limit the efficacy of part-time work.

Economists often talk about something called "returns to scale," which basically means how much additional benefit you gain from additional inputs. Because most activities involve start-up costs, there are often increasing returns up to an optimum point. After that, returns diminish, because demand is not infinite, and the inputs can be more profitably used for other things. For instance, it is just as easy to make a pan of brownies as it is to make one brownie, and if you have kids, they will definitely lap up that whole first dozen. However, if you make a dozen pans of brownies, you'll run out of space in the fridge and your family will get so sick of brownies they'll start hankering for fruit. The brownies will go stale and you'll have to dump them, meaning that the eggs you used for the last few pans would have been more profitably employed as breakfast.

So it goes with work hours. In order to do 1 hour of work, you need to get to your workplace and—even if you work from home—figure out what you should be doing and start attacking the problem. All of these actions involve effort, which means that if you only worked 1 hour per week, you wouldn't get much out of it. But the second, third, and fourth hours are more productive. Each hour has additional benefits as you roll through your projects and get in a groove, or start seeking out new opportunities. At some point, these benefits stop accruing because you lose intensity, but right up until that point, every additional hour can generate a huge return. And unfortunately, for many reasons, including cultural assumptions, procrastination, and workplace distractions, a number of people who otherwise love their work stop before that point.

The ideal workweek for feeling like you're getting somewhere varies among people. Given that the overwhelming majority of workers clock fewer than 60 hours per week, I'd wager that the point of diminishing returns is almost universally less than that. That's certainly the impression I've gotten from visiting or interviewing people at some dysfunctional workplaces where you can show up at 8:00 p.m. and people are clearly in leisure mode—lingering over takeout, shooting the breeze, wandering the hallways—but won't go home because the culture says success means staying late. For me, the point of diminishing returns is 45–50 hours per week, which is on the high end and is a function of my stubborn refusal to specialize. Many others do better with less. But from talking with hundreds of people about their careers for this book and other projects, I have learned that in most fields, it is very difficult to get to this state of forward momentum—where you are improving at your craft, seeking out new opportunities, and making a name for yourself—working fewer than 30 of your 168 hours.

This is actually a lot, because these are real hours—not lingering-over-takeout-face-time hours or hours spent on calls you didn't need to be on, or responding to e-mail you didn't need to read. I suspect one reason New York's mayor, Michael Bloomberg, persists in telling graduating classes in his stump commencement speech that "it never hurts to be the first one in in the morning—and the last one to leave" is that this is the only way you can clock 30 hours of real work in some offices! People interrupt you all day or you put off your most important work until 5:00 p.m., and then you finally get serious. You may stay until 10:00 p.m., but you only really worked 5 hours. A 60-hour workweek can easily consist of only 25 hours of real work if you're not careful.

But that's the problem. Most people aren't. A few are hypervigilant, and can get by with less. But if you're working only 20 hours per week and trying to build a Big Career, these hours can't look anything like what other people think of as work. A single stray phone call, a slow-loading Web page or a printer on the fritz can throw the whole week off. Every minute has to be planned and full so that you not only do the stuff of your job, but also the long-range planning and prospecting and occasional "inefficient" networking that leads to opportunities down the road. Leah Ingram tries to confine her workweek to the time her children are in school, which, if you subtract the hour she spends walking the dog briskly every morning, leaves her with 25 hours. To fit the bulk of her work into that time, she often sets a kitchen timer for 30 minutes and races through assignments on turbospeed. When it dings, she looks up to breathe or goes to the bathroom, then puts her head back down for several more sprints during the day. There is zero downtime. There is little time for e-mail during those hours. This explains why, when I got to know her a few years ago after she had taken on a project editing an education magazine and assigned me a few pieces, much of my e-mail from her came time-stamped at hours like 9:36 p.m., 7:09 p.m., or 8:32 p.m. These e-mail sessions probably came out to at least an hour a day, or 5 hours a week, which puts us back up to 30 hours.

Now, in most work-life-balance books, working at 9:36 p.m. falls in the "horror story" category. But no boss was making Ingram answer e-mail at night. Like me, she works for herself. If she'd wanted to work fewer hours, she could easily have stopped blogging. But if she hadn't worked those extra hours on the margins—those hours with increasing returns—she wouldn't have sold her book. She'd be a much less happy person about life in general if she hadn't achieved that breakthrough. When people feel like they're moving forward in their jobs, this gives them a lot of zeal for the rest of their 168 hours. This includes being more present for their families when they are around, and watching less TV.

If you're not convinced by that fuzzy argument that working more can sometimes help your personal life in addition to your career, then let me try using numbers.

Working the 30–60 hours per week most people find necessary to achieve a career breakthrough still leaves you with plenty of time for other things. If you work 60 hours a week and sleep 8 hours a night, this leaves 52 hours a week, or nearly 7.5 hours per day, for other things. A 50-hour week leaves 62 hours, or about 9 hours per day, and a 40-hour week leaves 72 hours, or more than 10 per day.

This is a lot of time. It's so much time that it's unclear what's "balanced" about working just 20 hours for pay, and thus having 92 waking, nonworking hours to fill with other things. Just as several of the people profiled in Chapter 4 found that they could force themselves to be more effective at work by limiting their total work hours, I believe that limiting your total nonworking hours forces certain efficiencies there as well, most notably on the housework front. There is more about this in the next few chapters, but suffice to say, if you think in the context of 168-hour weeks, a 40-hour workweek comes a lot closer to being balanced between your professional life and personal time than, say, one of 15 hours.

So, if you really do want to take your career to the next level, take a good look at your hours from the time diary you kept in Chapter 1 and tallied in Chapter 2. Are you spending enough time focused on your professional craft?

If an honest accounting of your weekly hour total is under 30, or it's over 30 but you don't feel like you have time to plan and prospect for opportunities, see if you can add 1–2 focused hours per day. You can do this either by clearing your calendar of non-core-competency activities at work, or by scheduling a shift when your kids go to bed or during their weekend activities.

Another solution is to trade off kid time with your spouse, or spring for a few more hours of child care. If you choose high-quality care, and are truly focused on being present with your children during the times you're not working, then your kids might like the variety. You may be surprised at how quickly you will earn that investment back. Lyn Franklin Hoyt of Nashville, Tennessee, co-owns a business called Berkeley Tandem, which designs and sells framed recognition products such as employee-of-the-month wall plaques. When we first talked in 2008, she had around 20 hours of child care per week, so that was how much she worked. When we talked again in early 2009, she had added more child care and was hitting 30 hours per week on a regular basis. Net result? Berkeley Tandem's revenue had jumped 30 percent since she started putting in the additional time.

Spin a Good Story

In this competitive age, everyone knows you need to be "The Brand Called You" (as Tom Peters announced in a 1997 cover story for *Fast Company*) to have a prayer at a coherent career that won't be outsourced to India. And so business blogs teem with tips on personal branding— the idea of creating and marketing an image that will follow you through your career. As I'm writing this in 2009, the gurus all agree that you should promote yourself via social media such as Facebook, Twitter, and LinkedIn. This is probably wise advice, and I'm sure I'll be visible on all three places when this book comes out.

But the electronic world shifts quickly, so rather than create a how-to that will be dated in 10 months, I want to talk more about the philosophy of personal branding and what it should and shouldn't mean. What a lot of this comes down to is that people are hungry for authentic stories. Since our prehistoric days around the campfire, humans have had a deep desire for narratives, and particularly amid the information clutter we encounter now, we are drawn to identities and images that have been honed over a lifetime. We want stories that make sense. People who get profiled prominently in the media or talked about a lot in their companies—and often launched to the next level in their careers in the process—tend to be able to spin good yarns about why they're doing what they're doing.

As a journalist, I admit that I am sometimes cynical about this. Real lives rarely follow the kinds of paths that make for completely coherent narratives. But we seek out epiphanies all the same, and so stories are a great tool. People do many things in their lives, and you can choose events and thoughts from your past, and choose certain projects in the present and the future, that make for better story lines.

Mary Mazzio, for instance, is a former Olympic rower who had built a successful legal career, making partner at the firm now known as Brown Rudnick. She always wanted to be in the movie business, though, and so, a little over a decade ago, after writing scripts on the side for years, she decided it was time to take this part of her professional identity to the next level.

She gave serious thought to her personal brand—that is, what she wanted to be known for. She had always been drawn to stories of people who overcame obstacles to create a new path for themselves, failing multiple times in the process. She could identify one such story in her own life; as she says, "I fought to get on the Olympic team tooth and nail." Before finally being chosen in 1992, "I was cut more times than you can shake a pair of scissors at."

So for her first major film (mostly executed while she was on maternity leave from her law firm), she hunted for a story that conveyed this theme, and that would capitalize on her unique knowledge. She chose the story of Chris Ernst, an Olympian and rower at Yale who fought to get women's sports taken seriously at this storied university. Mazzio trusted that her personal connection to rowing would intrigue people who heard about the project. "You have to be able to articulate the compelling nature of what you do," she says. If you can't excite a reporter in 20 seconds, or you can't excite an investor in 20 seconds, then you're unlikely to *ever* excite them.

Fortunately, Mazzio's personal narrative, coupled with the quality of the film that became known as *A Hero for Daisy*, grabbed people's attention, and the film was shown nationally on ESPN and Oxygen.

She has continued this idea of advancing her personal brand with the subsequent films released by her production company, 50 Eggs. *Apple Pie* (2002) featured the stories of mothers of professional athletes; Mazzio could talk about her own mother's influence on her Olympic dreams and her experiences as a mom as well. *Lemonade Stories* (2004) tweaked this format to focus on mothers of famous entrepreneurs such as Richard Branson; by this point, Mazzio could talk about her own experiences starting a company, and how the lessons she learned from the moms she filmed changed her parenting style. Her most recent film, *TEN9EIGHT* (2009), features the stories of young inner-city entrepreneurs who have overcome long odds, sometimes failing as many times as Mazzio got cut from the Olympic team. There are literally millions of stories a documentary filmmaker could tell; by choosing ones that gave her a great personal answer to the question of why she cared about the topic, Mazzio increased the odds that her films would stand out in a crowded market.

No matter what your line of work, you, too, can spin a story about it that will help take your career to the next level. Carve out an hour or two of your next 168 hours to ponder this question. How do you want people to perceive you? If someone were to write a profile of you for a company newsletter or, for that matter, *The New Yorker*, what would you hope it would say? Ask your trusted friends and family members what they see as your story. Ask family members in particular for memories that lend credence to this platform. For instance, if you are a consultant who's into optimizing business revenue, your mom might remind you that you used to check the weather forecast as a kid and would choose the hottest days for putting a lemonade stand up near construction sites. If you're a litigator who perceives herself as taking on the big guys, your father might recall that as a toddler, you'd walk up to neighborhood dogs that were twice your size. If you own a small business, you already know that people always ask entrepreneurs why they took the plunge. Having a good answer can earn you the kind of attention and word-of-mouth marketing that will raise your revenue by an order of magnitude.

The best stories not only reach back to earlier events, they include the present. What activities could you do now that would challenge and excite you, and also enhance your brand and make for a better narrative? If you're a free agent looking to establish your credentials, you could start a professional organization devoted to your work, or take on a leadership role within one. You could write an article, blog, or book chronicling your expertise. If you're a doctor who wants to be known as an expert on public health, a stint volunteering somewhere exotic (for instance, a primary care clinic in Tanzania) will not only do good for the world, it will give you great stories.

I want to stress that you do have to be careful when creating these narratives. People are hungry for *authentic* tales. Phoniness is counterproductive. I avoid profiling people I perceive as too packaged. College admissions officers sigh as they talk about seventeen-year-olds who seem to have arranged to have life-changing experiences in order to write about them. The past few presidential campaigns have indulged more than necessary in the idea of personal narratives, with Senator John Kerry, for instance, widely viewed as overplaying his Vietnam adventures and President George W. Bush failing to convince many people that he was a cowboy from Midland. Some people really do have better stories than others. Mazzio really was on the 1992 Olympic rowing team. Like anything, you want to strike a balance—presenting your story in the best way possible while not claiming you're something you're not.

If you're not sure how to present your story, read a few books on publicity, or interview people in this field, and spend some time thinking back through your formative experiences. Chances are, there are a few that might be worth highlighting, and things you can do now that will cement the coherence of your story. None of this requires that you post twenty times a day on Twitter. But in a cluttered world, if you want to achieve a career breakthrough while maintaining a personal life, it helps to have other people believe that your breakthrough is the next logical step in the story.

Be Open to Possibilities; Plan for Opportunities

Even if you're clear on where you're going, have figured out the metrics and gatekeepers, are working as hard as you have in your life and have a good story, career breakthroughs can still require luck. At a management consulting or law firm, it will be more challenging to make partner if some random economic catastrophe swallows a major client right before your evaluation. The Boogie Wipes creators Julie Pickens and Mindee Doney, profiled in Chapter 3, are great businesswomen with innovative products, but a key reason their sales zoomed to $5 million in 2 years is that they got their goods into Wal-Mart. This retailing giant accepts only a tiny fraction of the new products that come its way; with such low odds, there are plenty of good products designed by great businesswomen that *don't* make it.

You cannot remove randomness from the universe. You can, however, use your 168 hours to stack the odds in your favor. To do this, you have to place many bets, and leave nothing you can control to chance.

In other words, you have to be open to possibilities, and plan for opportunities.

That's the message I got from the story of Leanne Shear and Tracey Toomey, who met while bartending at Onieal's on Grand Street in Manhattan in 2002. Neither was thrilled to be slinging cocktails; Shear was an aspiring writer and Toomey an aspiring actress, with "aspiring" in this case meaning broke. That need for cash drove them even closer together. They soon discovered that they had "incredible business chemistry," according to Shear, with an ability to talk up each other's tips from the moneyed (and often borderline insane) patrons whose stories they absorbed as they served them drinks. "We became best friends almost immediately," Shear says. One night while taking out the trash, the two started talking about writing a book together chronicling their experiences.

That could have been the end of it—a passing fancy—except that Shear and Toomey made a critical decision. They didn't keep quiet about their idea. They talked about it with each other; they talked about it with various patrons. Sure enough, one night two men sat down at the bar. One of them made several inappropriate comments to Toomey. After he left, his companion apologized and said he was simply having drinks with the man for business reasons. Toomey asked what line of work required such care and feeding of difficult people, and the man said he was a literary agent. "Oh," Toomey said. "*We're* writing a book." This wasn't true in the strictest sense—"we hadn't yet written anything"—but the man asked her what it was about, and she regaled the tales. He said it sounded like good material. Would Toomey and Shear be available to meet a colleague of his who represented such work?

They agreed immediately, and spent the next week furiously writing down ideas to present to Elisabeth Weed, who now runs her own literary agency in New York. She encouraged them to fictionalize their material and aim straight for the then-hot genre of urban chick lit laced with satire (à la *The Devil Wears Prada, The Nanny Diaries*). If they acted fast, they might be able to cash in on the trend.

This was nothing but an opportunity—an offer by an agent to represent them, but with no guarantee it would work. Still, Shear and Toomey decided to give it their best shot. They knew they needed more material, and the focus to write. So they took off for the Hamptons to bartend for the summer at Star Room, a club. They'd work until 4:00 a.m. most nights, and then haul themselves to Starbucks in the morning. "We just wrote all summer long," Shear says. They hammered out a process for leveraging both of their skills. Toomey, the actress, was better at dialogue. Shear, the writer, was better at description. They'd brainstorm ideas for a chapter, turn that into a detailed outline, then each go off and crank out a version. They'd compare versions, and then spend 2–3 days splicing together the best parts of each. Over the summer, they produced more than a hundred pages. Weed edited the work and shopped it around. They got a meeting with the Broadway Books division of Random House. Shear and Toomey walked into a room full of suits and proceeded to sell themselves as media-savvy young women whose own bartending experiences would make a great backstory for anyone looking to publicize the book (see the section, above, about spinning a good yarn). Random House bought that pitch, and bought the book, *The Perfect Manhattan*, for six figures, a rare sum for first novels.

There is a lot of being in the right place at the right time in this story, but Shear and Toomey certainly helped their fairy godmother along. Though neither wanted to be bartending, rather than view it as a setback ("You're supposed to be on Broadway and you're behind the bar!" as Toomey puts it), they turned that reality into a career-building project, and used their working hours effectively by talking with people they'd never meet otherwise. They used the situation to get better at their crafts, studying the way characters acted and told their stories. When opportunities did present themselves, they did everything they could to plan for the possibility of success, even if that meant keeping up a bleary-eyed schedule of writing in Starbucks rather than zonking out on the beach.

You don't have to bartend to be open to possibilities, but as Shear and Toomey did, it helps to step outside your comfort zone. You can talk to people in line at the coffee shop or while picking up your kids at day care. Ask to join a group of coworkers you don't know well for lunch. Mention your plans and projects to other people at events. I wound up interviewing Shear and Toomey because I decided to show up at a 1-800-Flowers media event on a slow day of writing in spring 2009, and mentioned this book project to someone who ran the Celebrations Web site, which Shear and Toomey blog for on occasion. How random is that? Send an e-mail to someone you haven't talked with in ages. Nine out of ten times, reaching out won't result in anything, but it's like planting seeds. The more seeds you plant and water, the better the chances that one will sprout.

When seeds do sprout, obviously, you need to know what to do with them. That's what I mean by planning for possibilities. Lots of people ponder what they'd do if things went wrong. Try to spend an equal number of your 168 hours pondering what you'd do if things went *right*. If the CEO of your company called you into her office tomorrow and said she was so impressed with your work that she wanted to put you in charge of your dream project, do you know what you would ask for? If you sat next to your dream client on a flight, or a literary agent at a bar, could you toss a casual pitch over peanuts?

There is a lot of randomness in the universe, but truly lucky people recognize that fairy godmothers are lazy. If taking your career to the next level will require your fairy godmother to tip her wand, make sure the wand is pointed at you, and that you're standing as close to her as possible, so all she has to do is nudge the thing like a bored barfly fiddling with a cocktail glass.

Be Ready to Ride the Wave

Of course, if you follow all these steps, there's a reasonable chance you may achieve your breakthrough. Then what?

This is a question Leanne Shear, in particular, has grappled with. She wanted to be a writer, and while she's thrilled to get the chance— "Tracey and I didn't have to pay dues," she says—she freely admits that *The Perfect Manhattan* is not Proust. And while she doesn't want to be Proust, she doesn't want to be a flash in the pan, either. She wants to be taken seriously. So, after a flurry of publicity for *The Perfect Manhattan* and some follow-on work (such as a nonfiction book called *Cocktail Therapy* prescribing a drink for every woe), she and Toomey have slowed down before crashing the market with other chick-lit books. Shear's been spending some of her 168 hours working with established writers to hone her craft, and figuring out ways to turn her early success into a "slow burn career," rather than one that flames out.

This is worth keeping in mind. After the champagne goes flat, the balloons deflate, and the confetti gets swept into the trash, you still have to get out of bed the next morning. You still have to know what you want your 168 hours to look like. You will have to figure out how to spend your time as you're managing a $1 million company rather than a $100,000 company, or after the Nobel Prize ceremony, or after you return home from living underwater for two weeks.

That last one was a major career breakthrough for Sylvia Earle, the ocean explorer we met in Chapter 3. Back in 1970, she was chosen as one of fifty scientists given the opportunity to live in underwater habitats dubbed the "Tektite Hiltons" amid the coral reefs of Lameshur Bay near the Virgin Islands. She led an all-female team; in 1970 the project directors thought a coed team would invite too much speculation. It's not clear anyone would have had much interest in shenanigans, though. After 21 hours in a decompression chamber, Earle was able to spend 336 hours underwater, exploring the ocean "not just as passing-through visitors, but as day to day residents," she wrote in *Sea Change*. She got to know specific barracudas, and five gray angelfish who, every morning, began "their slow waltz around the mounds of coral, pausing now and then to nibble a bit of sponge or nose at a lump of algal debris."

She loved the peacefulness of being underwater. She returned to the surface, though, to media coverage resembling a shark feeding frenzy. She and her fellow female aquanauts were whisked to Chicago for a ticker-tape parade, and were invited to join Pat Nixon (not Richard, she notes) for a lunch at the White House. She was interviewed by Barbara Walters and Hugh Downs, and wrote a piece for *National Geographic* about her experiences. She had to figure out what to do with this sudden fame. "It quickly became apparent to me that it might be possible to bounce from the light and entertaining"—such as whether she ate fish sticks underwater—"to more serious topics," she wrote. And so she decided to use her platform to share what would turn out to be her life's work: a message that the world's oceans were in deep trouble, dangerously depleted, and needed to be saved.

Only you can answer what you will do to ride the wave of your breakthrough, though I can offer one suggestion: take at least a few minutes every week to be grateful. Earle speaks with awe of what she's been able to do. "It just gets better," she told me in 2009, nearly 40 years after that big break under the sea. I try to write my gratitude for my smaller victories in my journal sometimes. Psychologists find that we tend to revert to our previous happiness levels within a few months of major events. While that's comforting in the case of a divorce or amputation, it's not so great if the event was good. Things that were once uncertain seem, in retrospect, to be inevitable. You can choose, however, to rekindle some of the joy you felt after winning that promotion or landing that record deal. Simply remind yourself of where you once were, and where you are now, and the gulf between them that's as wide as the ocean blue.

How to Achieve a Career Breakthrough

You *can* take your career to the next level while investing in the rest of your life. But doing this requires more thought than simply working around the clock. Ask yourself these questions:

- What would the next level look like for you? Picture it as vividly as possible.
- Do you know anyone else who has achieved a similar breakthrough? What steps did he/she take? Who were the decision makers? What do these people care about?
- How many of your working hours are you spending focused on the "stuff" of your professional craft?
- Do you have time to plan and prospect?
- If not, go back to Chapter 4 and see if you can figure out ways to create more space in your professional calendar. If this won't work, see if you can add a focused hour or two per day (5–10 per week). How could you make this happen?
- How would you use this time?
- What is your story? Why does achieving the next level make sense? If someone were to write a profile of you, what would it say?
- Do other people know about your goals?
- What "seeds" can you plant to advance your career in the future?
- If you were given a chance opportunity to achieve your breakthrough, would you be prepared to seize it? What needs to happen for you to be prepared?
- If you did achieve your breakthrough, what would you do next?

PART

3

@ HOME

· 6 ·

The New Home Economics

Walk into the cleaning supplies aisle of many grocery stores these days, and you'll soon bump into a woman named Mrs. Meyer. Cartoon images of her keeping house peek out from sleek bottles of Mrs. Meyer's Lemon Verbana All Purpose Cleaner, as if she intends to inspire you to get that last spot of dust off the shelves. When I first heard about Mrs. Meyer, I thought she sounded like a brilliant marketing invention. A more grandmotherly Mr. Clean perhaps, designed to intrigue consumers hungry for authenticity in a world of packaged goods.

But it turns out that Mrs. Meyer is actually a real person. Thelma Meyer is an empty-nester now, which means her life is much calmer than it was back in 1965 when she presided over one fairly clean Iowa house and a brood of nine rambunctious children.

Clearly, this involved a lot of work. Despite her more recent role as the face of a line of cleaning products, Mrs. Meyer was relaxed about housekeeping—"My house has never been my top priority," she told me in an interview recently—but still, "you were just kind of busy all day." Since she didn't own a dishwasher until she delivered baby number five, there were always plates to be scrubbed and dried. She did own a washing machine, thank goodness—she did more than fifteen loads of laundry a week—but without a highly functional dryer, she wound up pinning plenty of wet clothes onto the clothesline outside. She swept the floors and wiped down the kitchen sink every day. She dusted the banisters, light fixtures, furniture, and shelves every week, a task that grew in scope as the babies came and her husband, Vern, expanded their two-bedroom Cape Cod into a five-bedroom house with an upstairs family room (which, she confesses, she didn't bother to inspect too often).

The regular maintenance of caring for nine children and a home vacuumed up time. While she doesn't call it drudgery ("It was just something that had to be done," she says), it was laborious. The children helped, but given her family's finances and the culture of the era, even her "leisure" pursuits kept her busy. When the little ones napped, she sewed dresses for the girls or made her own maternity clothes. She gardened to supplement the family food budget. When her friends came over to play bridge, she baked lots of treats, which the kids crawled over one another to lap up the next morning.

All this labor left little time for other things. For instance, when I asked how she managed to spend time playing with each of the nine kids, she laughed. "That's something that probably did not get done," she said. She did what she could, getting one in the car on an errand, or two reading stories and saying prayers together before bedtime, but these modern notions of intense individual attention would have seemed foreign in the Meyer mid-century household.

While Mrs. Meyer's brood was large, it wasn't too rare for the time. Her sister had thirteen children. The total U.S. fertility rate— the number of babies the average woman could expect to have over her lifetime—hit an average of almost four children per woman in the 1950s. Judging by my collection of old *Good Housekeeping* magazines from the era, Mrs. Meyer's housekeeping labors were also par for the course. When we talked, Mrs. Meyer described elaborate rituals for cleaning the Venetian blinds in the bathtub and washing fiberglass drapes. The December 1958 *Good Housekeeping* contains these instructions on the proper care for electric blankets:

Fill washer with lukewarm suds, or use cold water and a cold-water
   wool-washing detergent. Let blanket soak 10 to 15 minutes.
   Then agitate 1 to 3 minutes.

Spin just long enough for water to drain from washer; fill again
   for rinsing. Agitate 1 minute; spin again. If blanket still looks
   sudsy, repeat rinse.

Spread blanket over two parallel clotheslines to dry. When it's
   almost dry, brush lightly to lift nap. Press binding with iron set
   at "synthetic" or "rayon."

In addition to these elaborate cleaning rituals, women of the 1950s
and 1960s spent a lot of time baking for their bridge groups and friends.
That same December 1958 issue of *Good Housekeeping* contains half a
dozen recipes in a section called "And Now to Go with Coffee." The
most intriguing, one End-of-the-Rainbow Cake, is actually a 2-day
ordeal that, though allowing for the use of white cake mix, calls for the
industrious housewife to tint crushed pineapple pale yellow; brighten
raspberry jam with red coloring; tint whipped cream green; and mix egg
whites, sugar, water, corn syrup, and salt in a double boiler over rapidly
boiling water until they form a stiff peak (7–10 minutes), only to find
out, in the last step, that the cake must refrigerate for at least 6 hours.

The editors of the magazine also assumed everyone sewed. A "Needlework" page discusses what to do should you discover to your "horror" that you have nothing to wear to a Christmas party. "Well, here's
an easy solution," the text reads. "An outrageously flattering little party
top you can make in a morning." What follows is a pattern calling for
stitching on four (and three-quarters) yards of Franken Trimming
metallic gold and black braid to some wool squares of fabric, "mitering
corners," and securing the edges with seam-binding.

Women of the era certainly knew that housekeeping could be labor
intensive. Though the modern habit of warning readers how much
hands-on time and total time each project takes was years away, in
December 1965, *Good Housekeeping* ran an article titled "75 Ways to Save
Time During the Holidays." But even this list implies a level of standards

that seems foreign now. Number 24 on the list is "Cut raisins and dates with kitchen shears" (I have been racking my brain to figure out why raisins might need to be smaller than they already are). Number 29 is "sift dry ingredients on waxed paper, not in bowls." If you are undertaking such serious recipes, you clearly don't want anything to go wrong, which may be why Number 35 is "Provide interesting toys or books for small children to keep them out of the kitchen," Christmas-cookie baking being far too serious an enterprise to share with your offspring.

Mrs. Meyer had a slightly different philosophy; not living up to women's magazine ideals is nothing new. For instance, from the time baby number three, a little girl named Monica, could hold a spoon, Mrs. Meyer allowed her to cook and clean alongside Mommy. Mrs. Meyer remembers that Monica was quite good at it. "She was really a homemaker," she says. "She really wanted to follow in my footsteps in cleaning."

But Monica (Meyer) Nassif, founder of the Caldrea Company, which launched the Mrs. Meyer brand of home products, did not grow up to spend a high proportion of her time cleaning. Indeed, her life has looked very little like Mrs. Meyer's. From children to careers to housework, Nassif's life, and the popularity of her products, has shown how drastically the economics of home and family—and how we use our 168 hours—have changed over the years.

Social science statistics are inherently fuzzy, but we do know this: women today, like Nassif, spend a lot more time working for pay than they did 40 years ago when Mrs. Meyer was running her home. In 1965, 38.5 percent of women aged twenty-five to thirty-four were in the labor force (that is, doing or seeking paid work), as were 46.1 percent of women aged thirty-five to forty-four. By 2005, those numbers were up to 73.9 percent and 75.8 percent respectively. This rise has cut across all demographic groups. The vast majority of mothers of young kids are now in the labor force to some extent, and even most moms married to men earning more than $120,000 a year work outside the home.

Here's another statistic we know is true from time-diary studies: moms—and dads—spend more time interacting with their children these days than they did in 1965. According to an analysis of the old Americans' Use of Time Study done by University of Maryland researchers (and different than the modern BLS American Time Use Study), in 1965, married moms spent a total of 10.6 hours per week on child care (9.1 on routine activities like dressing and bathing; 1.5 on interactive ones including reading and playing). Married fathers spent 2.6 hours (1.3 on routine, 1.2 on interactive, with some rounding issues causing the slight total discrepancy). By 2000, this had risen to 12.9 hours total for married mothers (9.5 and 3.3) and 6.5 hours for married fathers (4.1 and 2.4).

While these are all smaller numbers than one might imagine, and probably less than ideal, what this means from a broad societal perspective is that both moms and dads have doubled the proportion of their 168 hours spent on what we might recognize as "quality" parenting over the 40 years since Mrs. Meyer's children were little. According to statistics averaged from the 2003 to 2006 American Time Use Surveys, married moms in dual-career couples spend 2.3 hours per week on reading, playing, and educational activities these days—a small number, to be sure, but still a higher number than the 1965 figure, when the majority of women were not in the workforce.

In other words, the hours that women, overall, spend at paying work and the quality time they spend with their kids have risen in tandem. Men, likewise, for all the talk of overwork, have more than doubled the hours they spend with their children, compared with 1950s dads who left work at 5:00 p.m. and read the paper (or so the narrative goes; by some counts, fathers work slightly fewer hours for pay now than they did 40–50 years ago, though since moms are working much more, family tallies are higher).

This is what I mean by the "new home economics." As adults, overall, in two-parent families have spent more time working for pay, the time they spend interacting with their kids has also increased.

Since weeks still contain the exact same 168 hours they had in the 1950s and 1960s, this is a fascinating development in terms of resource allocation. It raises questions about exactly how people spend their time and the differences in ways that people who are in the workforce and are not in the workforce spent their 168 hours in the past and now.

I would argue that, over the last 40 years, as a higher proportion of parents' time in two-parent families has been compensated at market rates, parental time overall has become more valuable. Consequently, parents allocate this valuable time differently during their nonworking hours than people did in the past. This gives rise to the new home economics, which in turn casts old arguments about the trade-offs involved in personal and professional achievement in a very different light. Just like modern corporations, parents are starting to focus on their core competencies at home—the things they do best, and that others cannot do nearly as well. There is plenty of room for improvement, and this chapter looks at ways to fill the hours we do have with our families in the most effective ways possible, but there is also less reason for angst about the American family—at least the two-parent version of it—than many pundits seem to believe.

To understand the new home economics, it is important to understand what, exactly, people do with the hours they are not working for pay. One of the big benefits of the American Time Use Survey and other historic time-diary studies is that they give insight into this question. A big chunk of people's time is spent sleeping, and some other amount of time is leisure (predominantly watching TV, as we'll see in Chapter 8). Then, to use the ATUS categories, there is housework, which can include cleaning, cooking, laundry, yard work, household administration, and "caring for family members"—which usually means children.

Over time, the way parents have allocated their non-market-work hours has shifted considerably. The biggest change in the new home economics has been time devoted to housework. This has fallen precipitously—almost in half over 40 years.

One reason for this is that we are having fewer children. None of Mrs. Meyer's nine children has nine kids themselves. Nassif, for instance, has two. As anyone who watches TLC's endless shows on megafamilies can attest, you achieve economies of scale with large broods. But still, more children take more time for their simple upkeep: doing their laundry, shopping for them, and doing their dishes. These are not activities that particularly nurture their souls or brains, and indeed, may crowd out time for such things. From the 1950s to the 1970s, the total U.S. fertility rate fell from nearly 4 children per woman to a low of 1.74. There has been an uptick since, to 2.12 children per woman in 2007. Still, it's a sign of the times that recent headlines about the return of "large" families have started the "large" level at three. Three would have been "small" in 1955.

But this doesn't explain everything. In theory, it takes more time to help four children get dressed than two children, yet modern moms still spend the same total amount of time on the physical care of children as they did in 1965. So everything related to the care of children has not dropped proportionally. Instead, it appears that it is solely our housekeeping standards that have borne the brunt of the decline—to the point where women who run households today often do not seem to be speaking the same language as the raisin-cutting *Good Housekeeping* editors of yore.

"I don't know how women who work full-time ever get their houses clean," Mrs. Meyer told me, confessing that when she went back to work part-time as a nurse when her kids were older, "my house probably went to the dogs." It's a good thing she was telling me this on the phone since, while my house doesn't look horrible, by the standards outlined in her new book, *Mrs. Meyer's Clean Home: No-Nonsense Advice that Will Inspire You to Clean Like the Dickens*, my house went to the dogs a long time ago.

For instance, I have never done a proper spring cleaning. I have never—as her book instructs—cleaned the windows inside and out with a solution of equal parts white vinegar and water. I have never vacuumed the walls and ceilings, or rented a carpet cleaner from a hardware store. I've never waxed my wood furniture or steam-cleaned the upholstery. To be transparent, I do pay a cleaning service to come in and give my apartment a good scrub from time to time, but I have a home office, so I see what the process involves, and it doesn't seem to include many of the most laborious tasks Mrs. Meyer describes, either. Sweeping the floors is more of a weekly thing than a daily thing. I do cook—easy two-pot meals that take a maximum of 30 minutes. But having coffee with a friend involves going to Starbucks, where the plethora of baked goods means I don't have to spend 2 days constructing an End-of-the-Rainbow cake or, for that matter, 20 minutes baking Toll House cookies out of premade dough.

Messes bother me less than they bother many other folks, but my casual attitude is borne out in time-diary data. In 1965, married mothers spent 34.5 hours on household tasks including mopping, chopping, and laundry. In 2008, moms of minor children spent 16 to 17 hours weekly on these things. Moms like me, in dual-career couples, spent (according to 2003–2006 data) a bit over 14 hours. Men did more than in 1965, but when you add men's and women's hours, you still don't get the totals from Mrs. Meyer's day.

Most people, when asked to guess the reason for the decline, point to labor-saving devices. One hundred years ago, moms of large broods could spend whole days bent over washboards or baking bread from scratch. *Really* from scratch. On a trip to Scotland not too long ago, I spent some time wandering around the primitive croft (tenant farm) houses on the Isle of Skye. A sign in one noted that it was not uncommon for mothers to go outside at dawn and hack down some oats, grind them by hand, and turn them into bread or oatmeal before the kids left for school. But this turns out not to be the full explanation for time use in mid-century households like Mrs. Meyer's. By the 1950s and 1960s, my old *Good Housekeeping* magazines came packed with ads for prepared foods such as Kraft salad dressings and Betty Crocker Scalloped Potatoes, as well as KitchenAid dishwashers and auto-cleaning Frigidaire ovens. Certainly, not everyone had dryers and dishwashers—Mrs. Meyer didn't when she embarked on her homemaking adventure—but many people did.

In theory, all these devices and conveniences should have saved women time. But they didn't, for a simple reason. A packaged cake mix doesn't lighten your load if you proceed to incorporate it into a 2-day recipe that involves tinting raspberry jam more red than it already is. A washing machine doesn't save you time if you then fill those hours with elaborate rituals for brushing an electric blanket's nap.

The reality is that time—all 168 hours of it—has to be filled with something. If you are not working for pay, then you need something else to do. The obvious answer for moms (or dads) would be to spend that time playing with their children, just as we assume that stay-at-home moms today spend a lot of time interacting with their kids. They do spend more time with their kids than moms who work for pay, and for many people, that statistic, right there, should be the end of the argument in terms of what is best for children. But I want to float the idea that "a lot" isn't necessarily the right phrase, on average, for two reasons.

First, children spend very few years in that preschool age range when they're actually in their homes, demanding an adult's attention, for lengthy periods of time. Even Mrs. Meyer with her nine children only had a baby at home full-time for about 15 years. Modern women with two or three kids will spend less than a decade in this state, and given the rise of preschool for two- to four-year-olds, and children's napping schedules, even women who are not in the workforce will have many waking hours that would not be available for interacting with kids long before the children are in school. Then, when children do start school and other activities, this reduces the time available for parental interaction even more. Children who are at school (or on the bus or playing sports) from 8:00 a.m. to 3:00 p.m. each day spend about 35 hours a week out of the home—perhaps not coincidentally, the same amount that the average mom with a full-time job works. Many homemakers reenter the paid workforce when their children start school. But others don't, either because they don't want to or because they encounter obstacles such as a lack of flexibility or discrimination in their attempts to restart their careers. Regardless, by the time they are in school, children of homemakers and children of employed moms do not have appreciably different levels of interaction with their parents. Indeed, one 2002 calculation from a study of children's time found that kids' schedules look pretty much the same regardless of maternal employment—from time spent watching TV to the not-so-impressive 0.5 weekly hours kids in each family type spend in "household conversations."

Second, there is the reality of human nature. Just as people with paid jobs don't spend 100 percent of their time on the substance of their work, the average stay-at-home parent doesn't spend 100 percent of his or her available time on that main job of nurturing children. Married stay-at-home moms with kids under age six spend, on average, 22.5 hours per week on child care as a primary activity, in total. That's 3.21 hours per day for both physical care and playing. Some, obviously, do much more.

We all know moms who fill their children's days with fabulous opportunities for learning and exploration. But some do less, too. The kids may be there, in the adult's presence, which makes the parent feel "on," but the kids are watching videos (the average child aged two to eleven watches nearly 4 hours of TV per day, according to Nielsen, though time diaries put this number much lower), or playing independently. There is nothing wrong with playing independently; it's how children develop their imaginations and learn to be their own people. But this is not interactive time—particularly if Mom is in the next room checking e-mail—and hence this is another factor affecting the totals.

If you choose not to work for pay, or choose to work part-time, and you simply can't interact with your children 24/7, then you need to do something else with that portion of your 168 hours. Some stay-at-home parents volunteer extensively or undertake serious exercise programs or other hobbies. Jeremy Adam Smith's 2009 book, *The Daddy Shift*, documented that stay-at-home fathers often carve out time for projects such as woodworking or home renovation when their children are doing other things. In extremely high-income households, the at-home party may spend considerable time undertaking activities to advance the breadwinner's career (orchestrating dinner parties or accompanying the breadwinner to events). But housework is the easiest choice, and is the "hobby" many women choose. It seems more productive than watching TV, is cheaper than shopping, seems like it has to be done, and you don't have to leave home to do it.

Consequently, in the past at least, housework wound up expanding to fill the lion's share of the available time that children were at school or playing with friends. And so the cultural narrative made 1960s housewives feel that they really did need to bake something if company came over, and that electric blankets really did need to be ironed. Housework was a housewife's full-time job, and hence, there wasn't much time for paid work or, for that matter, playing with the kids. That's why the December 1965 *Good Housekeeping* instructed women on how to keep their children out of the kitchen *while they're baking Christmas cookies*, as if cookies needed to be baked for their own sake, as opposed to being something you do primarily because it's fun for your kids.

But here's the fascinating thing about the new home economics. At some point, women's labor-force participation rates rose to a level that changed this narrative. As women entered the workforce in droves, their time became more valuable. Literally. It rose to the level of the wages a woman could command. This may not seem fair. There are serious arguments to be made that caregiving is undervalued and should be respected far more than it is, both as a profession and in the family versions of it. But remember, that's not necessarily what women in the 1950s and 1960s were doing with their time. On average, moms of kids under age eighteen spent around 10 hours a week on child care. They spent 34.5 on house care.

And so, as women's time became more valuable, like corporations allocating their most precious resources to their highest-value use, women have had to make a choice about how to allocate their limited hours. They decided, in the aggregate, that children were more important than housework. This shouldn't be surprising. Moms love their kids. They want to spend time with them.

But here's how this wound up playing out: in order to hold time with kids at least constant as they began spending, on average, more time in the workforce, women had to indulge in a rapid decline in housework expectations. There is a big difference between 34.5 hours a week and 14 or so hours per week. That's enough time to work 4 hours per weekday for pay and not lose a second of time to read or play with your kids.

Since most two-income families aren't breeding typhoid in their toilets, I'd argue that those extra 20 hours turned out not to be particularly necessary. Women these days simply don't do many of the things women did 40 years ago. We don't cut raisins—with kitchen shears or otherwise. We don't polish our children's footwear, because our kids wear sneakers from Target, not saddle shoes that require upkeep. We don't iron our electric blankets, or any blankets for that matter. Indeed, I would argue that at least some of the time that modern stay-at-home moms spend on housework isn't really necessary either, though at least they're spending less time on these chores than in the past. Moms who are not in the workforce currently spend about 26 hours per week on housework, down from about 37 four decades ago. When standards go down, they go down for everyone, and stay-at-home moms are spillover beneficiaries of this trend. When Glenna Matthews, a seventy-something historian and the author of *Just a Housewife: The Rise and Fall of Domesticity,* was in her twenties, "Somebody who didn't like me came over one time and then a week later said, 'You think you're so hot but I've seen the dust under your bed,'" she told me in a 2008 interview for *Doublethink* magazine. These days? "It is inconceivable to me now that anybody would be talking about dust under your bed as a mark of shame."

Interestingly, at the same time that we have seen a decrease in house-keeping standards, we have seen a massive *increase* in parenting standards for women and men.

Some of this is laughable, especially among the yuppie set, says Paula Spencer, the *Woman's Day* "Momfidence" columnist, whose motto is "an Oreo never killed anybody." Spencer has made a career of mocking modern parental foibles. She ticks off the list: grinding baby food by hand, purchasing seat covers for shopping carts and hygienic gloves so babies never touch the dirty world, using flashcards with infants to aid language development, and enrolling a four-year-old in Pee Wee football so he won't be "behind on his skills" ("that's a phrase I hear a lot," she says). Parents drive children to the bus stop and monitor their homework assignments rather than help children learn to take care of themselves.

As Spencer notes, these new standards are not entirely benign. "I know enough women who have sort of puffed up the job of being a mom to absorb more hours than I can certainly fathom," she says—and not in ways that involve interacting with children. If you think parenting requires checking every arithmetic problem, making Valentines for every kid in your second-grader's class, and making all your own baby food, then it *will* be hard to hold a paying job. Fortunately, the evidence does not support the idea that any of this is necessary. Exhibit 1: Spencer's house—she's raised four normal kids while working 40–50 hours per week during the entirety of their childhoods.

Nonetheless, there is a lot to like about the new parenthood in the sense that many high-achieving parents are spending their non-market-work hours not on housework, but with their kids, and focused on their core competencies. These are the things that they do best, and that others cannot do nearly as well. For instance, someone else (for example, a bakery) can make baked goods for a get-together. Someone else can sew your kid's clothes—probably better, and certainly much faster, than you could. But that clothing manufacturer can't help your child become excited about books by reading him his favorite story with the voices he loves so much quite as well as you can.

That's the philosophy by which James Andersen operates. By day, Andersen is the managing partner of Clearview Capital, a private equity company, in Greenwich, Connecticut. At night, he and his wife divide their five boys into four book groups—the five- and seven-year-olds together, then the nine-, eleven-, and thirteen-year-olds separately. In recent years, they've tackled great literature for boys of all ages: *The Adventures of Huckleberry Finn, The Adventures of Tom Sawyer, 20,000 Leagues Under the Sea,* and other classic works. This reading time gives the boys a window into different parts of the world, with the promise dangled out there that when the boys turn thirteen, Andersen will take each of them, individually, somewhere they want to learn more about. For example, he and his oldest son read a lot of World War II books, so they planned to go to Normandy to see the site of the D-day landings.

Obviously, not every parent can afford to take their kids to France. But anyone can develop special rituals with their children that leverage that parental core competency of sharing values and making memories together. Take another look at your "List of 100 Dreams" from Chapter 2. Can you do any of these activities with your children? Ask your kids to make a "List of 100 Dreams," too, and try to figure out which activities they value and enjoy that can be done as a family. If you both love swimming, for instance, go to a community pool as often as you can. Any parent can bring the kids to the library. Any parent can make up stories with their kids, pray and discuss religious texts together, do hobbies together such as puzzles or making crafts, garden together, and visit local historic sites. As much as possible, try to share your expertise and passions, because when you're excited about something, chances are your kids will be, too. For instance, I love music, and so Jasper and I sing songs together, and I'm eagerly awaiting the New York Philharmonic's "Very Young People's Concerts" which target three-year-olds. You can exercise together. As Kevin Peter, the development director of Community Legal Services of Philadelphia, was training for the August 30, 2009, Ironman Louisville triathlon, he would sometimes have his eleven-year-old son join him as he did long runs, with the boy biking by his side. They ran a few 5Ks together. The two also commute together some mornings on the bus and train to school and Peter's office.

Young children naturally want to spend time with their parents, but even older children can be lured into the habit if you behave like you truly want to invest time with them. That means not checking your Blackberry every 3 minutes. The point is to treat your children as privileged clients. You have to think through the time you're going to spend together because it is valuable. If you don't, one of two things will happen.

The first trap is that you'll become a slave to the weeknight routine of dinner, bath time, and bed. As part of writing this book, I asked dozens of people to keep time logs, and you could set your clock by some parents' devotion to these rituals. That would be fine if it was working for everyone, and indeed, some kids require routine. But often, these logs would be accompanied by laments such as *I wish I felt more focused when I spend time with the kids. Sometimes I just feel like I'm trying to get through to bedtime.* We're all tired after work, and it's easy to succumb to the boredom and then feel bad because time with kids is supposed to be meaningful and fun.

In these cases, it may help to consciously shake things up. Choose two weeknights to bust the routine and get out of the house. Make plans ahead of time so everyone can look forward to them. After picking the kids up from day care or after-school care, have a dinnertime picnic at a park, or pack snacks and hit the playground if it's still light. Find a museum with evening hours. Build a campfire in the backyard and make s'mores. Go to a minor league ball game or some random nonfootball/nonbasketball college sport (so tickets are cheap and plentiful). Variety is the key here. Like Oreos, eating dinner on the fly a few times per week won't kill anyone. It's also a little-known fact of parenting that small children don't need to be bathed nightly. Just wipe off any obvious dirt, and you should be good for the next day.

The other trap you'll fall into if you don't plan your family time is that you'll watch massive amounts of TV. Television is OK in small doses, but it generally isn't a core competency in the way that making collages together might be for a family of artists, and (as we'll see in Chapter 8) isn't as pleasurable as people think.

Of course, to truly treat your children as one of your core competencies, you have to actually be there with them for reasonable chunks of time, even if you have a demanding job. Andersen has been known to leave the office at 5:00 p.m. to serve as an assistant Little League coach for some of his sons' teams. Because of his travel schedule, he couldn't commit to being a head coach, but he still figured out a way he could volunteer, and gets to practices as often as he can. "I generally don't work a lot on weekends," he says. "Almost everything can wait until Monday." When he's traveling, he pulls together a drawing or poem about "a day in the life of Daddy" to fax to the boys. He switched from a BlackBerry to an iPhone so he could e-mail photos from his trips including, when we touched base recently, a warehouse/factory he was visiting in France. "That way they get a real sense of where I am and what I'm doing."

Likewise, you can find these opportunities for nurturing anywhere, even in a full schedule. Get up 15–20 minutes before your children so you're ready and the mornings aren't rushed. If it takes you much longer than 20 minutes to get ready, then you need to adjust your hairstyle or wardrobe or showering habits as soon as possible. When the mornings aren't rushed, you can turn breakfast into a family meal. Discuss what everyone plans to accomplish that day over your cereal and coffee. Use the morning time to fit in some family reading or projects such as puzzles or building giant Lego towers. Have evening conferences when you're putting the kids to bed to discuss how the day went. Use this time to strategize new ways to deal with school issues, friend issues, or the vagaries of teenage life.

To do this, you'll have to organize your work life in a way that reflects the existence of your children. There are tips in Chapter 4 on compressing work into less time so you don't blow through these valuable evening hours when the kids are awake and home from school. But if this compression isn't enough, then your best bet for creating time with your kids is to shift your work hours to open up chunks of time.

Here's how this usually works for the core-competency parent: Treat the hours between 5:00 and 8:00 p.m. (or 5:30 and 8:30, or 6:00 and 9:00 if you've got night owls) as sacred. This is family time. Block it out on your calendar. Use it to plan activities with your kids that leverage the things you do best. But then, a few nights per week, open up the hours of 8:00–10:00 or 11:00, after your kids go to bed, for work.

This is important. If you're one of the few people whose jobs honestly require 12-hour days, 5 days per week, there is a huge difference between working from 8:00 a.m. to 8:00 p.m. compared with working from 8:00 a.m. to 5:00 p.m. and then 8:00 to 11:00 p.m. In one world, you do not see your children much at all, though you will have more time to watch TV. In the other, you can spend as much time interacting with your children as the average stay-at-home parent, even as you work more hours than the vast majority of Americans.

This is particularly important if you are parenting on your own. Maureen Beddis of Alexandria, Virginia, works full-time as a senior director at the Vision Council, a nonprofit that promotes better vision care. She is the mom of a one-year-old daughter named Abby, has a baby on the way, and her "first baby" is a Husky-Lab mix named Cyrus. It's a full plate anyway, but what makes this situation all the more complicated is that her husband, Chip, was, when I interviewed her, in the middle of a 400-day Army Reserve tour in Iraq (if you're wondering how the second pregnancy happened, he was home for a well-timed 2-week break in the middle).

She made it work by waking up around 5:30 a.m. to go play with Cyrus in the backyard, which functioned as both exercise and a way of relieving stress. Abby would wake up around 6:45, and they would spend the next hour together before leaving for day care and work. Beddis picked her daughter up again right at 5:00 p.m., went home for dinner, then would put Cyrus on the leash and Abby in the stroller and go for a nice long walk to explore various neighborhoods and parks together. At

7:30, Abby would go down for the night, and Beddis would spend the next 30 minutes dealing with housework or household management activities. Yes, this comes out to even less than the 14 hours most moms with full-time jobs put in; Beddis is a champion outsourcer. But she had a good reason for the compression—at 8:00 every weeknight, she would go back to work until at least 9:30. This schedule gave her, as a single parent, 8 hours to sleep, a full 50 hours to work, time to exercise and play with the dog, and 15–20 hours during the workweek with Abby. If she worked until 6:30 instead of 5:00, she would have had more leisure time, but she would have cut her time with her daughter in half.

Lots of parents make this choice. Years ago, Rick D'Angelo, who currently manages a $500 million private equity fund for WR Huff Asset Management, was a geophysicist trying to transition into management at Amoco, the oil company, while he and his wife were raising what ultimately totaled four children. He'd come home around 4:00 p.m. and spend a few hours playing with the kids. He studied for his MBA at night. He chose that as a strategic way to advance his career, rather than, say, playing golf with colleagues on weekends. "My hobbies consisted of playing with my kids," he says. It wound up working, and he was promoted soon enough.

As we discussed in Chapter 1, 168 hours is enough time to work 50 hours a week, sleep 8 hours a night, and still spend massive amounts of time with your children. But since all hours aren't created equally, making this come out right involves moving around chunks of hours like puzzle pieces. Split shifts are a good way to use the fact that young children sleep more than adults do to still get your work hours in.

But though plenty of parents have managed to advance their careers via this schedule, when I've suggested split shifts to people, I get some grumbling. At one consulting firm, the partners nodded in agreement that they could work this way. The associates were less sure. People with long commutes claim they simply can't get home early. Or everyone else at the office puts in face time in the evenings, going out to dinner with the clients or scheduling internal meetings, since the hours of 9:00–5:00 are for client time. Doctors and dentists claim that they have to keep their practices open in the evening hours or that they can't control their schedules. Some jobs require being at a certain place during a certain time with no flexibility to move work around. Moms and dads with stay-at-home partners say that their arrangement is that the at-home party covers this time, so the breadwinning party can advance his or her career or earn more money with overtime pay. Or here's my roadblock: I often get in a real groove with my writing right around 5:00 p.m. Knowing that a finished draft of whatever I'm working on is only an hour or two away, it is monstrously hard to stop.

There are a million excuses, and some of them may be good. If you have very young children who wake up at the crack of dawn, but don't have to be at school at a certain time, and you have a job that requires evening hours, you may find that you can re-create evening quality time in the morning. Often, if an office culture values putting in 8:00 p.m. face time, no one will notice if you don't show up until after 9:00 a.m.

But, in a broad sense, we can choose what to do with our lives. If it is worth it to you to spend time with your kids—and I believe this is the case for the vast majority of parents, including those with stay-at-home or primary-parent partners—you will figure out a way to do that. It doesn't have to happen every weekday, particularly if your spouse is covering some of the time, but it shouldn't *never* happen, either. So you will get a different job. You will work from home and nix the commute 2 days per week. You will assure the whiny part of your brain that you will still have 2 hours of creative energy left later in the evening. You will do better work between the hours of 8:00 and 11:00 p.m. than your colleagues do from 5:00 to 8:00 p.m. and get yourself promoted anyway. You will open your dental practice early and work with a partner who wants to cover the evening hours (or vice versa).

Or you'll change the job description. As I've been in my baby-making years, I've been fascinated to see how obstetric care has changed as women have come to dominate the field. It was once assumed that an OB needed to be available to work 24/7 since babies can come at any time. Consequently, these doctors needed stay-at-home wives to cover everything on the home front. Now many OBs work in pools where one of four or five doctors might deliver your baby. This reduces the on-call requirement for a practice to 1 or 2 nights a week, which is a far more family-friendly schedule. Perhaps some personal touch is lost, but many new moms are happy to be cared for by women, particularly women who understand exactly what labor feels like.

The new home economics has changed the way parents juggle time among children, work, and housework. Unfortunately, in all this, one extremely important thing can suffer: your marriage or partnership. According to time-diary studies, in 1975, married parents spent 12.4 hours with each other, without the kids, each week. By 2000, that was down to 9.1 hours.

This is a problem, and not just because nurturing this relationship is obviously a core competency—at least you hope no one can do it better! The hard truth is that being happy in this department has a massive multiplier effect on the rest of your life.

At least that's a lesson I take from the story of Empress Maria Theresa, who lived from 1717 to 1780. I have long been fascinated by this woman, who historians consider to be one of the most effective rulers of the Hapsburg Empire during its long history. During her 40-year reign, she instituted many social reforms, including a simplified tax structure that boosted the economy, education, and health reforms. Ruling an empire of 20 million people (back when world population was fewer than 800 million) made her one busy lady. That's why her marriage is such an interesting part of the story.

A marriage was arranged for Maria Theresa as a child, but when her prospective husband died early, she became one of the few monarchs of the eighteenth century to marry for love. And love her husband, Francis of Lorraine, she did. She bore sixteen children over the years (ten survived to adulthood). Think about that in light of the modern standards for "having it all." A ruler who was more or less the equivalent of the U.S. president for her era was pregnant or caring for a newborn for about half of her time in power. And though she certainly had an abundance of servants, by many accounts, she was quite involved in that care. She continued to correspond with her children at length, even after they grew up and she married them off to form strategic alliances with other European powers (though perhaps not so wisely in the case of her ill-fated daughter Marie Antoinette).

I don't mean to imply that Maria Theresa and Francis's marriage was perfect; there's evidence that Francis had affairs, among other transgressions. But given that many arranged marriages in that era featured the royals living completely separate lives by the end, you have to admire the sheer steaminess of this couple's setup. Even in an era when society expected monarchs to produce many heirs, I'd argue that a couple who bore sixteen children together had to be hot for each other—even after decades of marriage.

I don't think it's a coincidence that Maria Theresa was able to outshine the other Hapsburgs both professionally and personally. A good marriage gives you great energy for achieving success in all parts of life. It can help you keep up that energy even in the face of trials that would decimate other people.

That's what Doug and Cheryl Chumley discovered. The Chumleys met at Fort Stewart in Georgia, when he was in the Army Corps of Engineers and she was an army mechanic. They married a few years later and now have four children, ranging from age two to fourteen. Both work full-time. Cheryl is a reporter who covers the Prince William County government for the *News & Messenger* in Woodbridge, Virginia, and Doug is a mechanic for a Virginia golf course. In addition, Cheryl does a number of freelance projects on the side. She's training for a half marathon, though Doug isn't because in April 2008, when their youngest was still a baby, he suffered a massive heart attack. His heart stopped for 8 minutes, and the prognosis was bleak enough that the hospital dispatched counselors to the Chumley children. Doug survived, but various complications resulted in him losing his left leg above the knee.

Needless to say, this was not easy on the family. It still isn't. Doug has difficulty getting around, and Cheryl helps him with a lot of daily tasks. Still, less than a year after his heart attack, Doug was back at work, and Cheryl was also reaching new heights in her career. Marrying her "soul mate" has been key to that, she says. "If I had marital problems, all my hopes and dreams really wouldn't matter. I wouldn't have the focus to concentrate on it," she says. "My family situation is solid and I know it. There are no worries here, which leaves me open to pursue whatever else I want to do in life."

This kind of marriage does not just happen; Cheryl and Doug invest a lot of time in it. They commute together sometimes, turning what would otherwise be a chore into a date. They talk to each other three or four times a day on the phone. And, interestingly, they make more time for family intimacy by not enrolling their children in every activity under the sun. "I have four kids and they all play together, so it's not like they're ever lonely," Cheryl says. This gets at an important discovery: functioning as a taxi service is not a parental core competency in the way that eating dinner together or doing Bible studies together (frequent Chumley activities) are. Plus, it does little good to have your children enrolled in many different activities if the fragmentation means that Mom and Dad can't build the kind of happy marriage that children crave.

Just as with your children, you have to make time for your spouse. This is challenging because you can't control your partner's schedule. You can't force your spouse to make time for you. It's hard to get in the habit of planning dates when you're already planning a career breakthrough and planning activities with your children. This is definitely a component of my 168 hours that I'm trying to improve upon. My husband and I do try to talk by phone for a few minutes during the day. We also try to hire a sitter sometimes after the kids' bedtime so we can go out to dinner. We try to take at least one short adults-only trip per year (my mother-in-law graciously takes on kid duty). If hiring a sitter isn't an option, you can make in-home dates work. Hold off on eating dinner until the children go to bed, and then have a candlelit meal in which you can finish sentences without interruption. One father told me that he and his wife enlist their eight-year-old to run interference if any of their younger children attempt to leave their downstairs bedrooms once Mom and Dad have gone upstairs to take in a movie.

While movies are fine for weekends, you shouldn't watch them right before bed on a regular basis because TV interferes with sleep habits. A better idea? Schedule a "spouse conference" for the last half hour before bedtime. Talk through your days. Talk about your kids and talk about your dreams. If one of you is traveling, have the conference by phone. If you're both in your house, have the conference in your bed. What this leads to is up to you.

Over the past 40 years, Americans have drastically changed the way they allocate time to work, housework, and their families. Thanks to the new home economics, it turns out that careers and children have not competed with each other to the extent that most people believe they have for women's time. The true competition has turned out to be between paid work and housework, with women trading these off as they've entered the workforce. I'd say this is mostly a positive development. Our houses may be a little more rumpled, but the economy and the world as a whole have benefited from women's varied skills more than our electric blankets have benefited from ironing.

And here's an even more positive development: as women have discovered their core competencies outside the home, men have discovered the core competency of being dads. In 2008, according to the Families and Work Institute, young fathers under age twenty-nine spent 4.3 hours each *weekday* with their kids; dads aged twenty-nine to forty-two spent 3.1 hours (up from 2.4 and 1.9 hours in 1977). These are self-reported, non-time-diary numbers, so they are likely inflated, and they include all time spent together (such as time spent watching TV). But the trend is higher, and in fact, younger fathers now claim to spend more time with their children during the workweek than moms in their thirties. You can see this statistic illustrated on playgrounds, at day-care drop-offs, in pediatricians' offices, and in sheer child-care competence. When Jasper was a baby, one of my aunts asked me if my husband was willing to change diapers. It had never even *occurred* to me that he wouldn't be. While I won't claim that the child-care split in my house is entirely equitable (my husband might point out that our paychecks have yet to achieve equity either), I don't have to leave instructions when I go out. Michael knows which is the preferred blankie, the favored shoes and cereal, and the onset and duration of nap time.

In other words, while it's fashionable to complain about how little men do at home, I believe this complaint is a bit misguided. A big

source of the tension is that men don't do m
ing. Though they doubled the amount of tim
work between 1965 and 2000 (4.4 hours per wee
time diaries), this is about half the time married n
chores, averaged across women who are both in an
force. But in dual-career couples, dads actually spend
playing with their kids than moms do. I think dads ha
here. Playing with your kids is a core competency. Va
rugs is not. There are tips in the next chapter about cuttin
time down to the bare minimum, so it ceases to be a burde
parent, but already, with housework standards falling as pre
as they have, "burden" is probably not quite the right word. Id
fact that dads don't do much housework should inspire, rath
infuriate, moms. It should lead us to figure out ways to spend m
our 168 hours on the things we do best.

I have written and spoken about the decline of housework, and the chan,
ing home economics that has parents ditching their kitchens for both the
office and the playground many times over the years. Inevitably, though,
someone asks, "But what about Martha Stewart?" The question is really
why, in our modern era, anyone can still make a mint talking to women
about making their own jam or constructing elaborate centerpieces from
colored tissue paper, silk flowers, candles, and who knows what else.

At first blush, the projects in *Martha Stewart Living*, or the Caldrea
Company's decision to promote a book touting Mrs. Meyer's instructions for vacuuming the ceiling, seem startlingly retro. But the answer
is that the changing home economics has had some interesting
repercussions—which brings us back to the story of Monica Nassif.

Unlike her mother, Nassif worked the entire time her daughters were
little. Her husband actually took on the primary parenting role. While
this is rare, it's more common than it used to be. In 2008, according to
the Families and Work Institute, 49 percent of men claimed to take equal
or most of the responsibility for child care. This isn't just (all) wishful
thinking; a full 31 percent of their wives agreed that this was true.

ut what's most fascinating is why Nassif, like Martha Stewart, has
n able to make a bundle in her line of work. She started Caldrea in
9 after spending years as a consultant in the consumer goods space.
company legend goes, she was in Atlanta on a business trip, and
hile stopping by a store, she noticed a giant load of ugly, harsh clean-
ng products. Why, she wondered, couldn't these goods be as lovely
as the ones women demanded for their skin and hair? So she started
experimenting and soon began marketing a line of extremely high-
end cleaning products, such as a $9 Sea Salt Neroli scented countertop
cleanser and a $75 "cleaning-essentials set" in a retro silver mop bucket.
Caldrea promises that these treats will deliver the "premier home cleaning experience."

There is an irony to this. Women who can pay $75 for soap can pay
$75 to outsource the "cleaning experience" to someone else.

But this recasting of cleaning as "luxurious" or as fantasy (like Mrs.
Meyer's vacuumed ceilings, or *Real Simple*'s recent instructions to its
upper-income readers on how to make a grout cleaner of fresh lemon
and cream of tartar) was also, in some ways, inevitable. I would argue it
is actually a sign of how far women have come.

Once you no longer have to spend massive amounts of time doing
something—for example, cooking or cleaning—you can afford to be
nostalgic about it. You can afford to treat it more as a leisure activity, indulged in the same way men go fishing, secure in the knowledge
that their families won't starve if they fail to catch something. Once,
women complained of being chained to the stove. Now, yuppie couples
who could eat out every night carefully select Whole Foods heirloom
tomatoes for their made-from-scratch pomodoro sauce. Their home
renovation projects elevate kitchens from hidden galleys to galleries of
high-end appliances—with some of those appliances used about as frequently as one would "use" the art in a museum. Now that women do
not have to sew clothes for themselves or their children, knitting has
become so hip as a hobby it's practically clichéd.

Nassif was the first entrepreneur to understand that the same thing
is happening to cleaning. A lemon-scented grout cleaner is nice to read

about when you're kicking your feet up with a magazine. And if you spend just 1.3 hours per week doing dishes, as opposed to 5.1 hours in 1965, why not indulge in "liquid loveliness" (as Caldrea touts its $9 dish soap) and turn the whole thing into aromatherapy? The fact that women have used the time they've saved by not baking End-of-the-Rainbow cakes to work for pay and play with their children is a huge feminist victory. That is no more undermined by pricey scented soap or the existence of TV shows about "good things" than the movement of men from the manufacturing to the knowledge economy is undermined by shows about woodworking. Last time I checked, few of us built our own houses.

In the new home economics, our cooking and cleaning fantasies are much like those roadside attractions known as Renaissance festivals. You wear fancy dresses and ride a pony, but you drive your car to get there. Likewise, an $899 Williams-Sonoma Miele Celebration Canister Vacuum does seem worth celebrating if—should the moment pass with the wind—you can always hand it over to Merry Maids or let the dust linger on the floor. Or ceiling. Mrs. Meyer may want to inspire you to clean like the Dickens, but trust me, if you don't, few will judge you for it.

Your Core Competencies at Home

For parents, nurturing children is a core competency. It is something you do best. Take a good look at your time logs from Chapter 1.

What blocks of low-impact time can be redeployed as high-impact time with your children? Be creative and think beyond nights and weekends. Weekday mornings work for some parents. If it works for your caregiver's schedule, the occasional weekday lunch may also be a place you can find time.

What activities can you do with your children during these blocks of time? Ask your children to create a "List of 100 Dreams" and see what matters to them. List some activities here:

1. _____

2. _____

3. _____

4. _____

5. _____

Which blocks of time can you commit to spending with your spouse/partner? What arrangements need to be made for that to happen?

· 7 ·

Don't Do Your Own Laundry

Recently, Sid Savara made a surprising discovery for a thirty-year-old single man: "I was spending *a lot* of time cooking," he says.

He didn't mean to be spending a lot of time cooking; he wasn't attempting anything as complicated as the End-of-the-Rainbow cake described in Chapter 6, and he wasn't getting many gourmet meals from his efforts. But this Honolulu-based software developer was feeling burned out from trying to combine his job with regular exercise and launching a rock band. So he studied his time and created a spreadsheet to log his 168 hours. He recorded them for the next three weeks.

When he added everything up, he realized that, in an attempt to avoid unhealthy take-out food, he was spending as much as *15 hours* per week on food-related tasks. He'd get in the car and battle after-work traffic to go to the grocery store because he didn't have anything in the house. He'd spend half an hour picking out items for the next day and waiting in line. At home, his failure to plan ahead meant he'd find himself waiting for the chicken to defrost or discovering midway through a recipe that he was missing a key ingredient. Then there was the active cooking time: chopping veggies, tending the stove, doing the dishes.

If he enjoyed shopping and chopping, this would be one thing. But he didn't. The lost hours were also particularly galling because they fell during that valuable postwork window when he could have been relaxing or doing something fun with family and friends. The only chunk of his food-chore time that he enjoyed was the eating.

So Savara did what any modern man would do: he went on Craig's List.

This Web portal, founded by the San Francisco IT guy Craig Newmark in 1995, is famous for many things like murder cases, personal ads, and no-fee apartment rentals. But the site also allows you to advertise gigs, projects, or your own skills for free (or close to it, in the case of employers listing payroll jobs). These low transaction costs result "in more jobs being listed than would be otherwise" in a newspaper that charges per line, the Craig's List CEO Jim Buckmaster told me in a 2008 interview. Because there are more jobs listed, there's more variety, and "when you have a wider variety of different kinds of employment opportunities, it stands to reason that you're going to fit more people into more different kinds of situations beyond the traditional 'I'm looking for a forty-hour-a-week job in an office complex somewhere in a cubicle.'"

So Savara placed an ad on the site hoping to find someone who would cook for him. "I thought I'd get one response, or two responses, but I was blown away," he says. Some responses tilted to the sketchy side. One catering company employee wanted to siphon off food from her events and moonlight on her employer's time (he nixed that one); a retired consultant, worth several million bucks and in Hawaii to surf, was learning to cook and wanted someone to cook for. But "he didn't need me," Savara says, and he worried that the millionaire would quit when he got bored.

So he finally settled on a mom who'd recently left her day job and was working as a personal chef. He pays her $60 per week plus the cost of groceries, and she makes him enough food for 12-15 basic meals, counting leftovers. (In general, personal chefs either cook in a client's home or in rented space in commercial kitchens where they cook in bulk for multiple clients). In theory, this is $60 added to Savara's budget, but in reality it isn't. His credit card bills have gone down. It turns out that not only is Savara's personal chef more efficient about buying groceries, "A great side effect is that I spend a lot less money on random things," Savara says—such as doughnuts that he didn't come in for, but which look oh-so-tempting in an end-cap display. All told, he saves about 10 hours per week, time he's used to practice the guitar and write more for his Web site.

Indeed, the arrangement worked so well that he's been experimenting with outsourcing his laundry, too. His current laundry service comes to his apartment and, for $7 per load, picks up his dirty clothes and returns them in 48 hours. This has been helpful to Savara because he has a tiny washing machine and a king-size bed. Washing his comforter was "literally an item on my to-do list for four months," because he never got around to hitting a commercial Laundromat. The poor dirty comforter sat there moldering in the hamper for an entire season. Then he gave it to the laundry service, and it returned 2 days later, "washed and smelling fresh."

It may strike you, reading Savara's story, that he has basically hired himself a wife. Indeed, it begs the question: If he were married, would he still be so gung-ho about outsourcing his chores?

He seemed like a pretty modern guy when I interviewed him, so maybe he would, but our cultural assumptions about which tasks men and women are "supposed" to do run deep. Dads mow the lawn; moms cook and clean. Around Mother's Day each year, Salary.com posts calculations on what you'd have to pay a mom on the open market for her domestic services. Based on survey answers, these services include food chores, cleaning, shopping, laundry, and general household management. Many a young groom is still asked, postnuptials, if he's enjoying his new wife's cooking. Those assumptions are the reason that the essayist Judy Syfers caused quite a stir in the premiere issue of *Ms.* (published in the early 1970s), with a piece called "I Want a Wife." She daydreamed about having a wife to manage dental appointments, "keep my clothes clean, ironed, mended, replaced when need be," plan the menus, "do the necessary grocery shopping, prepare the meals, serve them pleasantly, and then do the cleaning up," take care of the details of her social life, plan parties, and so on.

I wasn't around in the early 1970s, so I can't speak to the politics of the time. Certainly the essay has anachronisms. It seems that, back in the day, many husbands expected their wives to type their school papers. Dinner guests expected a hostess to provide ashtrays. But when I picked up the essay in 2007, I was most struck by two things. First, how few of Syfers's non-child-care chores I actually do, and second, how many of these chores can now be affordably outsourced—often to small businesses or sole proprietors who are better at these individual tasks than any wife could hope to be.

This is the core-competency principle again. Just as you have core competencies at work, you have core competencies in your personal life. Whether it's playing guitar in a rock band or nurturing your children, or both, you have things that you love and do best and that other people cannot do nearly as well.

For most of us, housework is not one of these core competencies. Chances are, someone else can do at least some of these tasks better than you can, or enjoys them more than you do. Though using a personal chef saves Savara 10 hours per week, it doesn't take the chef 10 hours to cook for him. Her work time clocks in at closer to 3–4 hours, because she plans meals, shops in bulk, and so forth.

But even if you don't mind cleaning, cooking, or laundry, or you are efficient at these things, the important point is that household chores have an opportunity cost. While big companies could likely do a fine job booking their own travel, many outsource this to corporate travel agencies in order to keep their employees focused on their core competencies of developing drugs or building airplanes, or whatever they happen to do. Likewise, even if you're a reasonable housekeeper, such chores take time away from activities that are among your core competencies. This is true even if you're a full-time parent. If you're a full-time parent, your job is nurturing your children, not housework.

Unfortunately, this calculation of opportunity cost often gets lost in the debate about outsourcing, or the best ways to pinch pennies in a down economy. On one hand, hauling your own clothes to the

Laundromat instead of paying for wash-and-fold, or buying whole frozen chickens instead of the chopped kind, seems like a good way to save cash. Aren't these optional perks? Savara's father, who owns a franchise of The Maids, a cleaning service, once thought that his business was a purely discretionary household expense too. That meant the target market would be well-off people who wanted pristine homes. He later learned that "clients don't hire [The Maids] because they do a better job," Savara says. "A normal person with enough time could make the house spotless." The problem is that "most people do their heavy cleaning on Saturday or Sunday, which is family time. So they're not buying a clean home, they're buying their weekend back." If you spend a lot of hours working from Monday to Friday, that's worth more than The Maids' prices. "Almost every month they have someone—let's say the wife—call and cancel the service. Then the husband will call and start it up again and say 'We canceled the cable instead.'"

The truth is, money, like time, is a choice—and often a related choice. Just as you need a "work team" to support your career, you need a "home team" to help you focus on your core competencies and save time in your personal life. If you're rolling in cash, this may literally be a team. At a party not long ago, I started talking with a mom of several young children who ran a hedge fund in her spare time. Her husband bragged about how involved his wife was in their children's lives. So I questioned her to the point of social awkwardness on how she'd achieved such domestic and professional bliss. The answer was pretty straightforward: this family had roughly four full-time equivalents on the payroll, including people to run their errands and a full-time male housekeeper who came from 11:00 a.m. to 7:00 p.m. every day to clean, do laundry, cook dinner, and clean up afterwards. It was Syfers's dream come true (minus the ashtray part). Of course, by the time you figure in payroll taxes and such, all this domestic support was probably costing the family about $200,000 a year.

More practically for most of us, having a "home team" will involve creative use of the growing household-services industry and some smart planning—the same minimize/outsource/ignore strategies we talked about in Chapter 4. If vacuuming is not among your core competencies, better to own a smaller house and pay someone who specializes in cleaning to vacuum it than own a bigger house and lose your weekends chasing dust balls. Or you can take the free approach: developing selective vision and looking right past the dust balls until they are big enough to support commercial agriculture.

Fortunately, it is relatively easy to hack the hours devoted to housework, shopping (for all consumer goods), food prep, and other such things well down from the 31 hours the American Time Use Survey finds that dual-income couples with kids devote to them.

The first step is to go back to the time diaries from Chapter 1, and figure out the hours that you and your family devote to household activities. If you're like most people, you spend the lion's share of your time on these four chore categories:

Laundry and "wardrobe maintenance"
Food: menu planning, shopping, cooking, cleanup
Housekeeping, including lawn and garden care
Household management—a.k.a. "the little things that kill you"

Look at the hours for each. Is one consuming a disproportionate share of time? Maybe they're even, but one steals more family time than others. After all, you can pay bills after the kids go to bed, but the lawn has to be mowed when it's light. Or maybe you detest one aspect of housework, and want it off your plate first. The rest of this chapter will look at strategies for dealing with all these things. Building up such a support team in your personal life may be more difficult than doing so at work, but the payoff is high in terms of saved time, hassle, and sometimes cash.

Laundry and Wardrobe Maintenance

We all have to wear clothes, but obtaining them can be inefficient. Think about it—how much time and money did you spend concocting your current wardrobe? According to the Bureau of Labor Statistics, the average American family, with annual household expenditures of around $50,000, spends close to $1,900 of that on "apparel and services." That's a reasonable amount of money, especially if you consider what percentage of those clothes people actually wear. If you're like most of us, the answer for adults is less than half, which raises an important question: What else could you have done with the time you spent earning money to buy clothes you don't like?

I shudder to think about this question when I look at my own wardrobe. Due to a combination of shortsighted frugality and total style blindness, I have never been good about dressing myself. I have a closet full of cheap clothes I don't really like, and what little I do know about fashion has come from studying magazines and the TLC show *What Not to Wear*.

Writing this book, however, gave me a professional excuse to tackle the problem. Since my two sons were born at different times of the year, I needed new maternity clothes for my second pregnancy. So I decided to do something I'd long fantasized about: hire a personal shopper.

Finding one was easy enough. I Googled "personal shopper" and "NYC" and soon located Lindsay Weiner, a *What Not to Wear* veteran and Fashion Institute of Technology grad who now owns a company called Style Me NY. Unlike me, Weiner was drawn to fashion from an early age; while her all-girls school in Washington, D.C., required a uniform, "I used to get in trouble for trying to spice up my outfit," she says. She would pair red shoes with her navy shorts, which "looked so much better than the brown shoes we were supposed to wear." When she was bored in class, she would mentally make over the teachers. So I asked her to help me buy a summer maternity wardrobe.

It was like no other shopping experience I've ever had.

A few days before we met, she sent me a questionnaire in which I described what I liked wearing and what I didn't. Then she met me in the Starbucks on Grand and Broadway in SoHo, with an itinerary loaded into her Blackberry. First stop? The little-known maternity section on the third floor of TopShop (the U.K. fashion import), which, needless to say, I would never have found on my own. She talked me into trying on some skinny jeans I wouldn't have had the courage to pick up; they turned out to be too skinny and a saleswoman was sent scurrying to find another size. In the meantime, Weiner organized the piles of clothing, took things off the hanger, and even held them the right way so all I had to do was stick my head in. She talked me into trying on a shirt I thought would wash me out (it didn't). She nudged me toward a fun purple tank top, rather than a more functional white one. While we waited in line to pay for, among other things, the skinny jeans that turned out to look less ridiculous than I'd imagined, she held the clothes for me, and then insisted on carrying the bags.

Next stop: a maternity boutique that sold suits. Inexplicably, it was closed at 3:00 p.m. on a Monday afternoon. Weiner acted personally offended and apologized profusely. From there it was on to Anthropologie and Tahari, where we also struck out, mostly because even the stretchy stuff wasn't cut right for my belly. But no matter. She recovered. We hit another maternity boutique for a dressy shirt, then cabbed it up to Belly Dance Maternity, where we hit the jackpot. She found the exact right pair of black dress pants from a pile, nudged me toward an A-line skirt rather than a pencil skirt, yanked a stunning cobalt dress from a pile of other colors I might have tried on first, flatteringly claimed I didn't even look pregnant in a wrap sweater I never would have picked out but loved, then talked me out of buying a $50 dressy turquoise shirt just because it fit. It was nothing special, she said. All I had to do was change clothes when instructed and pull out my credit card (and write Weiner a check). I came home three hours later with bags full of clothes I was actually excited to own, which is saying something given the sheer horror of much maternity wear.

I interviewed Weiner afterward and found some parallels with her work and my own. Because everyone does have to write a little in their lives, most people think they do it just fine. They're wrong. Likewise, with clothes, "just because you like it doesn't mean it works on you," she says. There is a corollary: "Just because it fits doesn't mean you should wear it." There are oceans of bad clothes out there. There are also oceans of bad ideas, such as that if you're larger, you should wear baggy clothes, or if you're young, it's OK to look like a stuffed sausage in a pair of jeans. Also, "there are some things that stay in style, but many things that don't." She once went through a woman's closet and had to chuck outfits from the early 1980s. On the other hand, with professional help, no one is hopeless. She once went shopping with a sixteen-year-old boy whose mom called her in desperation. He enjoyed the experience too. Who wouldn't enjoy shopping if someone could make it efficient and fun?

Hiring a personal shopper isn't cheap, so it's most practical if you're buying lots of clothes—for instance, if you've just landed a new job or lost weight. I paid about $400 for Weiner's time, though some department stores will perform similar services for free, as long as you buy your clothes from that store. On a more ongoing basis, here's a lower-budget way to outsource the task of styling. Find a boutique store that appeals to you (Ann Taylor Loft, Banana Republic), and figure out your size. Then, every season, buy two outfits straight off the mannequin. Down to the handbag or tie. These mannequins are professionally styled and will save you the trouble of figuring out what works together. They may also save you some money. After all, if you buy $1,500 of clothes a year, and only wear $750 worth (or less), anything that helps you shop smarter is more cash straight to the household bottom line.

Of course, once you own those fabulous clothes, you have to clean them. I'd argue that this is a good chore for outsourcing, too. You don't do your own dry cleaning. You don't do your own tailoring. So why not take it one step further and outsource your laundry?

That's what Savara does. So, interestingly, does Sarah Wagner, a Philadelphia-based stay-at-home mom. She watches what she spends, but as she told me when we talked in 2008, she simply hates spending her afternoons stuck in the laundry room, dealing with the Sisyphean task of cleaning clothes that just get dirty again. "Folding the laundry requires uninterrupted time that I don't have," she says. "If I stop mid-load, the kids and dog will inevitably trample my work."

So she contacted a business called We Wash It Laundry that usually caters to Philadelphia college students. It turned out that We Wash It does pickup, wash and fold, and delivery for private homes as well as dorms. They charge $1.10 per pound. For Wagner, this comes out to

$25–35 per week. Given the time she saves, this is a small luxury on a per hour basis.

"A lot of my friends cannot believe I don't do my own laundry," she says. They tell her it only takes a little bit of time (though they haven't added up the hours). They tell her to just put the kids in front of a DVD while she folds shirts. But "I don't want to spend less time with my children," Wagner says. "I want to spend less time doing housework." After all, families may have fond memories of cooking together, but no one waxes nostalgic that "Mom always had piles of laundry in a basket."

She's on to something, though I recognize that sending out the laundry is not a typical American habit. I started doing it solely because my first apartment building in New York City lacked a washer-dryer. There was a Laundromat across the street, but when I walked over with my bag and coins, I noticed a sign saying they would do it for me for about fifty cents a pound. I ran the numbers and decided to buy myself back my Saturdays by drinking less on Saturday nights and using the saved cash to outsource this chore. My plan was to continue this, and when I moved with my new husband to a high-rise with a laundry service in the basement, we often paid the dollar per pound for our own clothes (though we did our baby's clothes ourselves, since he required special detergent). Then, when Jasper was a year old, we moved to a bigger apartment. This apartment had a washer and dryer. Around the same time, I purchased some canvas army-surplus-type bags to replace the torn bags we had been sending to the laundry service. Michael laughed at the purchase. I believe his exact words were, "That's funny, since now we'll never have to use them."

I was a bit worried by this statement. To me, the fact that we possessed a washer and dryer didn't mean we had to change anything about our routine. After all, we own a juicer, too, and don't use that. Did my husband now expect me to spend hours each weekend doing this chore I hated?

The answer was no, though the end result wasn't necessarily better from a life-management perspective. Michael decided that *he* would do the laundry, so now Saturdays often find him trotting around the apartment with a laundry basket. I've come up with a few strategies to minimize the job. The kids can rewear any pajamas or pants that did not suffer an active diaper blowout. We own enough underwear and socks that we can go weeks between loads. I rewear my exercise clothes. Why do I care if my sports bras smell when I start running if they're just going to smell more five miles later? But when Michael's traveling, I sometimes haul out the canvas bags. After all, the laundry service even matches my socks.

"I am surprised that more people don't do this," Wagner says. Certainly, it's easier to outsource laundry in Manhattan, where so many people lack laundry rooms that there's a competitively priced wash-and-fold business every few blocks, though Wagner and Savara managed to find such services in Philadelphia and Honolulu, respectively. If you're looking for a service in your area, check with your dry cleaner first; they might do the job. If you strike out there, Google your zip code or city name and "wash and fold" or "pickup and delivery laundry service." I found several businesses around the country this way, with fun names such as Alabaster Cleaners in San Francisco, and The Clothesline in Milford, Connecticut. A few national dry-cleaning franchises, such as Pressed4Time, do this in some areas, and if you live near a university, there might be a student service. Or you can go Craig's List cruising for someone looking to moonlight—though you will need to talk with your accountant about the tax ramifications if the person you're hiring is operating as an individual rather than as a business, or if the laundry is done in your home rather than in a commercial Laundromat.

Food Chores

Savara hired someone to cook for him, and the personal chef business has grown rapidly over the last few years, but this is far from the only way to outsource the food chores that gobble vast hours if you're not careful. According to the American Time Use Survey, married moms and dads in dual full-time-career couples spend a combined 9.24 hours per week on grocery shopping, food preparation, and cleanup. By contrast, they spend about 3 hours per week, total, playing with their children. Lest you think this time allocation is unique to working parents, married stay-at-home moms likewise spend more than three times as many minutes grocery shopping, cooking, and doing dishes each week as they do playing with their kids.

One way to chop these hours drastically is to hire a commercial meal delivery service such as Jenny Craig, Zone Chefs, or Nu-Kitchen to bring the bulk of your food to your door. There may also be independent delivery services in your area, sometimes catering to certain dietary restrictions. When Wendy Kagan and Michael Belfiore of Woodstock, New York, welcomed their daughter, Amelie, several years ago, they started using a vegan meal delivery service because "cooking was at the bottom of the totem pole at that point," Kagan says. For $93.50, the service delivered enough meals to take two adults from Tuesday through Friday, which "ended up being cheaper than takeout." There was, of course, no requirement to actually be vegan to sign up.

The Kagan-Belfiore clan got a good deal at $93.50 for 4 days (and indeed, Kagan reports the price has gone up since); Nu-Kitchen charges $7.95 for breakfast and $11.50 each for lunch and dinner. If you have more than one mouth to feed in your household, that's going to add up fast. So for most families, I find the best option for outsourcing food chores is to use online grocery shopping as strategically as possible.

Though online grocery shopping was one of the great hopes of Web 1.0, it didn't catch on at first. Webvan lost something around $1 billion before going bankrupt in 2001. But nearly a decade later, retailers have worked out most of the kinks, with established players such as Fresh Direct in New York having forecasted double-digit growth in 2009.

There are several genius parts of online grocery shopping. For starters, you can shop late at night or during what would otherwise be wasted time at work while waiting for a call. You need not get in the car and wait in check-out lines during rush hour.

But that's just the obvious time saver. More crafty? Some online platforms let you quickly refill your cart from the shopping lists you've used before. Many of us purchase the same items nearly every time we go shopping. Think about how much of your grocery shopping time is spent wheeling your cart around the store picking up staples like milk or Cheerios. If you always buy something, automate it.

By far, though, the biggest genius element is the plethora of ready-made foods that smart online grocers offer. If you don't have a delivery service in your area, a stop every 2–4 weeks at Trader Joe's or another store that specializes in ready-made foods can also work when supplemented by quick in-between stops for milk and fresh produce. Fresh Direct sells dishes from trendy New York restaurants such as lamb chops with goat cheese orzo, and tequila chicken with mushrooms. I also buy premarinated meat, prechopped veggie mixes, and frozen lunches and breakfast treats such as scones. All I have to do is turn on the stove or microwave. If you buy in bulk for your freezer, and keep enough other staples such as instant rice and interesting sauces in your pantry, you can mix and match and never be more than 15 minutes of hands-on time away from a meal. I mean a good, healthy home-cooked meal that's a pleasure to eat. Some recent stand-outs in our house:

> Teriyaki pork tenderloin and asparagus with mushroom risotto (ingredients: premarinated tenderloin, bunch of asparagus, box of mushroom risotto, and extra mushrooms to mix in)
>
> Salmon with soy-maple glaze and green beans and brown rice (ingredients: frozen salmon, soy sauce, maple syrup, green beans, boil-in-bag brown rice)
>
> BBQ pork chops with peaches and toasted pine nut couscous (ingredients: frozen pork chops, barbeque sauce, chopped-up peaches, box of flavored couscous)
>
> Angel hair pasta with mushroom marinara sauce and salad (ingredients: pasta, jar of sauce, extra mushrooms to mix in, whatever random ingredients we have for a salad)
>
> Red pepper pizza (ingredients: frozen pizza, chopped-up red pepper on top)
>
> Baked chicken with apples and leeks (ingredients: get ready for this . . . chicken breasts, apples, and leeks). If we're feeling especially decadent, we might start with lobster bisque soup (ingredients: can of lobster bisque soup).

Almost all of these ingredients are staples that can be kept around or frozen (even the veggies and some of the fruit) so you don't have to think things through ahead of time. If you keep your meals simple, you won't even have many dishes—just plates, silverware, and at most two or three pots. If you detest loading and emptying the dishwasher, have your children do it. Or use paper plates and utensils, and then write a check to your favorite environmental charity as atonement. Fifteen minutes is nothing. Domino's can't get to your house faster. You'll do better, from a time perspective, than going out to eat.

Not that there's anything wrong with going out to eat. Americans spend about half our food dollars in restaurants or cafeterias these days, up from a quarter in 1955. This is an easy way to outsource food chores, and I definitely recommend sending kids to school with lunch money rather than a packed lunch, unless they wish to pack their lunches themselves. Menus have improved since the meatloaf surprise days of your youth, and you are not going to be able to make a good lunch for less than a school lunch costs. Plus, since most schools don't give kids access to a fridge or a microwave, the school lunch is the only way they're going to get something fresh and hot. If your office cafeteria serves tasty grub, feel free to use it, though keep in mind that you can lose vast amounts of time getting there and lingering over mediocre soup. Also, you can eat at your desk, but you can't run or bike at your desk, and lunchtime is often a good opportunity for office workers to fit in a workout (see Chapter 8 for more on this). If I don't have a meeting scheduled for the lunch hour, I rarely find it worth the lost work time to walk to a burrito restaurant when I can heat up a frozen burrito in the microwave. It's the same issue with Starbucks. I can make coffee just as I like it at home in less time than I waste standing in the rush hour 7:45 line giving my order to the nice but harried lady with the headset.

Indeed, the problem with America's restaurant addiction—aside from rising obesity and consumer debt—is that a great many of our food dollars are spent in restaurants that aren't really that good, but we're choosing just because we think they're convenient. As of 2009, we were spending about $35 per week for every man, woman, and child on commercial food services. Personally, rather than go out to eat three times a week someplace where the tabs are $10–15 a person, someplace where I have to deal with waiting in line at a counter or the stress of my toddler throwing his fork at the waitress, I'd rather make 15-minute meals at home and spend the money once every week or two on a babysitter and a real dinner someplace nice.

But this is a personal choice. The *168 Hours* approach to time management is to get rid of the chores you hate or that consume a lot of time, so you can focus your time on the things you do best. If you love going out to eat and hate cooking, then you have to figure out a way to make that work for your budget and your waistline—maybe by moonlighting or going to the gym during the hours you save.

Housekeeping

You know how to outsource at least part of this task. You call a cleaning service such as Merry Maids or The Maids (incidentally, both founded in Nebraska in 1979) and schedule a weekly or biweekly scrub-down. Give the service a copy of your key, set up a recurring payment, and you won't have to think about it. In general, unless you're looking for someone to come in multiple times per week (that is, someone who really would be a household employee), it's more efficient to hire a service than an individual, because the service will take care of payroll taxes and preemployment screening. If you have an average-size house, expect to pay somewhere around $100 a cleaning, meaning you'll pay $2,500 to have your house cleaned every other week for a year.

This is not a small chunk of change, though of course, cost is relative. The average family has gotten their heads around paying $876 per year for the convenience of cell phone service, often without giving up the landline. People spend vast sums on clothes they never wear. The average cable bill in the United States is now around $71 a month, or $852 a year, and the average tax refund is now well over $2,000. Most families treat their refunds as windfalls and spend the money on things like new furniture. A smarter idea if you value your weekend time or hate cleaning would be to adjust your withholding so the money shows up in your paycheck, and rather than buy new furniture, pay a service to clean the furniture you have.

The key thing to keep in mind with outsourcing the major household cleaning tasks, though, is that you might not save as much time as some of the folks who send me e-mail about how *of course* it would be easier to get things done *if only I had a cleaning service* seem to think. It takes about 4 professional man-hours to clean my 1,600 square feet of living space every two weeks. While we are not that efficient, I doubt it would take my husband or me more than 5 or 6 hours every 2 weeks to do the mopping, vacuuming, dusting, and toilet scrubbing that a cleaning service handles. That's 2.5–3.0 hours per 168-hour week (in a world in which the average American watches that amount of television daily). Yet in 2000, married mothers spent 5.1 hours per week on core cleaning chores, and married fathers spent 1.8, coming out to about 7 hours per family. So what fills the balance?

It's hard to tease the answer out perfectly, but I think a big part of it is the daily maintenance tasks of keeping everything picked up: putting away kids' toys, putting away clothes, throwing away mail, wiping up spills. The easiest way to cut down this time is to stop caring what your house looks like. If you *do* care what your house looks like, you probably can't lop this to zero without hiring a full-time housekeeper like the hedge fund manager I cornered at that party.

But there is one shortcut to making daily maintenance less overwhelming: an uncluttered house looks clean with less effort than one overflowing with piles. Every professional decorator will tell you this. No matter how much time you spend vacuuming your ceilings and washing your windows, what makes a house look clean is clear horizontal surfaces. That means having almost nothing on the counters, coffee table, dining room table, desks, and so on. Your drawers, cupboards, and closets can be as stuffed as you want. Feel free to throw the pile of mail in there if company's coming over! But when you have clear surfaces, you can make your house look tolerable between biweekly scrubbings with a madcap 15- or 20-minute blitz per day.

I know this. Yet, personally, I have found it quite difficult to get to this decluttered state. At times, my house has looked like a "before" scene on TLC's *Clean Sweep*. I've always been a messy person, albeit one with enough self-awareness to recognize that. My husband is no better. So, back when my husband, son, and I were living in a one-bedroom apartment, and I had to throw out two bags of trash from my desk because I couldn't find a document from the IRS that I needed, I decided to call a professional organizer.

The field of professional organizing is relatively new, and is thoroughly a creation of the modern era. In the past, there was no job title for someone who would help "see to it that my personal things are kept in their proper place so that I can find what I need the minute I need it," as Judy Syfers wrote in her famous *Ms.* essay. Standolyn Robertson, past president of the National Association of Professional Organizers and owner of the organizing service Things in Place, told me that, years ago, she described her vision of organizing closets to a high school mentor. He told her, "You want to be a wife."

But that wasn't quite it. Organizing is a skill, just as composing advertising jingles is a skill. In theory anyone can do it, but some people do it much better than others. The hilarity of professional organizing is not that it exists, it's that in the past all women were expected to have this skill among their core competencies.

Given the messy state of my house, I was pretty sure it wasn't among mine. Or at least that's what I thought until I met Janine Sarna-Jones, the New York–based owner of Organize Me. She came to my house for an assessment. For 2 hours, as I studied her methods, she studied my home office and kid space systems, and my commitment to actually doing things differently. She examined my teeming bookshelf warily. She opened the coat closet and asked if I had any idea what was in there. She noted the stack of Pampers boxes supporting a basket with diapers, wipes, and a trash can at changing table level. She took notes.

Then she sat me down on the sofa.

"Here's the scoop," she said. "You guys have done an amazing job." I raised my eyebrows. She explained. We had managed to create a nursery in the former dining alcove of our one-bedroom apartment that looked pretty good. Actually, it looked good because we hired someone else to choose the furniture for it, but that is what it is. We had proven ourselves able to go through stuff and throw things out. Despite our busy schedules, we'd kept our kid well fed (I guess the bar on organization is low). We were not disorganized. We had a more specific problem: "You guys are lazy," she said. Quite simply, if our messiness bothered us, we would have done something about it. As it is, we had been able to walk, every day, past the car seat and bouncy seat our son had outgrown, knowing full well that there was a storage space in Long Island City that had been leased to us. And yet we put off hailing a cab and going back out there for so long that eventually we were expecting another kid and needed the infant stuff again. "You get eighty percent there," she said, "and then the last twenty percent you say, screw it."

I've never been one for accepting 80 percent, and over the year since the assessment, we've uncluttered our new, larger home in bits and pieces. If you're looking for practical guidance, I recommend checking out the Fly Lady's Web site (FlyLady.net). Her colorful suggestions include the "27 Fling Boogie," which means going through your house with a trash bag and throwing out twenty-seven things. Why twenty-seven? It's a big enough number to make progress, and an odd enough number to make it a game, especially if you boogie to some music at the same time. Spend 15 minutes each day for a month tackling some horizontal hot spot. Anyone can find 105 minutes in their 168 hours, particularly if you break it up into 5-minute chunks.

In my 5-minute chunks, I created a mail station. I designated a nice shiny tray as my husband's pocket-emptying zone, where his wallet and keys are supposed to go when he gets home from work so they don't get splattered over the kitchen counter. I found a waterproof bag for my son's tub toys and toy baskets for his other things, so he can help pick up. In one of the big shocks of my life, I found out recently that he likes doing this. At our first parent-teacher nursery school conference (don't laugh), his teacher informed us that whenever they sing the cleanup song, he is the enforcer, racing to put his toys away and then making sure all the other children clean up as well. This realization has given new urgency to the decluttering. Apparently junk really stresses my toddler out.

I won't claim any of this has been easy. One of the reasons I've resisted decluttering is that I worried I might need something later on. This has turned out to be true. Rather than move my fire-hazard collection of magazines to my new apartment, I threw 95 percent of them in the recycling bin. Then, when I was writing this book, I realized I needed a story that I had, in fact, dumped. I only had a vague recollection of when it had run. It took me 20 minutes of Web searching to figure out the issue date. Then it cost me $20 to order the issue from a collector. Not nothing, but in the grand scheme of things, I guess anything that can be solved in 20 minutes with $20 is not really a problem.

The net result of having clear horizontal surfaces and bins for stuff all over the place is that cleaning is not overwhelming. It takes less than 20 minutes a day to keep it under control. Just don't open my closets. Trust me on this one.

The Little Things That Kill You

You can develop good systems for outsourcing the recurring laundry, food prep, and scrubbing chores of life. What causes tension in many families, though, is the random things that don't happen often but take time when they do. Someone has to schedule and wait for the plumber. Someone has to take the books to the library, confirm that the hotel you'll be visiting on vacation allows late check-in, and schedule everyone's eye doctor appointments. I suspect one of the reasons women think they do more housework than they actually log is the mental overhead caused by "the random, miscellaneous things that kill you," as Kathryn Bowsher, the San Francisco–based founder of Act One Marketing, puts it.

Bowsher spends a lot of time building her company, which specializes in commercial strategy for development-stage drugs and medical devices. When she's not working, she likes to relax with family and friends, rather than attend to household details. So, like Judy Syfers, Bowsher found herself wishing, a few years ago, that she had the Perfect Wife.

Fortunately, she found one. His name is Ed Daly, and when I interviewed him in 2007 for *USA Today*, he was running a company called The Perfect Wife out in the Bay Area. Daly fell into the business about 10 years ago when he was in a career transition or, as he puts it "freaking out," asking "What am I going to do with my life?" A busy woman who lived on his street hired him to do some shopping for her, and then to switch out an old cabinet. He did such a good job that she asked if she could hire him for a few weeks to get her life in order. She took to calling him "the perfect wife" and gave his name and phone number to several girlfriends, who paid him to run their errands as well. And so he began hauling shoes to the cobbler. He would order replacement salad plates and make bed skirts. He planned parties, waited for plumbers and, for $35 an hour ("A lot of people tell me I should be charging more"), did anything else that there's "not enough hours in the day to do."

He's part of a growing industry of folks who will do these little things that kill you. There are concierge services such as Ask Sunday, the comically named "Yes, Your Highness!" service here in New York City, Red Butler, Circles, and various members of the International Concierge and Errand Association (ICEA). For a certain fee per month or request (sometimes offered as a corporate benefit), these services will schedule doctor appointments and find someone to water your plants, or otherwise fulfill Syfers's dream of having a wife who will "take care of the details of my social life." They will do this even if the details of your social life are weird; Chris Sterling, a spokesman for Red Butler, tells me that his company once fulfilled a request for a client who was staying at a hotel in New York and wanted a strawberry milk bath. Red Butler called someone to go out and buy Strawberry Quik ASAP.

Some people have success outsourcing their life maintenance by hiring virtual assistants through portals such as oDesk or eLance. You can also hire a "live" personal assistant or household manager if you're wealthy enough and your life is overwhelming; a number of agencies will help you find such a person. But for most people, simply contracting with someone like Daly or a concierge service will work if, as Daly notes, these people "don't want to come home at night and put a bicycle together for their son. They want to spend time with their son."

Of course, even if you book someone like Daly's services, you still have to tell him what to do. That means someone has to at least remember that antique sofas need to be appraised, Elvis impersonators need to be called, or whatever your needs happen to be. In two-income families, that someone is still, more often than not, the female half of the couple. But there is a big difference between spending all Saturday on the phone with clowns, and tossing a list at Daly that says "venue, balloons, entertainment, favors, cake." That, he can work with, because he wants to make your life, as he told me, "seamless." Problem solving is his core competency—something he enjoys in the same way Kathryn Bowsher enjoys building her company.

So, given that there are people out there willing to make your home life seamless for relatively small chunks of change, it raises the question of why more people don't do what Sid Savara, Sarah Wagner, Kathryn Bowsher, and others do. When I've suggested black-belt-level household outsourcing to people, I've gotten a few reactions.

The first, reflexive one is that it's too expensive, which isn't the case nearly as often as people think it is. You *can* spend $200,000 a year like the hedge fund family, but most people can get by with an outsourcing budget that is orders of magnitude less—and more in keeping with normal American budgets, which somehow manage to accommodate monthly $400 car payments (because we have to have new cars, not used ones), big air-conditioning bills because people feel entitled to freeze during the summer, or, for that matter, $25.95 books on time management. The only reason we consider household outsourcing expensive is that we, as a society, largely expect women to do these things for free. We may expect men to do some household tasks for free, like mow the lawn, but interestingly, lawn care turns out to be among the most highly outsourced of household chores. The National Gardening Association found that 30 percent of all U.S. households hired some sort of lawn or landscape service in 2006. By contrast, Merry Maids, the dominant player in the household cleaning industry, handles just 300,000 North American homes per month. It seems that men are wise to something. As it is, categories of women's work are disappearing, too. No one expects women to sew their children's clothes anymore. We outsource this to various factories around the world. No one expects women to milk their own cows or churn their own butter. We outsource these tasks to farms and manufacturers who can do it faster, better, and cheaper.

Including the opportunity cost of time is the only step forward in logic necessary to justify outsourcing laundry, cleaning, and food preparation alongside sewing. Indeed, if you run the numbers, you'll see that the rise of small businesses devoted to these tasks, and the moonlighting culture of the Craig's List economy, makes outsourcing far more accessible to the modern middle (or at least upper-middle) class than the maids, butlers, and laundresses of yore. Given the efficiency differences between Sid Savara and his personal chef, he manages to buy back his time at $6 per hour, which is less than Hawaii's minimum wage. He can definitely earn more than that by spending those additional hours working. Savara's chef, on the other hand, earns $15-20/hour. This is the same phenomenon that leads countries to trade goods with one another. The economy as a whole grows, and utility rises, when everyone focuses on what he or she does best relative to other market participants.

The second reaction is that some people really, truly enjoy housework, or at least parts of it. While I try to order the workhorse staples of my grocery list online, if my family has rented a car and ventured into suburbia, my husband and I can spend hours wandering the aisles of fancy or specialty grocery stores, tossing bags of frozen octopus or packages of raw milk cheeses into our cart. We consider this fun. Plenty of people enjoy gardening. And maybe some people out there really, really love laundry. If this is you, embrace it. Consider it leisure time, and indulge in pricey scented detergent, roll around in clean sheets, and dog-ear your copy of Cheryl Mendelson's *Laundry: The Home Comforts*

Book of Caring for Clothes and Linens. Better yet, if this is a core competency for you, then start a business doing other people's laundry. There's plenty of space in the Craig's List economy for more laundry experts, personal chefs, professional organizers, and other people who excel at household chores.

But the last objection is the one I find the strangest. Some people—women more often than men—get a little offended when I suggest outsourcing and say something along these lines: *It's my job to take care of my family.*

It certainly is a parental core competency to care for a family, but culturally, many people still believe that "caring for a family" means cooking, scrubbing, vacuuming, lunch packing, weeding, and laundry, in addition to the emotional work of nurturing children's brains and souls. For years, all these labors have been roped into the job description of "mom" or occasionally "dad." But does it make you a better parent to stand there in the kitchen every morning packing elaborate lunches that will get soggy when $2-3 for the hot school lunch would suffice? Is that really what kids need? Or do we have a situation like in the Gospels, when Martha was obsessed with cooking for Jesus, and got upset that Mary sat and listened?

We all have 168 hours a week. Time spent doing one thing is time not spent doing another. I would argue that unless you are making a conscious point of involving your kids with an activity such as laundry—a reasonable idea if they're ten, not so easy if they're two—doing loads of it is taking time away from them. Freed from unnecessary domestic burdens, we become better parents and people.

"I find it so interesting that it is commonplace in our society to outsource child care, but the burdensome routines of keeping house are, for the most part, not outsourced," Sarah Wagner says. Finding a laundry service has let her spend more relaxed time with her little ones without dreading that Sisyphean chore, just as outsourcing food prep has let Savara spend more time on his core competencies of working and playing the guitar. Says Wagner, "We have all been happier ever since."

Nixing Household Chores

Look at your time logs from Chapter 1. How much time do you and your spouse spend on these tasks?

	ME	SPOUSE/ PARTNER	TOTAL
Laundry			
Food Chores			
Housekeeping/ Lawn			
Household Management			

Which tasks do each of you like most?

Which tasks do you like least?

How could you ignore, minimize, or outsource these tasks?

· 8 ·

A Full Life

One of the most insightful fashion stories I ever read appeared in, of all places, *The Wall Street Journal*. For some reason a few years ago, the paper had dispatched a style reporter to the investment banker Herbert Allen's annual Sun Valley gathering of media moguls, where a surprising discovery was made: these corporate titans had no idea how to dress outside the office. "While media big shots may be used to getting their suits tailored, they often buy casual clothes off the rack and don't pay enough attention to style or fit," the paper noted. "The upshot: Executives who appear put together at the office can look uncharacteristically disheveled in a casual setting." Barry Diller showed up at the event in drawstring pants with a red-and-black zip-up cardigan and clashing orange polo shirt. Rupert Murdoch wore the same cable-knit tennis sweater 2 days in a row. Michael Bloomberg wore boat shoes with white socks. Geraldine Laybourne of Oxygen Media didn't match at all, and blamed her husband, who she said normally inspected her clothes.

Of course, it's always fun to mock CEOs, but I can sympathize with their plight. While the world of work is changing, the suit-and-tie rules of fashion are a lot clearer than the ones for our days off. The same is true for how we use our time. Work hours are often a blur of go-go-go from one scheduled deadline to the next. Then you come home for the evening or weekend. Now what? We feel like the businessmen-turned-hostages and the hostage-takers in Ann Patchett's novel *Bel Canto*, finding ourselves suddenly locked up in a strange Latin American vice presidential mansion, unsure what to do with our hours. "Without exception, these were men who were largely unfamiliar with the concept of free time," Patchett wrote. "The ones who were very rich stayed at their offices late into the evening. They sat in the backseats of cars and dictated letters while their drivers shepherded them home. The ones who were young and very poor worked just as hard, albeit at a different kind of work. There was wood to be cut or sweet potatoes to be dug out of the ground. There were drills to be learned with the guns, how to run, how to hide. Now a great, unfamiliar idleness had fallen on them and they sat and they stared at one another, their fingers drumming incessantly on the arms of chairs . . ."

Likewise, long weekend hours can easily disappear into chores, Blackberry breaks, shuttling children around, and checking what's on TV. Then, suddenly, it's Sunday night and you feel about as relaxed and rejuvenated as you would in a clashing cardigan and polo shirt, or in the middle of a Latin American hostage situation.

Of course, some people—in fiction and real life—seem to have a better handle on these things. One of the *Bel Canto* captives, a Japanese executive named Tetsuya Kato, happens to play the piano well enough to entertain even his captors. His secret? "He continued his lessons and practiced for an hour every morning before boarding the train for work," Patchett wrote.

He's not the only one making that sort of commitment with his leisure time. Consider the (nonfictional) story of Alexi Panos, who not only seems to have a good handle on these things, she has a better handle on her wardrobe than Diller, Murdoch, et al. Panos is the cohost of Sportsnet New York's *Beer Money* and a model who has appeared in *Runner's World*, *Health*, and *Cosmopolitan*, and in campaigns for Nautica and so forth. These gigs are her full-time job, but she also has another "full-time" project (as she puts it)—running a nonprofit called E.P.I.C., which stands for "Everyday People Initiating Change."

I've interviewed a reasonable number of philanthropy-minded actors and models over the years, and at first blush, the genesis of EPIC sounds much like the rest. In an earlier career iteration as a singer half a decade ago, Panos was in South Africa on a concert tour. She saw the grinding poverty of the townships. She noted the contrast to the rock star life she was living. And so she wanted to do something. Like many people from developed countries first learning about the woes of Africa, she figured that "something" would involve raising money for AIDS treatments or hunger prevention.

But what makes this story more interesting is that she and a friend, Tennille Amor (who'd lived in Egypt and had some African contacts), decided to do their field research first. They wound up in the Tanzanian village of Kawe, not too far from Dar es Salaam. As in much of eastern Africa, the architecture in this part of Tanzania is a mix of concrete-and-tin houses and mud-and-grass huts, and the lack of good sewage systems and drinking water breeds problems Westerners seldom imagine. Dirt roads flood with excrement and pollution when it rains. The standing pools of water contaminate everything and attract mosquitoes, which bring malaria. AIDS is certainly a problem, but it is far from the only problem.

So Panos and Amor took up residence with a host family, whose matriarch was a community leader. She helped them set up interviews with twenty other families. They went from hut to hut and "literally just asked questions—what's affecting you guys?" Panos says. "Everybody said water-borne diseases." Kids would die of diarrhea from drinking dirty water or become sick when cuts and scrapes got infected and could not get cleaned. In the absence of reliable local water supplies, children might spend hours per day walking to faraway (but often still contaminated) water sources, and hence have a difficult time cramming schooling into their 168 hours.

Panos and Amor did not expect this answer, but to their credit, they decided to chuck their preconceived notions, and go with what the villagers told them.

This is how the cohost of *Beer Money* wound up in the well-drilling business. Upon coming back to the United States, Panos spent every spare hour she had between photo shoots reading about sanitation and nonprofit management and figuring out how to hire engineering crews in Africa. Over the past few years, EPIC has built five wells in Tanzania. It is a slow pace, but it is one they can sustain on their small budget, which Panos and Amor raise or kick in themselves, and a pace that ensures that the residents near each site have the tools and knowledge to repair everything. Africa is literally littered with the carcasses of broken wells from previous foreign aid projects. Panos doesn't want to be one of these monuments to inefficiency. She spends most of her vacations living in Tanzanian slums. Like the fictional piano player in *Bel Canto,* she carves out an hour every morning to do the administrative work of EPIC before the phone starts ringing with last-minute commercial or catalogue shoots. "No one's going to give you that hour," she says. "You have to make it for yourself."

When you do give structure and purpose to your leisure time, though—the equivalent of treating your weekend wardrobe with the respect you'd assign your weekday suit and tie—you can have the kind of full life that few of us think is possible. It's "very rewarding" to travel for a reason, Panos says, to go to Africa and see five wells that exist solely because this young model and actress decided to do something besides party during her nonworking hours. "Every time I go out there I kind of question why I come back [home]."

I am going to argue something a bit controversial in this chapter. I think time is too precious for us to be totally leisurely about leisure.

I say this knowing that there is plenty of thoughtful research out there about the importance of that most free-form of leisure activities known as play and particularly its sad decline among upper-class children. One *Time Out New York Kids* article quoted Susan Linn, author of *The Case for Make-Believe,* as saying that the average time six- to eight-year-olds spend in creative play declined by a third from 1997 to 2002. Social critics like to blame this on kids' being "overscheduled," though I think this is a more limited phenomenon than people make it out to be. Many children still spend way too many hours unsupervised, and if anything they don't have enough activities or homework in their lives.

Still, there is something to this decline in unstructured hours spent daydreaming. Adults, likewise, need unstructured time to truly relax and rejuvenate. Sometimes our best ideas about advancing our careers or solving personal problems spring out of these fallow hours. The point that I think gets missed in all these lamentations is that almost all of us *do* have adequate time in our 168 hours for play—and for the structured leisure activities such as sports, arts, or volunteer work that add meaning to life.

We are not particularly good about seizing this time, however, for a few reasons. Though we don't work as many hours as we think we do, many of us have jobs these days that could, in theory, occupy our brains for 168 hours a week. Some of us are entrepreneurs, and so we are always responsible for our businesses. Some of us have open-ended job descriptions—like serving multiple clients—which mean that we're always going from one project to the next. Regardless, if you are in the right job, you are going to love your job. And if you love your job, then you're going to want to spend lots of time thinking about it. I am writing this paragraph at 9:00 p.m., even though this book isn't due to my publisher for another few months, my son is asleep, there's a *People* magazine in the next room and not a soul on this planet telling me I can't touch it. Add in family responsibilities on top of this constant mental siren song of work, and it's easy to see why those alarmist surveys we've discussed in the rest of this book have claimed that Americans have just 16.5 hours of self-reported leisure time each week.

As with all quick-response surveys, though, this number is problematic. More sober time-use studies find that almost all Americans, including parents of young kids, have at least 30 hours of weekly free time. That's over 4 hours per day, even though the *Real Simple* article we talked about in Chapter 1 had people grasping at 15 free minutes to try a hammock or take a bath.

So why the discrepancy between perception and reality? It comes down to this: we don't use the time we have well. We don't spend much time thinking about what we'd like to do with our free time, even though no one would take a 30-hour-per-week job without clarifying the job description. Because we don't think through our leisure time, we often don't even recognize when it's appearing, and so we wind up spending big chunks of it in the most frictionless way possible: in front of the television.

When I say "big chunks," I mean big chunks. Nielsen's research numbers show that Americans spend, on average, more than 30 hours per week watching television, though "watching" may not be the right word. Recent American Time Use Survey results find that Americans report watching television as a primary activity closer to 20 hours per week. Still, this is a lot of hours. For many people, it is the lion's share of their leisure time. It's the equivalent of a part-time job, and it's more time than Michael Schidlowsky, the Google software engineer from Chapter 1, spends training for the Ironman Triathlon. Think about that. If the average person started exercising every time he was tempted to turn on the tube, he could be doing triathlons competitively within a few years.

Instead, most of us elect to become world-class couch potatoes. There are several reasons that television dominates our leisure time, and they are understandable reasons. First, TV is relatively cheap on a per-hour basis. Once you've sunk the cost of the set, the marginal cost of the cable bill is less than a dollar per hour the set is on. In a tough economy, this is hard to beat.

Second, television makes few demands of the watcher. Most shows are pleasant or entertaining, even for people who've never seen them before. Anyone of any skill level can sit on the couch, and the television doesn't care what you look like. It also doesn't care if you don't pay complete attention because you're cooking dinner or you're checking downstairs every 10 minutes to be sure your children haven't killed each other. You don't have to hire a sitter to turn the TV on.

Third, television is almost perfectly suited to fit the way many of us experience our leisure time these days—that is, in chunks too small to do much else of consequence. While going to an art museum might be invigorating, that requires a concentrated block of at least 2 hours. TV can make you feel relaxed in less than 30 minutes.

But it won't make you feel *too* relaxed, and therein lies the problem.

While television is pleasant, it does not make us feel particularly happy or rejuvenated, the way true recreation should. In one old study from 1985 called the Americans' Use of Time Project, on a 1–10 scale of enjoyment that went from taking the car to get repaired (4.6) to sex (9.3), people ranked television somewhere in the middle, at a 7.8. This is below playing with kids (8.8), reading books (8.3), talking with family (8.0), or playing sports, which turns out to be almost as good as sex, at 9.2. There are plenty of allegations about the nefariousness of television—that it interferes with sleep patterns, that the ads make people want things they don't need and teach children to whine for sugary cereals—but we do know this: because TV is so easy and so accessible, it often beats out activities that would bring a lot more joy to our lives, such as visiting (8.2), going for walks (8.3), sleeping or going to church (8.5 each), experiencing art or music each (9.0), or going fishing (9.1).

There are two ways to avoid falling prey to this crowding. The first is to not own a TV, though your computer can be equally abused. The more practical option is to plan ahead—that is, lower the transaction costs—and fill your leisure time with enough meaningful activities and constructive relaxation that TV doesn't become the default activity when you don't know what else to do. You do know what else to do, and you do these things first. TV can then fill in around the edges in a way that works for you and your family.

These are the rules for leveraging your leisure time to create a full life:

Choose a small number of activities that bring you the most happiness; one of these has to be exercise

Create blocks in your schedule for these activities

Commit enough time, energy, and resources to make them meaningful

Use the principle of alignment to build in more time with family and friends, or for leisure generally

Use bits of time for bits of joy

Focus Your Time

The first step to getting more out of your leisure time is to figure out what you would like to be doing with it. Go back to your "List of 100 Dreams" from Chapter 2. Once you've tried several of these activities, you'll find a few that you'd like to make into more regular features of your life—that is, things that can claim roughly 2–10 of your 168 hours.

For instance, I've always loved artistic endeavors. I like singing, dancing, playing the piano, and taking photos. I have also learned, through disastrous adult dance classes and the fact that I don't understand even the most basic functions on my camera, that I can be satisfied with occasional dabblings in most of these matters. But singing is a different story. Choral singing has a social component I like and introduces me to a wide variety of music. I discovered in college that I was willing to devote serious time to it. Not only was I willing to commit time, I was willing to beg in a dean's office to be allowed to transfer out of a certain section of a class in order to attend rehearsals.

So, after moving to New York City a few years ago, I tried three different choirs before deciding to commit to the Young New Yorkers' Chorus, which rehearses every Tuesday night and performs three concerts a year. It's become a big part of my life, and the choir even sang at my wedding. I eventually became the president and helped hire our current director. We launched an annual Competition for Young Composers in 2004, which commissions three new works each year from composers under age thirty-five, and gives these works their world premieres. YNYC consumes enough of my artistic and volunteer energy that I don't feel bad saying no to other volunteer opportunities that I think are worthwhile. If I believe something is a good cause, I write a check.

Likewise, as you go through your "List of 100 Dreams," choose a small number of activities—one, two, or at most three—that truly matter to you. If you've got kids who also need your attention, you're better off sticking closer to one or two than three, because doing fun activities with your family will be another major leisure-time commitment (see Chapter 6 for more about this). Encourage your kids to adopt the same philosophy. Contrary to popular belief, Princeton's and Harvard's admissions officers are not looking for scattershot résumés of two instruments, three sports, four volunteer activities, and five hobbies. That's not passion, that's ADD. Once you've chosen a narrow-enough focus, you can throw enough energy into your activities to get better and get somewhere—like building five wells in Tanzania that didn't exist before—and hence use your time to actually "recreate."

These activities can be anything you dream of—singing, acting, competitive bridge or chess, drawing caricatures, learning French, playing kickball, gardening, running a Boy Scout troop, volunteering at a soup kitchen, serving as a lay minister—except for one rule: one has to involve working up a sweat.

There is simply no way around this. For good health, exercise is non-negotiable, and in a sense it's a core competency. You definitely can't outsource it. The Center for Disease Control and Prevention's minimum guideline for lowering the risks of the worst consequences of inactivity is 150 minutes—2.5 hours—of moderate activity each week. If you think about it, 2.5 out of 168 hours really isn't that much. You can easily top this up a bit and reap even more benefits. "Doing three to five hours a week consistently will massively change your health," says Gordo Byrn, a Boulder, Colorado–based triathlon coach. I am inclined to believe Byrn on this because, in 1994, he was an out-of-shape finance guy who tried to run three miles and had to walk home. In 2004, he finished the Ironman Canada in 8 hours and 29 minutes, ending with a blistering 2:46 marathon. He can run a faster marathon, but this was after swimming 2.4 miles and biking 112 miles.

Now, obviously, hitting a 2:46 marathon time will require more than 5 hours of training per week, but if 3–5 hours will revolutionize your health, consistently doing 5–9 hours will at least put you in near-peak amateur condition. This is only about 3–5 percent of your 168 hours. One approach is to commit to clocking 2.5 hours per week for a year, logging your time until you get in the habit, then bumping this up to 5 hours per week for the next year. If you decide that you enjoy this, and want to start doing races or long hikes, then you can bump it up again to 7 hours.

The physical activity (or activities) you choose is up to you, and you're best off choosing something you enjoy. "People have this concept in their minds that this isn't going to be fun," Byrn says. But "the people that actually get to the result are normally the ones that enjoy the process the most." If your sport of choice is snowshoeing or swimming and you live somewhere you can do this daily, great, but by far the most popular activity among people I interviewed for this book is running.

There are many reasons for this. For starters, you can see results in very little time. Not in the 20 minutes per week that exercise DVDs tout, but in short amounts of time nonetheless. Indeed, you simply can't devote that much time to it. "That's the beauty of running," Byrn says. "Because of the pounding there's only so much of it you can do. A normal person can only run about an hour a day—about seven to seven and a half hours a week."

I don't quite hit that. For me a great week is about 4–5 hours of running, and 1–2 hours of cross-training, though if you'd told me 10 years ago that I would someday type this sentence, I would have thought you were nuts. I started running consistently only a few years ago, in November 2004, after watching Paula Radcliffe's hard-fought victory in the New York City marathon. I'd just gotten married 2 months before, and since Michael had run cross-country in high school, running seemed like an activity we could do together. It wasn't easy for me. Even though I took many dance classes as a child, and would go to aerobics classes or use the elliptical machines at the gyms I joined over the years, I had a hard time running two miles. But I ran slowly and kept at it, and by spring, I could do a five-mile "long run." Michael and I signed up for a half marathon in Virginia Beach on our first wedding anniversary. On September 4, 2005, we took our places at the starting line, and started trudging along. I remember thinking, around mile 7, how amazed I was that I was even able to run that far. We finished with a two-mile sprint along the boardwalk and collapsed onto the sand. Even untying my shoes was painful, but by that point, I had the running bug.

Several years later, I'm still pretty infatuated. Few activities release the kinds of endorphins running does. I like that you don't need much equipment or anyone else to play. I like that a mere 5 hours per week keeps my usual weight about seven or eight pounds below where it was at the end of high school. I like that, as Joyce Carol Oates once wrote, "The structural problems I set for myself in writing, in a long, snarled, frustrating, and sometimes despairing morning of work . . . I can usually unsnarl by running in the afternoon." I like that I get a workout at whatever pace I can handle.

That's been important as my life situation has changed and I've found other reasons to be inspired by Paula Radcliffe. I learned I was pregnant with Jasper in September 2006. In October 2006, Radcliffe, then 6 months pregnant with her daughter, Isla, was photographed running a 10K in London. She was later photographed running, 8 months pregnant, for *Vogue*. Her decision to keep running through her pregnancy helped inspire me to do the same. It was a wonderful decision for myself and my baby. Jasper clocked in at a sturdy 7.5 pounds at birth, and was so healthy and eating so well that we got to leave the hospital early. We walked home. And let this be written on my tombstone: I showed up at an event less than a week after giving birth wearing my nonmaternity jeans. I started running again 2 weeks after delivery and found that 9 months of training with a stowaway had actually made me faster, much like a cyclist training at altitude. With all these upsides, it was an easy decision to run through my second pregnancy—this time, even more seriously. I trained for and ran the ten-mile Broad Street Run in Philadelphia when I was five months along. Passersby in my neighborhood often gave me strange glances as I, 8 months pregnant, did stair repeats in nearby Tudor City, but Sam was born just as hearty as his big brother. And so we got to leave the hospital early again for what I've begun to think of as a family tradition: walking home.

Of course, running during pregnancy number two was more difficult, logistically, than running during pregnancy number one, given that the second time around I had an extrauterine baby to care for. This leads to the second rule for creating a full life in your leisure time.

Create a Block Schedule

If you have a busy life, you simply can't leave your most meaningful leisure activities to chance. After all, you wouldn't just hope to meet an important client, maybe, someday, when you got around to it and all the stars aligned. You'd call her up, schedule the meeting for a time when you were focused and had child care, and you'd plan what would happen during that meeting.

So it goes with other things. Once you've created a spreadsheet documenting how you spend your 168 hours, go through and find times that you can block out for your leisure activities. Make sure you have a good sense of how long each will take. A run may only require an hour; a painting class will require more time. Figure out how many times you plan to do the activity per week. If you plan to exercise 4 hours per week, for instance, and take a painting class at a neighborhood center and volunteer at a local food bank with your teens, you might block off three 1-hour slots during the week and one 1-hour slot on Sunday (for workouts), one 2-hour slot on Wednesday nights (for the class), and one 2-hour slot on Saturday (for the food bank shift). If you think about it, this shouldn't be too hard. We aren't talking vast amounts of time. Those three activities together would consume 8 of your 168 hours—far less time than I'm guessing you watch TV—yet would massively boost your quality of life.

Certain blocks of time work better for some people than others. Since I work for myself and work at home, I usually carve out time to run in the late morning or early afternoon, otherwise known as lunch time. This tends to be when I need a break. It also happens to be a time I have regular, reliable child care. Even on days that are packed with meetings or calls, I make sure to create an open block of 45–60 minutes around lunchtime so I can squeeze a workout in. If you can't seem to find an open block, try stacking phone calls or meetings closer together to free up space (over time, promising people 20 minutes instead of 30 really adds up). If you work at an office, eat lunch at your desk 2 or 3 days a week and exercise when other people drift down to the cafeteria.

If a midday break doesn't work for you, or doesn't work regularly, then you may need to wake up earlier to build in time for your pursuits. Many people feel more motivated in the early hours anyway. "As much as possible, train in the morning, before you get busy, and before you're given an excuse to miss your workout," Byrn says. "There's always a reason to skip a four o'clock workout, and it's going to be a good reason, too."

You can do other activities in the morning time slot besides exercise. Panos sticks her EPIC work there. You don't have to wake up early every day, though you can if you discover you like it. Michelle Girasole, a business owner and mom of two who lives in Wickford, Rhode Island, wakes up around 5:00 a.m. 6 days per week, while the rest of her family is still sleeping. On 4 of those days, she walks along the beach for an hour. On the others, she reads. Waking up early sounds like it would involve sleep deprivation, but this isn't necessarily true. Many people wile away the hours from 10:00 p.m. to midnight watching late-night TV. Television doesn't really relax you. Go to bed instead, and shift that free time to the morning, when you'll have more energy to tackle a work-out, or a novel-writing or painting session.

If you've got kids or an unpredictable job, evenings can get complicated, though with 168 hours per week, there's plenty of time for leisure activities then, too. One workable option for families is to give each parent a weeknight "off." Girasole plays in a volleyball league on Thursday nights and her husband mountain-bikes on Tuesdays. The other parent can use this time for special activities with the kids, such as taking everyone to the park or the pool. The important caveat for this option is that both parents have to commit to the plan. Nothing will breed resentment like one party always missing his improv class because the other party "has" to work late. If you suspect this will be a problem for your family, hire a regular sitter instead.

Weekends require a different mind-set when it comes to scheduling, because often you're not trying to carve out time, you're debating how to spend far less structured hours. Some families turn their weekends into a death march of children's sporting events and errands. Other people don't have anything planned and see their weekends disappear into hours of TV watching, Web surfing, or inefficient bursts of work (for example, checking your Blackberry every hour). You want to strike a balance because there's no reason to plan every minute. Weekends are great for spending downtime reading a good book on the porch or sitting in the park if the weather's lovely, or even just enjoying your house if you don't see it often during the workweek. Weekends are also great times for doing the longer family activities that even the most efficient full-time workers won't have time for Monday to Friday. After talking to people who get a lot out of their weekends, I've found that they have a few principles in common.

First, they spend at least a few minutes thinking about what they'd like to do, and getting input from other family members as well. At Sunday-night family dinners, or while you're traveling back from a weekend away, discuss what everyone liked about that weekend, and what they'd like to do during future weekends. Assign responsibility for any necessary research or reservations. Then check in again during a midweek family breakfast or dinner conference to cement plans. You can do this even if the "family" consists of just you or you and a significant other, or you and roommates and friends. While you can always leave yourself open to last-minute opportunities, having at least one fun activity planned for the weekend gives you something to look forward to during the week. With any luck, once you establish this habit, your family members will get competitive over who can bring the best ideas to these meetings. They'll start hunting through listings for local festivals, nearby historic sites, church activities, dance classes, volunteer opportunities, or even projects such as scrap-booking or hosting a multi-age tea party that you could do at home.

Second, weekend masters know that extracurricular activities aren't just for kids. Adults are entitled to their fun, too. Since exercise is nonnegotiable, be sure to schedule at least one longer workout of 1–4 hours every weekend. Mornings tend to be good for this since you'll be fresher. Run someplace interesting you wouldn't go during the week, or do something like swimming that may require more travel than hitting the treadmill in your basement. If you've got kids, trade off childcare responsibilities with your spouse, or bring them along. Buy an old jogging stroller off Craig's List. Go for a family hike or a long run/bike ride to a picnic spot with your kids. Parents can also do solo activities on weekends if there's downtime that works for your family. At a Columbia University Graduate School of Business conference I attended recently, one Barclays Capital bigwig (and mom of three) told an audience that she signed up for professional cooking classes at 8:00 a.m. on a Saturday morning. While a two-year-old might want to play with you then, a teenager definitely doesn't, and such a commitment will give you a piece of yourself back, she said.

Commit Enough Time, Energy, and Resources to Make Your Activities Meaningful

Justin Honaman works for Coca-Cola Customer Business Solutions in Atlanta. This company, coowned by Coke and the Coke bottlers, helps merchants figure out their product mixes and promotions. Honaman likes his job, but a few years ago, in his early thirties, he "really had an itch to get back into music." He'd played the piano as a kid, and people at his church told him he had a good voice. So after reading a newspaper story about a local executive who did some serious singing on the side, he asked the man for the name of his voice coach.

Honaman started taking lessons. He learned about breathing techniques, and how to sing other people's music. A few months in, he decided to start writing his own melodies for fun. His days were already packed with meetings and the like. So he carved out time to jot down ideas while traveling, at night, during breaks in meetings, while exercising, and on weekends. He became a bit obsessed. He filled pages and pages of notebooks. Any time an image popped into his head—white sand on Caribbean beaches, stories his dad told him about flying helicopters in Vietnam—he wrote it down or called himself and left a voice mail.

He came up with melodies in his head and used the piano to develop chord progressions. "At first I was very verbose," he says. But he listened critically to the songs he heard on the radio, and figured out what worked and what didn't. He learned to build a song around one simple concept, such as his fondness for tailgating before autumn football games. This turned into a country song he called "Saturday in the South." He honed his own vocal performance technique more through his lessons, practicing, and leading a youth music program at his church. He sang his songs for friends, who thought they sounded decent.

Honaman was elated with this feedback. Indeed, he was having so much fun with his new hobby, that it "changed the way that I operate at work, to have this creative component." He wasn't about to quit his day job and move to Nashville to try to become a country music star, but by committing some serious resources to his new passion, he figured he could purchase at least part of the Nashville experience.

So he started researching country music producers and interviewed several. A few gave him a definite "this guy works for Coke—he's not really a country music guy" brush-off. But others were more pragmatic. Finally, he hired one and flew up to Nashville to work with him on turning his melodies into more standard song formats, such as you'd hear on a country radio station. The producer helped Honaman record his pieces a cappella, then hired professional musicians and background singers to fill out the tracks. The resulting album, *Saturday in the South*, is now for sale online, and a few of the tracks have gotten some airplay. He enjoyed the experience so much that he's now working on a second album. "If I had never done it, I'd have so many regrets," he says. At first, his coworkers found it a little strange that this guy in a suit sitting across from them in meetings kept talking about flying to Nashville on weekends, but some got inspired to take their own hobbies to a new level as a result.

And why not? As we talked about in Chapter 3, people are happiest when they are in a state of "flow," throwing themselves into something that challenges them to the extent of their abilities.

It is wonderful to feel this way at your paid job. It's wonderful to feel this way as you pursue other passions, too. If you like to run, you could simply pound out 45 minutes, 5 days per week. Or you could log your miles and times, analyze how you can improve, sign up for half marathons in fun places, check out books from the library on training programs, read *Runner's World,* and join a running club for the fellowship. If you think your local food bank does a good job, you could show up to volunteer once a quarter and write a check at Christmas. Or you could volunteer every week, join the board, and brainstorm ways—partnerships with local farms? cooking classes?—to better serve the clients. In either case, the first option will still improve your leisure time. But though you can't make such a deep commitment to many activities, the latter option will bring far more meaning to your leisure hours for the few activities you do choose.

Align Your Time

You may be wondering where friends and socializing fit into all this, and that's a good question.

When you're busy building a career, raising a family, and trying to stay in shape as well, it's easy to let friendships slide. Some may need to go; there's no more point in spending time with acquaintances you don't care for than there is in spending time on leisure activities that don't make you happy. But it would be a mistake to chuck all of them, and not just because spending time with friends is fun. A growing body of research is showing that friendships are intensely important for health and human coping. Women with breast cancer who lack close friends are more likely to die from the disease than those who are more socially integrated. There's some evidence that close friendships can help slow brain deterioration as we age. People with strong friendships get fewer colds, and their burdens feel lighter. Literally. A few years ago, for a study published in 2008 in the *Journal of Experimental Social Psychology,* researchers asked thirty-four University of Virginia students to wear weighted backpacks and estimate the incline of a steep (26-degree) hill. The guesses were wildly inaccurate, which is no surprise. People have as hard a time estimating angles as they do estimating how many hours they work or sleep. What is surprising is that students who were standing next to their friends perceived the hill as much less steep than students who stood alone did. When asked to estimate the angle, those with friends said 47 degrees (compared with 55 degrees for solo walk-ers), and "the longer friends knew each other, the less steep the hill appeared," the researchers wrote.

This creates a bit of a paradox. Living a full life in your 168 hours can sometimes be stressful. Friends take away much of this stress, but it's hard to find time to nurture these relationships. Indeed, finding time can be stressful. So what are you supposed to do?

The answer, I believe, is to engage in a special form of multitasking.

Multitasking gets a bad reputation in time-management literature for a reason. On a neurological basis, the human brain does not really process multiple tasks at once; instead, it toggles back and forth, los-ing time on every switch. The more complex the tasks, the more time lost. Though we're only talking fractions of a second this is, of course, plenty of time to crash your car if you're trying to drive and send a text message.

On a more macrobehavioral level, people are easily distracted and have trouble refocusing. One 2007 study of Microsoft workers found that when they responded to e-mail or instant messaging alerts, it took them, on average, nearly 10 minutes to deal with their in-boxes or mes-sages, and another 10–15 minutes to really get back into their original tasks. About a quarter of task suspensions resulted in a 2-hour gap, *or longer,* before workers resumed the original task. In other words, if you are working on a project, but check your e-mail every time the alarm dings or the urge strikes (easily every 10 minutes if you get fifty e-mails a day), you will never finish what you are doing. Multitasking is, more often than not, inefficient single-tasking. I particularly saw this in the time logs a few parents who worked from home kept for me for this project. Some thought working from home would be a good way to save money on child care. It isn't. Their work projects took forever and their kids got annoyed that Mommy and Daddy weren't fully present. As Lord Chesterfield, the eighteenth-century British statesman and writer, once noted, "There is time enough for everything in the course of the day if you do but one thing at once; but there is not time enough in the year if you will do two things at a time."

But there is one exception to this problem of multitasking, which is what I call "alignment." If you combine activities that utilize different parts of your brain, particularly if one doesn't require much active mental engagement, you can deepen relationships while filling your time with meaningful things, or fit more time for leisure pursuits into your day, generally.

This is what naturally happens when you share a meal with a friend. You're talking while eating, which you have to do anyway. This alignment is much more possible—and better for your relationship—than trying to talk with a friend while talking on a conference call or posting on Facebook at the same time. A running or biking partner will make the miles go faster. My little brother held a "birthday hike" for all his friends on his twenty-fifth birthday. Though volunteering usually does require active mental engagement, you can use transportation or transition times during these activities to interact with friends, or join a charity board with a family member as a way to stay close while working on something you both care about. Encourage your kids to choose activities that involve friends whose parents you really like. A bleary-eyed, coffee-clutching early Saturday trip to the playground is definitely better if you turn it into a playdate. If you are still going to a grocery store in person, rather than shopping online, go at the same time as a friend. Go over the activities you currently have in your 168 hours, and the ones you'd like to include, and figure out which might be good targets for alignment. Even a phone call while you're doing dishes can help you stay in touch.

Incidentally, you don't have to limit your alignment just to your leisure hours. Some very happy, productive people achieve the ultimate in alignment by going into business with their friends (or spouses). Others practice alignment with colleagues that they like. When I was working at *USA Today,* my boss drove me home most days. I kept her entertained in traffic, and she looked out for me at the office.

You can also use alignment to build leisure activities into your workdays. One of the more interesting work-alignment tactics I came across while writing this book was that of Sheryl Woodhouse-Keese, who owns an earth-friendly stationery outfit called Twisted Limb Paperworks in Bloomington, Indiana. Woodhouse-Keese put her headquarters

on a ten-acre farm (her house is at the other end), and started growing tomatoes, cucumbers, peppers, herbs, melons, and so forth. But,
of course, there turned out to be a huge overlap between people who
wanted to work at a recycled paper stationery company, and people
who are interested in small scale, sustainable agriculture. So, quickly,
the farm "turned from my personal garden into an employee garden,"
Woodhouse-Keese says. Now, many Twisted Limb Paperworks employees take their breaks in the garden while pulling weeds, and load up
bags of produce into their trunks rather than stopping by the grocery
store on the way home. While the employees don't necessarily use the
garden as a social outlet or place for meetings (as Woodhouse-Keese
points out, it gets hot in the summer), its existence lets everyone fit
gardening into their lives in a way that might not otherwise be possible
given how busy employees at small businesses tend to be.

The important thing to remember with work alignment, though, is
that unless you're involving your whole family (for example, your kids
play with a colleague's kids on the playground), be sure to combine
activities during your standard work hours as often as possible. Unfortunately, the more usual approach is to tack stuff on, like Saturday golf
dates with clients, or team happy hours and dinners. There is no reason
you can't play golf with a client on a Thursday morning. If you'd just be
sitting in a conference room or on the phone together anyway, why not?
You'll probably come up with better ideas on the links.

Use Bits of Time for Bits of Joy

You can carve out blocks of time for regular exercise, or for volunteer, religious, or artistic commitments during your 168 hours. But
what about those small bits of free time that appear during our weeks?
I'm talking about those 30-minute chunks when the car pool hasn't
brought your kids home from soccer practice yet, or while dinner is in
the oven, or even while you're on the train commuting to work. While
you can combine some of these chunks into more meaningful blocks
with good schedule control, that won't get rid of all of them. One of the

reasons smoking remains as popular as it does is that lighting up a cigarette provides a portable 10 minutes of pleasure and relaxation for less than fifty cents a pop. Television, likewise, can be enjoyed in 23-minute TiVo'd increments at any point.

For more meaningful options, though, go back through your "List of 100 Dreams" and choose elements of a few to incorporate into your days. Make two lists: one of activities that take half an hour or less, and another of activities that take less than 10 minutes. Then, figure out ways you can make these two sets of activities as easy as lighting up a cigarette or turning on the TV any time a bit of leisure shows up on your schedule.

For instance, on the half-hour front, as noted in Chapter 1, Jill Starishevsky writes poems on her commute from Manhattan to the Bronx. For that, she needs to have a piece of paper and a pen in her briefcase.

What else can you do while going to or from work? If you're taking mass transit like Starishevsky, you're golden. When I used to ride the express bus from Bethesda, Maryland, to Tyson's Corner, Virginia, in the mornings, I worked my way through a list of the top novels of the twentieth century as the bus worked its way through traffic. I almost— almost—missed that excuse to read when I started working from home in New York. If you're driving, you can listen to audiobooks with a purpose: all the works of Shakespeare, perhaps, or a course on the history of the Bible. You can listen to the great symphonies or operas you've always meant to become familiar with. People waste incredible amounts of time commuting. Even if you're just in the car half an hour every morning and evening 5 days a week, you could work through Wagner's entire Ring Cycle in a month. Then listen to it all again and become familiar with the themes. But to do that, you have to plan. You have to get to the library or buy these CDs or mp3s. You don't want to get stuck listening to morning drivetime radio shock jocks when you meant to listen to Wagner just because you failed to take action.

Noncommuting time opens up more options. In less than half an hour, you can handwrite notes to three elderly relatives, if you have stationery, stamps, and their addresses on hand. You can take a bubble bath, if you've got the bubbles. If you're artsy, carry your camera around with you and take some pictures, or bring a pencil and notebook and sketch the plants in your doctor's waiting room. Keep a Kindle in your briefcase so you can read a few more pages in that Michael Crichton novel or jump over to Jane Austen if you're looking for a change of pace. Pop in an instructional yoga DVD and learn some new poses. Go for a walk and really observe your surroundings. Maybe there's inspiration there for a song, a poem, a blog post, or even a solution to a knotty work problem. Play hide-and-seek in the backyard with your kids. Make collages with them. In 30 minutes you can practice a musical instrument, sing Christmas carols, or learn some folk songs. You can call a friend. You can nap. You can research your next vacation, or even plan a fantasy one for the no doubt distinct possibility that someone will call up and offer you a $25,000 voucher that can be used only for travel.

The 1–10-minute list is trickier, but there are still options beyond hauling out the Blackberry. Theresa Daytner from Chapter 1 reads Hardy Boys novels with her sons in 10-minute spurts before school opens. While waiting for items to heat up in the microwave, I am now in the habit of dropping to the floor and holding a plank pose or doing push-ups instead of flipping through the Pottery Barn catalogue. Payoffs include stronger arms and abs, and less desire for pricey throw pillows. You can pray while waiting for the elevator, or write in your journal while waiting to pick up your kids from school. You can brainstorm new ideas for your "List of 100 Dreams." You can read a poem or religious texts—if you have them handy. Keep a coffee-table art book somewhere in your office, and study a painting while you're waiting for a colleague to join a conference call. Keep a folder of images that make you happy on your computer: your kids as toddlers, pictures from your wedding or honeymoon, landscape photos of places you'd like to go. Send your spouse a romantic text message. Send your kids a funny one just to check in. Use the time to check your schedule and make a restaurant reservation somewhere your family has been hoping to try.

Or . . . you can watch TV. But make sure you control it, rather than it controlling you. Decide ahead of time how much television you want to watch during any given week. Seven hours—1 hour a day—is plenty.

That includes movies or children's videos; despite the popular belief among some parents, in an era in which marketers slap movie characters on every product imaginable, there is nothing more worthy or moral about a DVD than a television show. Choose the few programs you enjoy most, and TiVo or record them. Watch them at a time that is convenient for you. Fast-forward through the commercials, snuggle with your kids or partner while you're watching, and turn the TV off as soon as your chosen program is done.

Getting in the habit of thinking through your leisure time takes some practice. It certainly isn't easy for me to remember to stick leisure planning on my to-do list. I do OK with running because it's a near-daily habit, and choir because it requires a commitment at the same time every week. But filling the free time of my evenings and weekends is a different matter. Indeed, ironic as it sounds, I got so busy this week cranking out this 9,000-word chapter on how to master one's leisure time that I forgot until late Thursday that the calendar was about to smack into Memorial Day weekend. Three-day summer weekends are a rare and precious thing. A quick glance at the weather revealed that it was going to be a glorious string of May days. I was determined not to lose the weekend to chores, TV, and inefficient bouts of work. So what were we going to do?

Figuring that late was better than never, my husband and I used Friday morning to mash together a plan. Here's what it wound up looking like. On Friday, Jasper had to be picked up early from day care, so rather than go home and plop him in front of *Elmo*, I decided to bring him to our apartment-complex pool, a place I'd been meaning to take more advantage of as soon as the weather got warm. Instead of watching TV after Jasper went to bed, I made a point of sitting on the balcony and reading *Mrs. Dalloway* for a blissful, uninterrupted hour. We extended Michael's work car rental, and on Saturday drove to Ocean Grove, New Jersey, a cute little seaside town 75 minutes from New York, where we'd rented a cottage for a week three years before. We hadn't even known we were expecting Jasper the last time we were there. This time we got to watch our toddler play in the sand, eat fries at Nagle's, and attempt to spoon rapidly melting soft-serve ice cream into his mouth. We drove back that night, then got everyone to church on Sunday morning. We made it to the Central Park petting zoo early enough that the peacocks were still strutting about with a boldness that is possible in the midst of ten slobbering toddlers, but not in the midst of a hundred. Jasper had a clear shot at feeding the lambs. I went for a run during Jasper's nap. Having done enough at that point to make the weekend feel "full," I let things go more free form, except that I tried, consciously, to fill open spaces by reading *Bel Canto* instead of *People* magazine's write-up on Bristol Palin's baby (OK, I read that, too). I tried to practice the principle of alignment by scheduling a playground play date for Jasper on Monday with a friend whose parents were expecting a second baby at the same time we were.

I did work some in concentrated bursts when I wouldn't be interrupted—1 hour very early on Sunday morning, 1.5 hours on Sunday night, two hours on Monday afternoon while Jasper slept, and another 2.5 after he went to bed. Yes, I know that working on weekends and vacation days is a work-life-balance faux pas, but to me, work-life balance means actually *balancing* the two; a day lacking contact with the printed word feels as strange as a day of working around the clock. As the famed-opera-singer-turned-hostage Roxanne Cross says in *Bel Canto,* "I don't know what to do with myself when I'm not singing. I don't have any talent for vacations." Still, all in all, I felt reasonably rejuvenated by the end of Memorial Day weekend. I felt motivated to tackle another tough workload, or at least to spend 15 minutes thinking through my next patch of leisure time. That way I wouldn't sit around as lost as the *Bel Canto* captives, with my fingers drumming incessantly on the arms of chairs.

Making the Most of Downtime

Time is too precious to be lackadaisical about leisure. Looking at your time logs and your "List of 100 Dreams," ask yourself a few questions:

What one to three leisure pursuits would I like to build, regularly, into my 168
   hours? (One of these should be exercise.)

How much of a weekly time commitment would each of these activities take?

Where can I stick these blocks of time into my schedule?

What weekend activities could my family do together? When can we plan our
   weekends?

Where can I find time for nurturing relationships with friends?

Create two lists of things that make you happy—one for 30-minute
activities, and one for activities that take 10 minutes or less:

IN 30 MINUTES, I CAN . . .

1. _____

2. _____

3. _____

4. _____

5. _____

6. _____

IN 10 MINUTES OR LESS, I CAN . . .

1. _____

2. _____

3. _____

4. _____

5. _____

6. _____

What tools or supplies do I need to seize these 1- to 30-minute chunks of time when they appear?

PART

4

168 HOURS,

DAY BY DAY

· 9 ·

The Hard Work
of Having It All

The key message of this book is that there is time for anything that matters, though I realize that in the middle of a crazy Tuesday, this can be hard to believe. Hours rush by and confound our attempts to be more relaxed and mindful of their abundance. We do the things we have to—sleep, work, feed the children—and don't make time for the things we want to do. Or we don't appreciate how well we are doing, and so we feel squeezed and claustrophobic in our own lives.

Kathryn Beaumont Murphy could be the poster girl for these time pressures facing modern professionals, and parents in particular. She went to law school after a decade-long career in journalism. She was happy with the switch, but since she acquired a husband and a baby girl along with a legal education, this meant that she was suddenly facing life as a first-year associate at a Boston law firm with a toddler in tow. She had no options for choosing a part-time position, and since she was so new to her firm, she didn't have much flexibility with her evenings if other people expected her to stick around. Of course, she did manage to get home sometimes—she learned that she was pregnant with baby number two during her first year on the job. She found my Web site and a post about seeking time-makeover guinea pigs after reading one of my columns. She sent me an e-mail saying, "I think I could really use your help."

"I often go to bed frustrated and in tears because I don't have 'time' for anything," she told me. "Not cooking, not cleaning, not answering e-mail, and certainly not other 'good-mom' things like downloading pictures or keeping a baby book or blog or something." If she made it through one "Talk of the Town" in *The New Yorker* before falling asleep, she felt lucky. Novels, she said, were not in the picture. "Weekends are especially frustrating, as I feel like I have to cram in a week's worth of grocery shopping, errands, and, of course, quality time with my daughter."

She was careful to qualify her gripes. "I realize that these are very much first-world problems, and my husband and I are very lucky to have great jobs in this economy," she said. They could afford a "home team," including child care, a cleaning service, and takeout whenever they didn't feel like cooking. "But it would be great to find a way to feel less panicked all the time."

I agreed that feeling panicked was a lousy way to experience life. So I asked Murphy to keep a time log for 168 hours, which she did for a week in the middle of July 2009.

This was her schedule ("E" is her daughter):

	MONDAY	TUESDAY	WEDNESDAY	THURSDAY	FRIDAY	SATURDAY	SUNDAY
5 a.m.							
			up @ 5:45				
6			yoga				
	up! shower		yoga		up! get baby up		6:45-715 - quick run
7	watch TV/read w/ E	up! shower	yoga	up at 7:15	shower	up @ 7	run
	leave for work	chat w/ nanny	yoga	run	breakfast, play w/ baby	play with E	take E to Starbucks
8	get Starbucks/ check e-mail	leave for work	get ready for work:	run	walk to work	go to gym	playground
	start working (research)	check news/e-mail	shower, breakfast	get ready for work	walk to work	gym (while Tim & E go to store!)	playground
9	research and write	procrastinate/ coffee	leave to walk to doctor	leave for work @ 9:20	go through e-mails	gym	playground
	research and write	coffee w/ work friend	doctor appt.	lv. for work/ stop by cleaners	go through e-mails	shower	feeling sick, so nap
10	research and write	research	doctor appt.	client meeting	research	drive to Arlington	nap
	research and write	research	doctor appt.	client meeting	research	visit family	nap
11	research and write	research	phone call w/ client	client meeting	research	visit family	nap
	lunch (read Kindle at lunch!)	research	phone call w/ client	client meeting	research	visit family	get up; read E book and put her down for nap

(continued)

	MONDAY	TUESDAY	WEDNESDAY	THURSDAY	FRIDAY	SATURDAY	SUNDAY
12 p.m.	lunch (read Kindle at lunch!)	lunch w/ work friend	summer assoc. lunch	summer assoc. lunch	lunch w/ friend	drive home	go to store
	lunch (read Kindle at lunch!)	lunch w/ work friend	summer assoc. lunch	summer assoc. lunch	research	E naps; I nap	store
1	phone call	lunch w/ work friend	summer assoc. lunch	summer assoc. lunch	research	nap	pack for b-day party
	phone call	research	respond to e-mail/ vml	e-mails/NYTimes online	research	nap	get ready for party
2	phone call	research	leave for client meeting	phone call w/ client	research	nap	leave for party
	check personal e-mails/phone calls	research	client meeting	phone call w/ client	research+ procrastination!	get ready for pool	leave for party
3	meeting w/ summer associate	research	client meeting	personal e-mails	meeting	spend afternoon at pool	E b-day party!
	meeting w/ summer associate	research	client meeting	research	research	pool	(at pool)
4	work/research	meeting/training	client meeting	research	time entry	pool	(we stay very late!)
	work/research	meeting/training	travel back from mtg	revisions	organized desk/ pay bills	pool	party
5	work/research	meeting/training	phone call	client mtg/ networking event	walk home	pool	party
	work/research	head home	phone call	client mtg/ networking event	walk home	pool	party
6	work/research	watch TV w/ E	tax dept summer clambake	client mtg/ networking event	E bed/bath	pool	party
	work/research	bath time	clambake	client mtg/ networking event	E bed/bath	drive home	party

	MONDAY	TUESDAY	WEDNESDAY	THURSDAY	FRIDAY	SATURDAY	SUNDAY
7	commute home	bedtime	clambake	client mtg/networking event	order pizza	give E bath	party
	read to E	work at home	play with E	client mtg/networking event	watch TV	order take-out salads!	party
8	make frozen pizza for dinner	work at home	tidy up house/get ready for bed	client mtg/networking event	watch TV	dinner	home: bathe E
	eat/watch TV	work at home	in bed/read	quick dinner/fill out paperwork	read in bed	watch TV	put E down
9	in bed/read	work at home	in bed/read	fill out benefits/loan paperwork	read in bed	in bed read	in bed! read
	read	surf internet	sleep!	read	read in bed	read	read
10	sleep!	read		read	sleep!	read	sleep
				sleep		read (it was a good book!)	
11						sleep	
12 a.m.							
1							
2							
3							
4							

I asked Murphy a few questions about her 168 hours. First, what did she like most? "I generally make time to exercise," she wrote back in an e-mail, and she did have time to take care of personal tasks during her workday. "Looking at my schedule for the past week, I did do a lot of reading, but that may be a factor of (1) the novelty of my new Kindle and (2) our TV is broken!"

Second, what did she want to do more of during her 168 hours? This one was easy: spend quality time with her daughter. "I find that during the week, our time is limited," she wrote. They spent a quick few minutes together in the morning while Murphy was trying to get dressed. Then, when she got home in the evening, she felt like she had to rush the bath-and-bedtime routine so she could work or clean or cook, though she confessed that she really never did the latter. "I'd like to cook dinner in the evenings and eat with my husband," she said. "I just don't know that that is a reality with our schedules."

Third, what did she want to get off her plate? Her first temptation was to say shopping, cooking, and cleaning, "but the reality is, I did very little of that this week," she told me. "I can't really think of something I want off my plate, except for a day of work!" But that wasn't an option at her current job—though we could look for ways to crunch her working hours.

Next, I asked her what she thought she spent too much time on, and she answered, "Checking my personal e-mail at work, reading the news at work," and puttering around a bit listlessly at night. Of course, part of this was simply being in the throes of early pregnancy, which is not known for increasing people's energy levels. She needed a lot of sleep, though she admitted that "honestly, I probably spend too much time getting ready for bed."

I went through Murphy's time log and added up her hours in the major categories ("sleep" for each day counts until the next morning; since people sleep different amounts each night, this makes some days come out to more or fewer than 24 hours. "Personal care" includes showering and eating). This doesn't come out to exactly 168 hours because it never does. Things get messy in recording, and categorizing is tough, particularly when people multitask. But we're close.

MONDAY

Work: 9.0, sleep: 9.0, travel: 1.0, TV: 1.0, personal e-mail: 0.5, reading: 2.5, reading to daughter: 0.5 (plus a little in the morning), housework: 0.5, personal care: 0.5

TUESDAY

Work: 11.0, sleep: 7.25, travel: 1.0, TV (plus child care): 0.5, reading: 0.5, child care plus management: 1.5, personal care: 0.5, Internet surfing: 0.5

WEDNESDAY

Work: 8.5, sleep: 9.75, exercise: 2.5, reading: 1.0, personal care: 2.5 (including medical care), playing with daughter: 0.5, housework: 0.5

THURSDAY

Work: 10.0, sleep: 8.0, exercise: 1.0, travel: 0.75, reading: 1.0, personal care: 0.5, housework plus administration: 1.25, personal e-mail: 0.5

FRIDAY

Work: 7.5, sleep: 9.5, exercise (her commute): 2.0, TV: 1.0, reading: 1.0, child care: 2.0, social: 0.5, personal care: 1.0

SATURDAY

Sleep: 9.75, exercise: 1.0, child care/family/social: 8.0, reading: 2, travel (solo): 0.5, personal care: 1.5, TV: 0.5

SUNDAY

Sleep: 10.5, exercise: 0.5, child care/family/social: 10.5, reading: 1.0, errands: 1.0

After studying her schedule for a while, I had a few observations. Murphy clearly had a busy life, but on the whole a very good life, filled with positive things.

On the career front, she worked 46 hours (not counting her commute or e-mail, phone calls, or lunches if she identified them as personal). This is a long week. Her office culture made it difficult to leave in the evenings, though I figured she might be able to find some flexibility during the day. I also noted that about 10 of her work hours were spent at social events. Lawyers do need to network with their clients and colleagues, but these could be trimmed if work got busier.

Despite her busy workweek, Murphy did manage to sleep. Thanks to her naps, she logged more than 63 hours, or roughly 9 per day. This would probably go down during her second trimester, freeing up time to do more work in the evenings or get up earlier in the mornings to spend time with her daughter.

She got a lot of exercise—a full 7 hours, or 1 hour per day. This is an amazing amount for a pregnant mom with a full-time job, or anyone for that matter. It was a nice split among yoga, brisk walking to and from work (a great idea, since she had to commute anyway), and running, with the variety helping to keep her totals high. Despite her fretting that novels were no longer in the picture, she read like a madwoman—9 hours—which meant the Kindle was a great investment in redeveloping this habit. She was right that she spent very little time on housework, household administration, or errands. In general, that's a good thing, though since she wanted to cook more meals for her family, this tally could go up.

She wasn't spending much time interacting with her daughter during the week—about 4.5 hours dealing with her care as a primary activity, though she spent more time around her (for instance, watching TV together). Since this number bothered her, she needed to find time in her schedule for more mother-daughter bonding. However, she did spend much of the weekend with her daughter and husband, clocking at least 18 hours on Saturday and Sunday hanging out with the two of them.

I gave Murphy a few suggestions:

• Don't fix the TV. I guessed that a big reason Murphy managed to read 9 hours, exercise 7 hours, and get enough sleep is that she watched television for only 3 hours. If watching TV had been easier, these totals could have been much different.

• Carve out time for her daughter through creative scheduling. Murphy did see her daughter most nights, but she was having trouble engineering relaxed, meaningful evenings together. As a first-year legal associate, many of her colleagues were in their late twenties and single. They preferred to sleep later and work later, so that's the schedule her office tended to keep.

But evenings aren't the only times parents can spend with children— especially young children who often wake up very early. Given that Murphy's time log revealed that she never started "real" work before 8:30 a.m., and sometimes later than that, I suggested she make two early mornings per week into mommy-and-me time. She could get up at 6:15 (after making sure she was in bed on time the night before) and be ready for work, albeit wearing jeans or other play clothes, by 6:30. Then she could get her daughter up and have a 2-hour block of time with her. She should use this time to really play with the girl, and think through what she wanted to do ahead of time. Read? Walk in the stroller? Go to a playground? Build forts out of pillow cushions? Do arts and crafts? Then she could zoom out the door at 8:30. I doubted anyone would even notice her slightly tardy arrival.

Another way to fit in kid time during the week was to look at down-time during the day. From her schedule, it looked like Murphy had some freedom to meet friends for lunch. If her daughter's schedule permitted it, she could be that "friend" on occasion. While this couldn't happen too often, it would be a nice treat for everyone, and it's unlikely that anyone would complain that she missed work for an hour.

• Take baby steps on dinner. Some people want to get food chores off their plates, but Murphy wanted to cook for her family. I suggested she aim for 2 nights per week as a manageable goal. She could try a few of the idiot-proof dinners I listed in Chapter 7, like angel hair pasta with marinara sauce and salad. Another option to scratch her cooking itch would be to make a stew or soup on Sunday and then reheat it twice during the week with crusty bread and a premade salad. Or she might try a slow cooker. If she borrowed one from a friend and tried using it twice over the next week, she could see if one—like the Kindle—would be a good investment. Regardless, she should make a list before her husband went grocery shopping, or use some downtime at work to order groceries online so she would have some very easy cooking options. Peapod delivers most regular grocery items in the greater Boston area.

• Stop panicking. Like many moms, Murphy was comparing herself to some mythical ideal of the "good mother" who never felt annoyed when her toddler removed the shoes she'd just put on, who cooked multicourse dinners every night, and who had all her photographs dated and categorized. I have never met this woman. Indeed, many women who *aren't* highly paid corporate tax attorneys never get around to making cute baby books or posting daily on their baby blogs. Despite her busy schedule and the fatigue of early pregnancy, Murphy had managed to give her daughter a great weekend of visiting with relatives, playing on the playground, going to the pool, and enjoying the fun of her birthday party as long as the little girl wanted.

Sometimes when we get really busy, it's easy to feel absent from our own lives. I thought it was great that Murphy was doing yoga to help center herself. But one other suggestion I had was that she use those times she walked to and from the office to focus her mind on something in particular rather than letting her thoughts wander. One good topic? Counting her blessings. ("I have an awesome job! I have a beautiful baby! I'm having another one! I'm in good shape!) I suggested she use another of the walks to picture where she'd be in 20 years, when life would be more relaxed. I had some empty nesters keep track of their 168 hours for this project, and I was amazed by the hours and hours of leisure time they were able to fit in.

So what did Murphy think of all this? "You're right that in the grand scheme of things, I'm super lucky and have more time than I think—it was really insightful to have someone else point that out," she said in an e-mail. The particular week she recorded her hours was "atypical in that it was somewhat slow," but "at the same time, overall, this global economic meltdown has made a first-year associate's hours much easier this year. I'm not working nearly as much as I feared or expected, and I have to remember to take advantage of that as long as I can."

She really liked the idea of carving out blocks of time in the morning to spend with her daughter. "It would be so easy to do, I wonder why I didn't think of it," she said. "I really like the suggestion of planning it in advance." Cooking would be more difficult (as she was composing this e-mail to me, apparently, her husband was out picking up take-out salads again) but she resolved to at least try a few easy meals.

Finally, she liked the idea of "finding time to focus on certain things: the present, the future. You're right in that I often feel absent from my life, which is actually pretty great. It's hard to feel like I can find the time to connect to it, so having someone else actually point out where I can take the time to do so is incredibly helpful." She printed out her schedule for the next few weeks, and looked at it to figure out where she could block off mornings with her daughter. "I'm really excited for that," she said.

Did it work? I checked in with Murphy a few times over the next 2 months. Tweaking her schedule was an ongoing project. "I haven't been as successful as I've wanted to be on the toddler morning time because work has all of a sudden gotten super busy," she told me 3 weeks after she kept the log, and so she found herself walking out the door at 7:30 a.m. On the other hand, "I've made up for it on the other end to some extent," keeping her daughter up a little later in the evenings and trying to be present and focused on bath time and reading before bed. She had also come up with another solution to carve out space: since her family moved to the suburbs a few weeks after she kept the time log, which lengthened her commute, she would work from home as her schedule permitted (ideally, 1 day per week), and use what would be commuting time and break time to interact with her child. By the time we exchanged e-mail a few weeks later, she'd actually carved out morning time, too—no longer overwhelmed by early pregnancy nausea, she was getting up earlier and spending a solid hour most mornings with her daughter. "Part of what we do is cook, believe it or not," she said. "She loves to pull up a stool and stir things," like eggs for breakfast or cookie dough for homemade cookies.

What proved to be the biggest winner for Murphy, however, was making a point of being "present during the day." During her commute

(now on the train), she began meditating about being thankful and setting goals. She had continued her TV strike, using the evenings to read
and relax and get organized for the next day. "Somehow, even if I'm
not doing my morning toddler time, this makes me feel less frantic"—
and better able to focus on her daughter in the evenings. Freed from
the unrealistic expectation that she would make elaborate feasts from
scratch every night, she was also succeeding in putting home-cooked
dinners on the table twice a week, "even if it's just pasta and sauce or an
omelet." Which is fine. When it comes to cooking, better to do something simple and use the saved time and energy to focus on your loved
ones than spend an hour hunched over risotto that needs to be stirred
constantly and then snap at said loved ones for dawdling on the way to
the table.

No one ever said having it all was easy. Getting the most out of your 168
hours is a process of evaluating where you are and where you want to
be. Maybe these are the same, but maybe they're not. If they aren't, then
you have to look at what stands in the way, and what can be changed.

To figure out how real people could implement the best practices I
learned while writing this book, I asked dozens of people like Murphy
to keep logs of their time. Then we hunted through their schedules and
tried to figure out ways to fill their time with the things they wanted
to have there, and remove the things that shouldn't be there. Two of
these "time makeovers" follow after this chapter; you can find others
at My168Hours.com. Obviously, people's schedules change from week
to week. But after seeing enough of these logs, I've realized that no one
ever thinks one particular set of 168 hours was typical. We tend to have
mental pictures of our lives and so every log comes with a caveat. One
of my favorites was from my little brother, a twenty-something software
engineer who works at Google's San Francisco office. He tallied up his
week and found that he was working 40 hours, exercising 11, sleeping
53, and spending a whopping 45 hours socializing, including 9 hours of
one-on-one get-togethers, 6 hours of hanging out with his roommates,
8 hours of group dinners, and 22 hours of parties. When I quizzed him
about this Paris Hilton–esque lifestyle, he quickly protested that it was

not a typical 168 hours. "It is very rare for me to have social activities every single night of the week," he said. I understood this to mean that he usually takes Tuesdays off.

Since this was for the makeover section, I gave him one tip to focus his leisure time—train for a biathlon; he did me one better and finished a short triathlon two months later—but mostly, I told him to enjoy himself. Most of us don't revel in the copious free time we have before we become parents, hit managerial levels at work, or start our own businesses. Of course, then people in these later stages of life complain that they have no free time, which isn't true either. It's just more complicated to take advantage of free hours and minutes when you're trying to build a career and raise a family. But plenty of things in life are difficult and we do them anyway. The point is that there is always time: 168 hours is incredibly vast. There is time for anything you really want to do. Once you realize that, you can move from panicking to looking at the data objectively, and then putting yourself in charge of getting the most out of your 168 hours.

Here is the process for doing your own "time makeover":

Log your time. Use the spreadsheet at the end of Chapter 1 (downloadable at My168Hours.com if you borrowed this book from the library), or a word-processing document or a little notebook if you want, and keep as complete a record as possible of 168 consecutive hours. Tally up the time spent on the major categories (sleep, work, interacting with children, and so on). If you think your totals are unusual, go ahead and record another week. But keep in mind that when things are important to us, we tend to find ways to fit them in. People who really value exercise take their running shoes along on business trips and stay in hotels with treadmills. People who really value interacting with their children set up times to call them, and write individual e-mails to each of them about their days. Keep a time log until you are satisfied that you have a complete picture of how you spend your time.

Create your "List of 100 Dreams." This was the exercise from Chapter 2 that the career coach Caroline Ceniza-Levine does with her clients.

Come up with as many answers as possible to the question of "What do I want to do (or do more of) with my time?" Sometimes the answers are profound—for example, win a Nobel Prize—and sometimes they're more basic, such as "cook dinner for my family two nights per week." For the longer projects, create a list of actionable steps, and how long each might take, in terms of hours if you can. A lifetime is simply 168 hours, repeated again and again, and creating a completely unedited list of anything that might be pleasurable or meaningful will help you figure out what matters to you, and hence should go in your schedule.

Identify your core competencies. There are the things you do best, and that other people cannot do nearly as well. If you're in the right job—one that taps your intrinsic motivations, gives you lots of autonomy, and challenges you to the extent of your abilities—one of these will probably be the substance of your paid work. Others likely include nurturing your family members and other loved ones, and nurturing your own soul, brain, and body in ways that you excel at and enjoy. Make a list of your core competencies. How many of your 168 hours are you devoting to these things? How many are you devoting to other things?

Start with a blank slate. This is more of a mental breakthrough than anything else. For Murphy's schedule, and for the time makeovers that follow (and those on the Web site), I kept the basic rhythms of people's weeks intact, because my experience is that people develop their habits for a reason. While we can all benefit from having someone else study our weeks and offer suggestions, "quit your job" or even "move somewhere else" are long-term projects that require complete personal ownership of the process. But if you are undertaking your own makeover, then you can really zero your time log. All those entries in your 168 hours? Except for sleeping and eating (and making sure your children do the same), you probably don't *have* to do any of them. Everything else on there is a choice. There may be extremely unpleasant consequences to making different choices, but they are choices all the same. If you plan to keep them in there, recognize that doing so is your decision.

Fill in your 168 hours with blocks of core-competency time. Broadly, figure out what hours you would like to be working, sleeping, nurturing your family and friends, and nurturing yourself—for example, engaging in structured leisure activities such as exercise, volunteering, or participating in religious activities. For longer-term projects on your "List of 100 Dreams," schedule in the blocks of time associated with each actionable step. For instance, if you want to run a half marathon, you'll need to schedule in roughly 5 hours of running each week for the next 3 months if you're already a runner, or 6 months if you're starting from a lower fitness level. If you'd like to start a business, figure out the hundreds of actionable steps as best you can (one early step: beg advice from someone else who's done it!) and how much time each will take.

Put these on your calendar first or at least look for open or low-impact spaces to schedule them in. For people with regular work hours such as 9:00–5:00 or 8:00–6:00, there are often open spaces for non-work core-competency activities in the morning, during a commute, during a lunch break, in the evenings, and on weekends. If you truly need to work 12 hours a day during weekdays, you're better off splitting your shifts (working 7:30–5:30 and then 8:30–10:30) to fit in other activities, but even if you do need to be gone from, say, 8:00 a.m. to 10:00 p.m., you could still fit in 45 minutes of reading to your children in the morning. Add in a brisk walk at lunch with a friend, and a half hour on the porch with your spouse watching the stars at night, and the day won't be a complete waste from a personal perspective. Plus, given that very few people work 14-hour days for many days in a row, you'll be able to fit in even more leisure and family activities on shorter workdays. There is always time somewhere.

Ignore, minimize, or outsource everything else. I asked all my time-makeover guinea pigs to identify activities they wanted to get off their plates, and to fill in the blank for the sentence "I spend way too much time on _____." If you keep an accurate log of your 168 hours, you will likely be surprised by the number of hours you spend on certain things. C. K. Lowe, a Boston-area writer, kept a log for me and called it "one mortifying experience." Having seen many other logs, I didn't think it was that bad, but she was embarrassed to learn that she was taking five or more Facebook and Twitter breaks per day, with these "breaks" sometimes coming a few minutes after starting a more serious project. Simply being aware of this helped; by the end of the week she was more focused. Other common culprits include TV, housework, running errands, checking e-mail, puttering around the house (for example, looking through the Crate and Barrel catalogue when you are not in the market for a sofa), and excessive personal care. You do need to get dressed in the morning, but this should not be a 30-minute, angst-ridden process.

Knock a few of these easy items off first, then look for ways to minimize more complicated time traps. Do your kids really love their extracurricular activities, or are they doing them to please you? Are you volunteering for too many causes, and so stealing time from the ones where you could make the most impact? Does your whole department really need to meet once per week or have that daily conference call? Maybe you can outsource creatively. If you teach high school English, for instance, you might negotiate for funds to hire English graduate students to help grade papers—and hence save yourself time while increasing the volume of writing your students do.

Fill bits of time with bits of joy. This was an exercise from Chapter 8. Make lists of things that make you happy or that you find meaningful, and that take 30 minutes or less, or even less than 10 minutes. Murphy decided to count her blessings during her commute. Lowe wanted to learn French, so I suggested redirecting one of her 15-minute Facebook breaks to a French-language Web site. Sure, 15 minutes isn't much, but human psychology is funny. We tend to underestimate how much time things will take in the short run, which is why people often run late. But we tend to overestimate how much time things take in the long run. If you spend 15 minutes a day, five times per week, honestly practicing French conversation with the intention of getting better, you will do just fine in Paris in a year.

Tune up as necessary. Life changes. Schedules change. Your "List of 100 Dreams" will change, too. Check in with yourself regularly—maybe once every 168 hours—to see if your weeks look like they should. If they don't, spending 1 of those 168 hours figuring out how to change what you can is much more effective than stewing during the other 167.

This last step is important because using your 168 hours to build the life you want will require some serious discipline. There will always be temptations to revert to the usual way of doing things. Consciously lowering your housekeeping standards is hard if you think people will judge you for having a less-than-perfect house. Getting up early to run is hard on cold mornings, and thinking through activities you'd like to do with your kids requires more effort than turning on the television. People will try to interrupt you during the times you've set aside to brainstorm new ideas. Your new business—launched to tap your core competencies—might have slower sales than you anticipated, which will eat at your resolve to stick with it. The head of your kid's school's booster club will decree that all parents must bake something for the bake sale, and seem impervious to your suggestion that you just write a check instead. Your grandmother might recall that even though she raised six kids, she had a homemade dinner on the table at 6:00 every night. She will probably say this on the phone to you as you're making a rush-hour, time-wasting trip to the grocery store because you forgot to plan a few easy meals for the week. Your coworker might say that while leaving the office at 5:00 p.m. is OK for moms, he's never seen a man do it—even though by working from 8:00 to 10:00 p.m., you're logging more hours than he is. Your spouse undermines your attempts to schedule regular dates by caving to other demands and claiming that he or she has no choice.

You should not expect this to be easy, at least not at first. Hopefully, the two time makeovers that follow this chapter, and the ones on the My168Hours.com Web site, will inspire you, but even if you find this process difficult, the good news is that we get better at things the more we practice. Part of practicing is evaluating where things have gone wrong and strategizing to get back on track. Over time—time lived in

168-hour weeks—creating a life where you have it all will no longer seem so hard. Any changes you can make and stick with are better than nothing, and will set off a virtuous cycle. When you turn off the TV at night in order to talk with your partner, you will sleep better. When you sleep better, you'll be more focused at work. When you're focused at work, you will get more done in less time and get home earlier. When you get home earlier, you'll have more energy to play with your kids. When you're having fun with your kids, TV will seem a lot less interesting. And so the cycle repeats itself, until finally the life you want is there in the 168 hours you've got.

More Time Makeovers

Brian Brandt: Finding Quiet Time and Couple Time in a Full Life

Brian Brandt is executive pastor of the multisite Grace Community Church in Texas. He's also the father of three children, ages thirteen, ten, and six, and is running a coaching and training business called Summit Solution Group on the side. At work, he spends a lot of time meeting the needs of the staff and congregation, and at home, he's focused on the kids. That accessibility is in the job description for both these roles, and he loves what he does, but he felt like his schedule was leaving little time for praying and nurturing his relationship with his wife, Ann. He wanted to find more time for these two activities, which he knew would make a big difference in his effectiveness both at work and home. He also wanted to be more efficient at work without sacrificing the ability to truly invest in the people he was mentoring and counseling. He wanted to find time to read, too.

Here's what his schedule looked like for a week in July 2009 (GCC is Grace Community Church, SSG is Summit Solution Group, LT refers to Leadership Tyler, a nonprofit community service organization for which he serves on the board, and FB is Facebook):

	MONDAY	TUESDAY	WEDNESDAY	THURSDAY	FRIDAY	SATURDAY	SUNDAY
5 a.m.	sleep/wake up	sleep	sleep/wake up & e-mail	sleep	sleep	woke up too early	sleep
5:30	e-mail/FB	sleep	FB/e-mail/SSG	FB/e-mail	FB/e-mail	watch TV/FB/e-mail	sleep
6	workout	checked e-mail	workout	get ready/drive	workout	watch TV/FB/e-mail	sleep
6:30	workout	SSG—research on city project	workout	tennis	workout	SSG—started writing article	sleep
7	workout/get ready for work	SSG—research for board training	workout/shower	tennis	shower/drive	SSG—writing article	ck news/e-mail/FB
7:30	drive to GCC b-fast mtg	Shower/shave/b-fast/drive	drive to work	GCC—drive/l-ship devpt./mentoring	GCC—mentoring	SSG—writing article	ck news/e-mail/FB
8	GCC—meet with global outreach pastor	GGC—prep for staff eval	GCC—meeting @ homeless shelter	GCC—mentoring	GCC—mentoring	SSG—writing article	watch TV with kids/work on breakfast
8:30	GCC—meet with global outreach pastor	GGC—assist staff	GCC—meeting @ homeless shelter	GCC—mentoring	GCC—mentoring	yard work	breakfast
9	GCC—e-mail/FB/touch base with staff	GGC—staff eval	GCC—meeting @ homeless shelter	GCC—mentoring	GCC—mentoring	yard work	work on article
9:30	GCC—e-mail/FB/touch base with staff	GGC—staff eval	drive to office/grab b-fast	GCC—mentoring	GCC—mentoring	yard work	work on article
10	GCC—deal with personnel issue	GGC—staff eval	GCC—meeting w/ employee	GCC—mentoring	GCC—e-mail/staff	breakfast/FB	get ready for church/watch storm with son

(continued)

	MONDAY	TUESDAY	WEDNESDAY	THURSDAY	FRIDAY	SATURDAY	SUNDAY
10:30	my family stopped in (very rare occasion)	SSG—branding on research project	GCC—meeting w/ employee	drive/GCC—e-mail	GCC—meet with asst/projects	pool with family	drive to church
11	GCC—work on Lindale project	GGC—respond to staff e-mail	GCC—concl. mtg/e-mail/drive to lunch elders mtg	GCC—lunch with staff	GCC—projects	pool with family	church service
11:30	GCC—work on Lindale project	SSG—prep for meeting with BGCET	GCC—elders lunch & interview candidate	GCC—PR plan for marriage event	GCC—projects	pool with family	church service
12 p.m.	Lunch with friend	GGC—prep for exec. team meeting	GCC—elders lunch & interview candidate	GCC—PR plan for marriage event	GCC	pool with family	church/drive home
12:30	Lunch with friend	drive—make phone calls	Helped employee who had a tree fall on their house	prep for evening	phone calls/e-mail	lunch	grill out/lunch
1	GCC—work on project	SSG—BGCET Board	Helped employee who had a tree fall on their house	GCC—discuss staff issues	lunch	family time	lunch
1:30	GCC—work on project	SSG—BGCET Board	Helped employee who had a tree fall on their house	e-mail	GCC—write reference	nap	nap with daughter
2	GCC—e-mail	drive—make phone calls	Helped employee who had a tree fall on their house	GCC—deal with staff issue	GCC—organizing e-comm		nap with daughter
2:30	GCC—discussions with staff	GCC—meet with DC (boss)	GCC—e-mail	GCC—e-mail/Facebook	GCC—scheduled phone mtg	nap	nap with daughter
3	GCC—prep for tomorrow's mtgs	GCC—meet with Xteam	GCC—returning phone calls	GCC—e-mail/meet with assistant	phone mtg/meet with LT board member	family time	workout with son
3:30	drive to mtg	GCC—staff conversations	GCC—phone calls/email/FB/twitter	GCC—staff issues	meet with LT board member	family time	workout with son

	MONDAY	TUESDAY	WEDNESDAY	THURSDAY	FRIDAY	SATURDAY	SUNDAY
4	SSG—meet with potential client	LT board planning/respond to e-mail	GCC—phone calls/email/FB/twitter	GCC	e-mail	family time	workout with son
4:30	SSG—meet with potential client	plan for Nexus/respond to e-mail	GCC—phone calls/email/FB/twitter	e-mail	GCC—wrap up the week/prep for next	FB/e-mail/start another article	workout with son
5	head home/return phone calls	drive home/family recap	drive home/fix dinner	attend chamber of commerce event	drive/calls	family time/grill out	shower/snack
5:30	grill out	Workout with son	dinner with kids	attend chamber of commerce event	date with Ann	grill out	drive to small group
6	eat dinner with family	workout with son	got ready for kids' sleepovers	drive home/visit with family	date with Ann	family supper	GCC—small group
6:30	TV with kids	workout/get ready for dinner	took kids to the pool	family time & TV	date/visit with kids	family games	GCC—small group
7	TV with kids/work on SSG article	played wii golf	pool	family time & TV	family game night	FB/e-mail/phone calls—GCC	GCC—small group
7:30	TV with kids/work on SSG article	dinner with the family	pool	put kids to bed	family game night	work on article/watch TV	GCC—small group
8	SSG—finish and turn in article	watch TV/thunderstorm with son	TV w/ family	watch movie with Ann	family game night	work on article/watch TV	stop in at friends for visit/drive
8:30	get kids ready for bed	put kids to bed	TV w/ family	watch movie with Ann	family game night	TV with family	tuck kids in
9	tuck kids in	TV/talk with Ann	GCC—reading prep for leadership devpt. program	watch movie with Ann	tuck kids in	tuck kids in	e-mail/FB/visit wife

(continued)

	MONDAY	TUESDAY	WEDNESDAY	THURSDAY	FRIDAY	SATURDAY	SUNDAY
9:30	TV/talk with Ann	TV/talk with Ann	GCC—reading prep for leadership devpt. program	watch movie with Ann	visit with Ann	TV/talk with Ann	e-mail/FB/visit wife
10	TV/talk with Ann	talk with Ann/Facebook	sleep	sleep	visit with Ann	TV/talk with Ann	sleep
10:30	sleep	sleep	sleep	sleep	sleep	sleep	sleep
11	sleep	sleep	sleep	sleep	sleep	sleep	sleep
11:30	sleep	sleep	sleep	sleep	sleep	sleep	sleep
12 a.m. 12:30	sleep	sleep	sleep	sleep	sleep	sleep	sleep
1	sleep	sleep	sleep	sleep	sleep	sleep	sleep
1:30	sleep	sleep	sleep	sleep	sleep	sleep	sleep
2	sleep	sleep	sleep	sleep	sleep	sleep	sleep
2:30	sleep	sleep	sleep	sleep	sleep	sleep	sleep
3	sleep	sleep	sleep	sleep	sleep	sleep	sleep
3:30	sleep	sleep	sleep	sleep	sleep	sleep	sleep
4	sleep	sleep	sleep	sleep	sleep	sleep	sleep
4:30	sleep	sleep	sleep	sleep	sleep	sleep	sleep

What Brandt Was Doing Right

Brandt was doing an admirable job fitting exercise into his busy schedule. Not only did he work out most mornings, he did active things on the weekend like going to the pool with his family. It was especially good to see that his son was his occasional exercise buddy—something they could try more often as a way to practice alignment. The family game night is a great idea. He also managed to do a short date with his wife, in addition to an evening spent watching a movie together. He kept his work time reasonable at somewhere between 50 and 55 hours (with the ambiguity arising over how to count the e-mail and Facebook time). This is hard in both his lines of work. As a pastor you really do need to deal with things like trees falling on houses and you need to be available on weekends, and when you are an entrepreneur, work can expand to fill all available space. He slept a reasonable amount, 52.5 hours according to my tally. Though he woke up quite early to get his workouts in, he made time for this by being in bed before 10:30 every night.

The Time Makeover Suggestions

Brandt needed to focus more during his time with Ann. Like many people, he had trouble categorizing some of his hours because he was trying to do multiple activities at once. He had entries like "e-mail/FB/visit wife." Distractions make us feel more pressed for time than we really are. I suggested that he turn off the TV for good when the kids went to bed and then spend at least 30 minutes really talking with his wife, and some of the rest of the time reading. Any e-mail could wait until the next morning.

A strong marriage is based not just on big blocks of time together, but on small, loving interactions. Brandt could try to call his wife more often during the day. If he found himself with a 5-minute lull, he could call to check how she was doing, or even just text "I love you" to her phone.

Brandt was doing a lot of great family stuff (like going to the pool and having a family game night) but I thought they could all challenge themselves to go TV-free on another night too. They could plan something positive for the freed-up space. One option might be a family book group. The older kids and adults could read separately, and someone could read with the little one, and all discuss the chapters during one night together. Many classic series, such as C. S. Lewis's Chronicles of Narnia, work for all ages.

Brandt was right that finding time to pray is extremely important for a pastor. So I suggested he make the time . . . when he was in the shower. We all have to shower anyway, so we may as well use these minutes. This is a matter of getting in the habit. One approach I suggested was to recite prayers for the first minute or two so he wouldn't have to think about what he meant to communicate until his mind was more centered. Some people pray while exercising, too—for instance, while running, praying for a different person every mile. Brandt wondered if there was a better way to approach his mentoring and counseling duties. Obviously it's hard to be "efficient" when dealing with quality interactions with other people. But there were a few things he could try to make such sessions more effective. He could set an end point up front by mentioning another commitment on his calendar or saying, "I'm really looking forward to our hour together." Also, if there were questions people always asked he could prepare a list of "Frequently Asked Questions" so people could prepare for these sessions and keep themselves focused on issues that were unique to them. As much as possible, he could try to stick to an agenda. I suggested he try not to toggle back and forth too much between his church and business duties. He didn't do a great deal of this, but if it was possible to focus on his business only during certain blocks of time, that would reduce transitions. He could carve out strategic thinking times for both roles—an hour or two with no distractions (no e-mail or phone or Twitter) where he would figure out what the big issues were and how he intended to solve these.

What Brandt Thought of These Suggestions

He was generally positive, if concerned that he wouldn't be able to avoid "toggling" at work. A few weeks later, though, he sent me an e-mail saying "I have a good report. I've been praying more as I shower, mow, and drive." One morning, he got up and "had a great hour just walking and praying with a beautiful sunrise as the backdrop." He'd decided to be more proactive about calling his wife. "It's not odd for me to need to drive 5–10 minutes to a meeting at some point during the day, so I've often used that time to make a quick call and touch base with her," he said. He made a point of setting an ending time for some of his meetings, especially his mentoring and coaching. "That's made a big difference without diluting the quality of the session," he said. It turned out, too, that he could toggle back and forth less between his roles. He blocked out time for specific projects and consciously decided not to skip over to other projects, check e-mail, or return phone calls until an aspect of the project was complete. He was also finally finding time to read, finishing two books since completing the time log. Rather than watching TV or checking e-mail at night, he'd open a book, and "I've also taken a book with me to the gym and read while riding the stationary bike," he said. "When you combine all of these together, they really do make a significant difference."

Andrew Reilley: Balancing (Not Blurring) Work and Family

Andrew Reilley of Savannah, Georgia, has a lot on his plate. Not only does he run a Web-site-building company called United WebWorks, he's a single father of three young boys, ages eight, seven, and five. While being self-employed creates a lot of flexibility, it introduces its own challenges, namely that he was "always working on at least two things at once," he told me. This was particularly an issue during the summer of 2009, when he recorded his 168 hours. He had almost no child care. He'd hired a nanny at one point whom the kids had liked, but when she unexpectedly quit, the trauma was tough on his boys and he was gun-shy about trying again. He wanted to get his work projects done in less time and he wanted more time to hang out with his children.

Here's what his 168 hours looked like for a week in July (UWW is United WebWorks, WBB is WebsiteBuildingBook.com—which is a site about constructing commercial Web sites—and BPS is BestPlasticSurgeon.biz, which recommends doctors. The latter two are supposed to become passive income streams for this single dad).

5 a.m.	TUESDAY	WEDNESDAY	THURSDAY	FRIDAY	SATURDAY	SUNDAY	MONDAY
5:30							
6							
6:30			lying in bed worrying				
7		snuggling with kids/snoozing	snuggling with kids/playing	snuggling with kids			
7:30	snuggled with kids						
8	showered & dressed everyone, breakfast		breakfast				work up to UWW work emergency
8:30	dishes, e-mail/kids playing in garage		WBB work/kids	shower/breakfast		snuggled with kids	fed kids breakfast
9	UWW work/kids	kids breakfast/talking to sister		UWW work	snuggled with kids		UWW work
9:30	glowing again work/kids	general work, reading e-mail/kids		travel to meeting		breakfast	
10	UWW work/kids	BPS/BCD cleanup/WBB work/ordered cigars				kid problems	
10:30	BPS work	UWW work/kids		UWW meeting	breakfast	Xbox repair problems	kids grocery shopping
11	laundry		WBB work/kids out		dog walking w/kids		
11:30		BPS work	WBB work/kids			dog walk with kids	UWW work

12 p.m.	TUESDAY	WEDNESDAY	THURSDAY	FRIDAY	SATURDAY	SUNDAY	MONDAY
12 p.m.	UWW work	play with kids		travel to meeting	WBB work	kids to Burger King	
12:30	BPS Work			BPS meeting			
1	make/served lunch	lunch for kids and me	lunch w/kids				pick up cousin K
1:30	dishes/made dinner	UWW work	WBB work/kids	banking errand/travel home	McDonald's with kids	kids to Pass Pro shops	
2	UWW work/kids	BPS work					UWW work
2:30	chatting with Hartford/writing congressman	UWW work/kids		WBB work/kids		kids to Cold Stone	
3	BPS work/cooking/eating	time with kids			misc work/kids/TV news		
3:30	thinking/chatting about WBB sales & watching news	working on all projects			shower		
4	reading news/getting kids ready for beach		video games with kids		played with kids in rain	UWW work	
4:30	taking kids to beach	WBB work/kids	kids playing in rain				
5		WBB work	took kids swimming/dinner	get kids ready to go out	napped/played inside		more shopping K b-day
5:30				dinner & ice cream			
6	pick up Thomson, take kids to dinner					kids dinner	K b-day party

(continued)

	TUESDAY	WEDNESDAY	THURSDAY	FRIDAY	SATURDAY	SUNDAY	MONDAY
6:30	Sugar Shack for ice cream				cleaned up house		
7	baths and PJs	grocery shopping with kids		BPS work/kids/TV	dishes	playing with kids	
7:30	made/ate dinner for/with kids			TV w/kids	ate dinner/cleaned up	watching movie with kids	
8	talk with neighbor/cousin K	watching news/sort of working	WBB work/kids/news		watched TV		
8:30	work on BPS/TV with kids			nap			
9	chatting with mom/client/vendor/watching news	playing with kids					
9:30			UWW work	played with kids			
10	BPS work	watching news/sort of working	games	put kids to bed	kids to bed	kids to bed	kids to bed
10:30				TV news/computer news	watch TV/misc work	UWW work	WBB work
11	closing computer for TV until sleep			video games with J (couldn't sleep)			UWW work
11:30					WBB work	bed	
12 a.m.							
12:30	sleep	sleep		TV until sleep		sleep	bed/TV
1			sleep				sleep
1:30					bed		
2				sleep	sleep		

	TUESDAY	WEDNESDAY	THURSDAY	FRIDAY	SATURDAY	SUNDAY	MONDAY
2:30							
3							
3:30							
4							
4:30							
TOTALS							
Sleep	7	6	6	7	6.5	7	7
Work	5.5	6.5	9.5	6	3	2	8
Family	3	5	5	6.5	9	10.5	4
Leisure (TV, sports/ exercise, socializing)	2	3.5	2.5			1	
Travel				2			
Housework	4	2	1	1	2	3	3
Other categories							

What Reilley Was Doing Right

For all Reilley worried that he was shortchanging his kids, he was doing a lot of fun things with them, such as going to the beach, playing in the rain, walking the dog together, and snuggling in the mornings. He was managing to do these things even though, by his calculations, he worked just over 40 hours during the week in question.

The Time-Makeover Suggestions

This admirable amount of balancing, though, raised the question: Why was he feeling so stressed out about his time? After talking with Reilley for a while, I learned that he felt like his work projects were taking forever. His kids were constantly interrupting him (hence entries like "Misc Work/Kids/TV News" and "UWW/Kids"). He'd lose his patience, and then they'd be unhappy with him—and inclined to interrupt even more. Since he was being pulled in multiple directions at once, he didn't think he was doing a good job on anything. The stress led to him watching TV late at night to unwind, which led to him sleeping less each night (6–7 hours) than was really ideal for someone caring for three active little boys.

Like many parents—particularly those who can work at home—Reilley was deluding himself about how much he could get done at one time. What he needed was concentrated blocks of time to work, and concentrated blocks of time with his kids. If he carved out time in his schedule for each, I wagered that not only would he need to work closer to 30 hours than 40, his kids would be happier too.

This would be easier when school started up (all three children would be in full-day school starting in the fall). He could work from 9:00 a.m. to 2:30 p.m. 3 days per week, and 9:00 to 4:00 or so 2 days per week by enrolling the children in an after-school program. He wanted the boys to be more involved in extracurricular activities anyway, so this schedule would give them more active time with their peers, while buying him 30 concentrated hours. If he needed to add a few more hours during a particularly crunched week, he could work a shift after the boys went to bed, or even while letting the boys watch a movie 2 nights per week.

I also suggested that he consider blocking off 2 of the hours that his children were in school for solo exercising. While Reilley was fitting a lot of activity into his life with the dog walking, pool trips, and playing outside, this "me time" would give him a chance to center himself and would probably help him sleep better. He could make up the work time at night by consciously choosing to turn off the TV and work on those two nights. I also suggested he skip TV on a few other nonworking nights and read instead. TV isn't nearly as relaxing as people think it is.

All this would give him more focused time to work, but what about spending time with the kids? As it was, big chunks of Reilley's time with his boys weren't the kinds of high-quality interactions he was hoping to have. He'd wave the kids off when they came in to ask a question while he was checking e-mail, or quickly fix them a snack or turn on the TV or Wii before rushing back to work on a client project. I suggested that he choose to completely shut down his computer (and other e-mail devices) from 2:30 until the kids' bedtime, or 4:00 until bedtime, depending on the day. If he was using his work time effectively, it was unlikely any crises would come up. He should make a point of using this time to do more activities with his kids like going to the pool, playing in the park, and so on. He should think these through ahead of time, and look for fun things in his community that the boys would enjoy. Evenings could be used for family dinners, homework, and reading.

This, of course, left the question of what to do with the rest of the summer. Since school was only a few weeks away, I suggested he simply try to do the best he could, creating concentrated blocks of time with his kids in the morning, and explaining to them that he would need to have quiet work time in the afternoons while they played in the backyard or in their rooms. Since he did use babysitters on occasion when he had meetings, I suggested Reilley enlist their help for a few hours to give him some adult recreation time. Parents are people, too, and when we take time for ourselves, we're better able to focus on our loved ones the rest of the time.

What Reilley Thought of the Makeover

Reilley agreed to try to reduce the multitasking and set aside specific times for work and for his kids. By the time we touched base a few weeks later, right before school started, he'd established a rhythm of spending about 3 hours a day running around on the beach with his boys. They'd come home ready for quiet time—which Dad would use to work. "The undivided attention they get greatly reduced the work interruptions," he said. "Best of all, my kids are much happier." Indeed, he was getting so much done and having so much fun that he was almost sad to see the school year begin.

Acknowledgments

Writing *168 Hours* took up many of my 168 hours each week over the course of 2 years, and would not have been possible without help from my "work team" and "home team."

On the work side, my agent, Emilie Stewart, thought this project was a great idea back when it was just that: an idea. We hashed out the basic concepts during a playdate in September 2007, and she stuck with the project through a solid year and a half of multiple book-proposal iterations until it finally sold in one of those strokes of luck that come from patience and planting seeds. Will Weisser, VP, Associate Publisher and Marketing Director at Portfolio, read a book review I'd written for *The American* of Geoff Colvin's *Talent Is Overrated*, e-mailed me out of the blue to say he'd enjoyed it, and asked if I had any book ideas. Funny you should ask, I said. He and the editor David Moldawer met with me, honed how we should present the material, came up with the 168 Hours angle, and decided to take a chance. Brooke Carey did an excellent job shepherding *168 Hours* through the editorial process, hacking out the passive voice and smoothing my prose. I am grateful for her genuine interest in the project; it's a lot easier to write when your editor is excited about the chapters you turn in. I also want to thank the rest of the team at Portfolio, including Beena Kamlani, Amy Hill, and Elyse Strongin, Neuwirth & Associates, who helped edit, design, and produce the book; Joe Perez, who designed the jacket; and Amanda Pritzker and Nick Owen, who helped publicize this project.

I'm grateful to the various editors who have run articles based on my time use, careers, and home economics fascinations over the past few years, including John Siniff and Glen Nishimura at *USA Today,* Naomi Riley at *The Wall Street Journal,* Ivan Oransky, who was formerly with *Scientific American,* Brian Anderson and the team at *City Journal,* Cheryl Miller of *Doublethink,* and the staff of *The Huffington Post.* Lisa Belkin graciously gave me a platform via her "Motherlode" blog at *The New York Times,* which helped drum up more interest in the book. I've also been blown away by the quality of sociological research on time use that's out there for anyone wishing to make use of it. The American Time Use Survey is an absolute gem, and the work done by various researchers (particularly John Robinson and Suzanne Bianchi) is eye-opening to anyone willing to think about American society and families in ways we haven't before.

I'm particularly indebted to all the people who agreed to be interviewed for this book, and to the people who kept logs of their 168 hours. While I found subjects through plenty of networking and research, the Help a Reporter Out service, run by Peter Shankman, certainly helped this reporter out by expanding my horizons and, in the process, helping me meet new friends. My team of test readers offered great insight on the manuscript and kept me from making stupid mistakes. Kristin Deasy, my research assistant, likewise checked the facts and lent her sharp eye to the project.

On the home team side, I could not have finished this project without help from Jasper's teachers, our babysitters, and from Kathryn, our nanny who joined us shortly before Sam was born. Despite living in Indiana, my parents, James and Mary Vanderkam, and my mother-in-law, Diane Conway, put in many hours and plane flights to lend a hand in keeping the Manhattan-based Vanderkam-Conway household running smoothly. My husband, Michael, shows again and again that it is possible to have a Career with a capital C and still be a partner in parenting and in managing a home. His weekend daddy-and-toddler excursions gave me extra hours to write every time I was approaching chapter deadlines. More important, though he inhabits an extremely competitive professional universe, he seems to believe that having a wife with her own ambitions makes his life more interesting. I am grateful for that.

While we don't usually think of small children as making big work projects *easier*, mine, in their own way, helped out. Sam's impending arrival kept me focused on meeting my deadlines; his birth 11 days before I turned in the manuscript gave me a good reason to be up in the middle of the night making final edits with whatever hand wasn't holding him. And Jasper's entrance into my life in 2007 is the whole reason I began thinking about how I choose to spend my hours in the first place. He is the reason I appreciate my 168 hours more. Shortly after I began writing this book, I had the opportunity to sing Rachmaninoff's *Vespers* with the Young New Yorkers' Chorus amid the gorgeous acoustics of Manhattan's Holy Trinity Church. One powerful phrase in movement four, as the harmony deepens and resolves, is translated from the Russian as "Thou art worthy at every moment. . . ." One summer night when my two-year-old was having trouble sleeping, I sat beside his crib, holding his hand. As his crying slowly became silence, and then became the deep breathing of slumber, the musical phrase popped into my head again. But this time the words were different: *Thou art worth every moment.* There in the dark nursery, I kept repeating that text. It sums up how I feel about this special little boy.

Notes

INTRODUCTION

4 **In September 2005** Louise Story, "Many Women at Elite Colleges Set Career Path to Motherhood," *New York Times,* Sept. 20, 2005.

4 **Likewise, the Princeton University student Amy Sennett** Amy Sennett, "A Choice of One's Own: Undergraduate Perceptions of Work-Family Conflict and the Realities of the Opt-Out Revolution," senior thesis presented in the Woodrow Wilson School of Public and International Affairs at Princeton University, April 10, 2006.

5 **I discovered the American Time Use Survey** The Bureau of Labor Statistics' annual American Time Use Survey, referenced throughout the book, is available online at http://www.bls.gov/tus/.

CHAPTER 1: The Myth of the Time Crunch

10 **Though a recent Men's Health article test-drove the "Uberman"** Grant Stoddard, "Is Sleep Really Necessary?" Available at http://www .menshealth.com/spotlight/sleep/8-hours.php

12 **Back in 1959, amid the rise of labor-saving technology** Quoted in Juliet Schor, *The Overworked American: The Unexpected Decline of Leisure* (New York: Basic Books, 1992), p. 4. Schor's book was originally published in 1991.

12 **By 1991, the sociologist Juliet Schor** Ibid.

13 **Now, Harvard Business Review runs anecdotes** Sylvia Ann Hewlett and Carolyn Buck Luce, "Extreme Jobs: The Dangerous Allure of the 70-Hour Workweek." *Harvard Business Review,* Dec. 1, 2006.

13 **We tell pollsters from the National Sleep Foundation** "Stressed-Out American Women Have No Time for Sleep," National Sleep Foundation's 2007 Sleep in America poll, March 6, 2007.

13 **About a third of Americans who work full-time** "Longer Work Days Leave Americans Nodding Off on the Job," National Sleep Foundation's 2008 Sleep in America poll, March 3, 2008.

13 **A recent Gallup poll found that 12 percent of employed Americans** Lymari Morales, "Self-Employed Workers Clock the Most Hours Each Week." Gallup, August 26, 2009.

13 **We say that we don't have enough time to exercise** "CDC: Most Meeting Exercise Guidelines," UPI.com, Dec. 4, 2008. Just shy of two thirds of Americans meet the recommendation to do 150 minutes per week, but only 49 percent meet the Healthy People 2010 guideline to do 30 minutes of moderate activity 5 days a week. The science is currently unclear on whether it matters if the activity is spread out or concentrated.

13 **The percentage of adults who vote in presidential elections** Joseph Schwartz, "Did You Vote This Year?" Directions Magazine, Nov. 2, 1998. Available at http://www.directionsmag.com/features.php?feature_id=4

13 **We say we are too busy to read** "Reading on the Rise: A New Chapter in American Literacy," National Endowment for the Arts, Jan. 12, 2009.

13 **Moms and dads who are in the workforce clock a lousy** "Married Parents' Use of Time Summary" from the American Time Use Survey, May 8, 2008; available at http://www.bls.gov/news.release/atus2.nr0 .htm This section of the ATUS summarizes how married parents who are in and out of the workforce spend their time, further broken down by age of youngest child and employment status of spouse. There is also a chart that separates out married mothers and fathers by employment status (not referencing the spouse). The numbers between these two charts are usually close—within a few hundredths of an hour—but because a small percentage of married moms are not in dual-income couples, and a small percentage of nonemployed moms have husbands who do not work full-time, there are occasional discrepancies. I have tried to be consistent in using the same chart within each section in this book.

14 **A full 92 percent of us say we believe in God** "Think You Know What Americans Believe About Religion? You Might Want to Think Again," The Pew Forum on Religion and Public Life, June 23, 2008.

14 **but only about 40 percent of us claim to attend religious services** "No Evidence Bad Times are Boosting Church Attendance," Gallup, Dec. 17, 2008.

14 **Actual attendance is probably less than half of that** ReligiousTolerance .org produced a good discussion of evidence that people lie about their church attendance, available at http://www.religioustolerance.org/ rel_rate.htm.

14 **a group called The Simplicity Forum launched "Take Back Your Time Day"** John de Graaf, ed. *Take Back Your Time: Fighting Overwork and Time Poverty in America* (San Francisco: Berrett-Koehler Publishers, 2003).

14 **could find only 12 minutes a day** Take Back Your Time 2003, p. 38.

14 **Some 80 percent of children** Ibid., p. 48.

14 **A reported 20–40 percent of pets** Ibid., p. 53.

14 **Medieval peasants, the cartoon illustrations** Ibid., p. 35.

14 **Of course, medieval peasants also experienced a 25-percent-plus** This is a figure that is widely repeated; for one discussion, see Shulamith Shahar, *Childhood in the Middle Ages* (London: Routledge, 1990), p. 149.

14 **For instance, the January 2007 issue of *Real Simple* magazine** "If You Had an Extra 15 Minutes in Your Day, How Would You Use It?" *Real Simple*, Jan. 2007, pp. 26–28.

17 **While such studies are more laborious** For a discussion of the benefits and drawbacks of time-diary studies, see John P. Robinson and Geoffrey Godbey, *Time for Life: The Surprising Ways Americans Use Their Time* (University Park: Pennsylvania State University Press, 1997), Chapter 4 ("Measuring How People Spend Time"), pp. 57–78.

17 **Americans sleep about 8 hours a night** American Time Use Survey, 2008. Actual average is 8.6. In 1965, according to the Americans' Use of Time Project, women slept 55–56 hours per week and men slept 54–60, averaging out to about 8. For more on this, see Robinson and Godbey, *Time for Life*, p. 112.

17 **even married moms and dads** ATUS, Married Parents' Use of Time Summary.

17 **Married, full-time working moms with school-aged kids still sleep 8.09 hours per night** ATUS, Married Parents' Use of Time, "Time Spent in Primary Activities" chart.

18 **in reality, the average parent who works full-time** Ibid.

18 **about 1.7 million Americans had "extreme" jobs** "Is the American Dream on Steroids?" Center for Work-Life Policy, Dec. 1, 2006.

18 **not as clean as we did in 1965** For the 37.4 hour figure, see Suzanne M. Bianchi, "Maternal Employment and Time with Children: Dramatic

Change or Surprising Continuity?" *Demography* 37.4 (2000), 401–14. The 34.5 hour number comes from the 1965–1966 Americans' Use of Time Study; calculated in Suzanne M. Bianchi, John P. Robinson, and Melissa A. Milkie, *Changing Rhythms of American Family Life* (The American Sociological Association's Rose Series in Sociology) (New York: Russell Sage Foundation, 2006), p. 93.

18 **even dads whose wives are not in the workforce** ATUS, Married Parents' Use of Time Summary.

18 **Many moms who work full-time worry** Ibid.

18 **Americans in general also watch a lot of television** "A2/M2 Three Screen Report," 4th Quarter 2008, Nielsen, puts the figure at 151 hours per month, or roughly 35 hours per week for all TV watchers.

19 **we overestimate—by something on the order of 100 percent** Bianchi, Robinson, and Milkie, *Changing Rhythms of American Family Life*, pp. 34–35.

20 **Indeed, back in the 1990s, when the University of Maryland** Robinson and Godbey, *Time for Life*, pp. 85–93.

20 **When I contacted Robinson recently** John Robinson, e-mail to author, April 13, 2009.

20 **some studies have found that people's estimates of an average week** Robinson and Godbey, *Time for Life*, p. 59.

20 **One widely repeated statement from *The Overworked American*** Schor, *The Overworked American*, p. 1.

22 **You can top the 17–18 hours the average stay-at-home mom** ATUS, Married Parents' Use of Time Summary; the two charts (SAHM with husband employed full-time, and SAHM without status of husband) give slightly different numbers.

22 **People who give generously of their time to causes** "The Health Benefits of Volunteering: A Review of Recent Research," Corporation for National and Community Research, 2007.

22 **Yet only about a quarter of Americans volunteer** *Volunteering in America, 2009,* produced by the U.S. government from census and other data; http://www.volunteeringinamerica.gov.

22 **Only about a third of these folks logs more than 100 hours** *Volunteering in America, 2008,* p. 2 of research highlights. If one quarter of Americans volunteer, and one third of these does more than 100 hours per year, that leaves more than 90 percent of Americans volunteering fewer than 100 hours per year (2 per week).

26 **Jill Starishevsky, a Bronx assistant district attorney** See ThePoemLady .com.

CHAPTER 2: Your Core Competencies

30 **"I'm a watcher," he told me when I interviewed him** Laura Vanderkam, "The Watcher: Roald Hoffmann," ScientificAmerican.com, May 12, 2008.

33 **"A job is, in essence, a bundle of tasks…"** Troy Smith and Jan Rivkin, "A Replication Study of Alan Blinder's 'How Many U.S. Jobs Might Be Offshorable?'" p. 16, available at http://www.hbs.edu/research/pdf/08-104.pdf.

33 **But in 1990, the management gurus** C. K. Prahalad and G. Hamel, "The Core Competence of the Corporation," *Harvard Business Review*, May-June 1990, pp. 79–91.

35 **In 2008, while much of retail was in free fall** "Wal-Mart Reports Financial Results for Fiscal Year and Fourth Quarter," Wal-Mart press release, Feb. 17, 2009. This is for fiscal year ending Jan. 31, 2009, so mostly 2008.

36 **In 2008, the ATUS used these** For the 2008 categories, see http://www.bls.gov/news.release/atus.t01.htm.

CHAPTER 3: The Right Job

53 **I interviewed the marine biologist Sylvia Earle** Laura Vanderkam, "Aquanaut Lives Under Water Researching Ocean's Bottom," *The Washington Times*, Aug. 16, 1998.

53 **That's currently the average retirement age** For one discussion, see Murray Gendell and Jacob S. Siegel, "Trends in Retirement Age by Sex: 1950–2005," *Monthly Labor Review*, July 1992. While the median age moves around, according to the Social Security Administration, the average recipient starts drawing benefits before age sixty-five.

54 **That affection comes through in Sea Change** Sylvia A. Earle, *Sea Change: A Message of the Oceans* (New York: Fawcett Books, 1995), pp. 14–15.

55 **As he writes, "For most people … the perfect job"** Timothy Ferriss, *The 4-Hour Workweek* (New York: Crown, 2007), pp. 9–10.

55 **According to one late 2006 survey** "National 'Dream Jobs' Survey Reveals Four out of Five U.S. Workers Are Still Searching for Their Dream Jobs," CareerBuilder.com, January 25, 2007.

56 **the 2002 General Social Survey (GSS) found that most people** Arthur C. Brooks, "I Love My Work," *The American*, September/October 2007.

57 **recounted his grandfather's 40 years of labor** Jeremy Adam Smith, *The Daddy Shift* (Boston: Beacon Press, 2009), pp. 11–12.

57 **85 percent of Americans have high school diplomas** "High School Graduation Rates Reach All-Time High," Census Bureau press release, June

29, 2004. This release also reported that 27 percent of Americans over age twenty-five had completed college.

57 **I serve on the Princeton University Alumni Council's** The committee has done several informal surveys of alumni approaching major reunions. This was for those approaching their twenty-fifth reunion in 2009 (the class of 1984).

57 **Instead, the surprising figure is that the 2002 GSS** Brooks, "I Love My Work."

58 **according to a 1997 *California Management Review*** T. M. Amabile, "Motivating Creativity in Organizations: On Doing What You Love and Loving What You Do," *California Management Review* 40:1 (fall 1997), 39–58.

59 **Or as the poet Anne Sexton once told her agent** Quoted in Teresa M. Amabile, *Creativity in Context* (Boulder, CO: Westview Press, 1996), p. 9.

59 **While fewer than one in six Americans told CareerBuilder.com** "National 'Dream Jobs' Survey" 2007.

60 **Ilan Kroo, for instance, now an aeronautics professor** Laura Vanderkam, "Flying Green: Ilan Kroo Helps Shape the Future of Sustainable Aviation," ScientificAmerican.com, Dec. 9, 2008.

61 **To study the effect of job conditions on work quality** Amabile, "Motivating Creativity in Organizations."

61 **According to a meta-analysis of forty-six studies** Ravi S. Gajendran and David A. Harrison, "The Good, the Bad, and the Unknown About Telecommuting: Meta-Analysis of Psychological Mediators and Individual Consequences," *Journal of Applied Psychology* 92:6 (2007), 1524–41.

62 **self-employed people tend to have more job satisfaction** This has been found in several studies. For one discussion, see Brett W. Pelham, "Business Owners Richer in Well-Being than Other Job Types," Gallup, Sept. 16, 2009.

62 **Decades ago . . . Csíkszentmihályi and his colleagues** Mihály Csíkszentmihályi, *Flow: The Psychology of Optimal Experience* (New York: Harper & Row, 1990) Wall .

63 **Hours pass by in minutes** Ibid., p. 49.

64 **The morning I began writing this chapter,** *The Wall Street Journal* Mary Pilon, "From Ordering Steak and Lobster, to Serving It," *The Wall Street Journal*, June 2, 2009.

64 **By the time I was revising this chapter, the situation** Jennifer Levitz, "Unemployed Hit the Road to Find Jobs," *The Wall Street Journal*, June 25, 2009.

65 **In a 2008 review of the literature** Julia K. Boehm and Sonja Lyubomirsky, "Does Happiness Promote Career Success?" *Journal of Career Assessment* 16:1 (2008), pp. 101–16.

65 **Some of this is sheer temperament** Sonja Lyubomirsky, *The How of Happiness: A Scientific Approach to Getting the Life Your Want* (New York: Penguin, 2007).

66 **Amabile and her colleagues once asked various corporate** Teresa Amabile, e-mail message to author, June 2, 2009.

66 **popularized the findings of studies by K. Anders Ericsson** K. Anders Ericsson, Ralf Th. Krampe, and Clemens Tesch-Römer, "The Role of Deliberate Practice in the Acquisition of Expert Performance," *Psychological Review* 100:3 (1993), 363–406.

67 **In 1896 the world record time for male marathoners** For a graph of falling marathon times, see http://www.marathonguide.com/history/records/index.cfm.

68 **One recent University of Maryland study found that** "Unhappy People Watch TV, Happy People Read/Socialize," University of Maryland press release, Nov. 14, 2008.

68 **Like Kroo, she was a finalist in the Westinghouse** Laura Vanderkam, "Lise Menn: Figuring Out Why Kids Say the Darndest Things," ScientificAmerican.com, Aug. 25, 2008.

72 **another of those Westinghouse finalists, Kraig Derstler** Laura Vanderkam, "Kraig Derstler: Digging Up Dinosaurs Is in His Bones," Scientific American.com, May 4, 2009.

73 **according to numbers that the comptroller's office** Interview with Frank Braconi, chief economist in the comptroller's office. For more on self-employment, see Laura Vanderkam, "The Promise and Peril of the Freelance Economy," *City Journal,* Winter 2009.

73 **The Bureau of Labor Statistics says that the national self-employment rate** Steven Hipple, "Self-Employment in the United States: An Update," *Monthly Labor Review,* July 2004.

73 **according to the Census Bureau, the number of "non-employer businesses"** "Census Bureau Reports Increase of Nearly 1 Million Nonemployer Businesses," Census Bureau press release, June 25, 2009.

74 **According to Kelly Services** "Freelance Ranks Growing as Economy Is Slowing, Kelly Services Survey Shows," Kelly Services press release, Jan. 28, 2009.

74 **For many people, going solo is about push *and* pull factors** See Laura Vanderkam, "Laid Off? Here's a Silver Lining," *USA Today,* March 25, 2009.

CHAPTER 4: Controlling Your Calendar

81 **In 2003, the country suffered 30.83 deaths** For Vietnam's infant mortality rate, via the CIA World Factbook, see http://www.indexmundi.com/vietnam/infant_mortality_rate.html.

84 **As Allen writes, "More and more people's jobs . . ."** David Allen, *Getting Things Done: The Art of Stress-Free Productivity* (New York: Penguin Books, 2001), p. 8.

91 **For the past few years, I've been following the career** Laura Vanderkam, "Being Stung by Bees: You Get Used to It—Carol Fassbinder-Orth," ScientificAmerican.com, May 19, 2008.

91 **A few years ago, Summers, now director of the White House's National Economic Council, famously claimed** Lawrence H. Summers, "Remarks at NBER Conference on Diversifying the Science and Engineering Workforce," Jan. 14, 2005.

92 **average office worker admits to wasting 1.7 hours** "Employees Waste 20% of Their Work Day According to Salary.com Survey," Salary.com press release, July 25, 2007.

101 **Harris created a blog called "New Voices of Philanthropy"** See http://www.TristaHarris.org.

103 **through focused "deliberate practice"** Geoff Colvin, *Talent Is Overrated: What Really Separates World-Class Performers from Everybody Else* (New York: Portfolio, 2008).

CHAPTER 5: Anatomy of a Breakthrough

108 **In 2009's *Womenomics*** Claire Shipman and Katty Kay, *Womenomics: Write Your Own Rules for Success* (New York: Harper Business, 2009), p. xiv.

109 **I recently attended an American Express competition** The Make Mine a Million $ Business program offers resources and contests for women business owners (participants have included Theresa Daytner from Chapter 1); see http://www.makemineamillion.org.

113 **the average American workweek is down to 33 hours** "Employment Situation Summary," Bureau of Labor Statistics, Sept. 4, 2009. This is for nonfarm, nonsupervisory private payrolls.

113 **A Pew Research Center survey found** "Fewer Mothers Prefer Full-Time Work," Pew Research Center, July 12, 2007.

115 **New York's mayor, Michael Bloomberg, persists** For one example, see "Mayor Michael Bloomberg's Commencement Remarks," Fordham University press release, May 16, 2009.

124 **Back in 1970, she was chosen as one of fifty scientists** Earle, *Sea Change*, pp. 65–77.

CHAPTER 6: The New Home Economics

130 **The total U.S. fertility rate** "Total Fertility Rates and Birth Rates, by Age of Mother and Race: United States, 1940-99," CDC chart, available at http://www.cdc.gov/nchs/data/statab/t991x07.pdf. In 1957, the TFR topped out at 3.767.

130 **The December 1958 *Good Housekeeping* contains** "The Real Why of Electric Blankets," *Good Housekeeping*, Dec. 1958 (vol. 147, no. 6), p. 137.

131 **The most intriguing, one End-of-the-Rainbow Cake** "And Now to Go with Coffee," *Good Housekeeping*, Dec. 1958 (vol. 147, no. 6), p. 91.

131 **A "Needlework" page discusses what to do** "Fashion to the Rescue," *Good Housekeeping*, Dec. 1958 (vol. 147, no. 6), pp. 52 and 206.

131 **in December 1965, *Good Housekeeping* ran an article** "75 Ways to Save Time During the Holidays," *Good Housekeeping*, Dec. 1965 (vol. 161, no. 6), pp. 163–64.

132 **In 1965, 38.5 percent of women aged twenty-five to thirty-four** "Employment Status of Women 16 Years and Over by Age, 1948–2005," labor force participation rate chart, Current Population Survey (obtained directly from BLS).

132 **majority of mothers of young kids are now in the labor force** David Cotter, Paula England, and Joan Hermsen, "Moms and Jobs: Trends in Mothers' Employment and Which Mothers Stay Home," fact sheet from the Council on Contemporary Families, May 10, 2007.

132 **most moms married to men earning more than $120,000 a year** Ibid.

132 **moms—and dads—spend more time interacting with their children** Bianchi, Robinson, and Milkie, *Changing Rhythms of American Family Life*, pp. 63–64.

133 **According to statistics averaged from the 2003 to 2006 American Time Use Surveys** ATUS, Married Parents' Use of Time Summary.

134 **From the 1950s to the 1970s, the total U.S. fertility rate** "Total Fertility Rates and Birth Rates, by Age of Mother and Race: United States, 1940–99," CDC.

135 **There has been an uptick since** "Births: Preliminary Data for 2007," National Vital Statistics Reports, vol. 57, no. 12, available at http://www.cdc.gov/nchs/data/nvsr/nvsr57/nvsr57_12.pdf.

135 **the standards outlined in her new book** Thelma Meyer, *Mrs. Meyer's Clean Home: No-Nonsense Advice That Will Inspire You to Clean Like the Dickens* (New York: Wellness Central, 2009).

136 **In 1965, married mothers spent 34.5 hours on household tasks** Bianchi, Robinson, and Milkie, *Changing Rhythms of American Family Life*, p. 93.

136 **In 2008, moms of minor children spent 16 to 17 hours on these things** "Time Spent in Primary Activities for the Civilian Population 18 Years and Over by Employment Status, Presence and Age of Youngest Household Child, and Sex, 2008 Annual Averages," American Time Use Survey

136 **Moms like me with full-time jobs spent** ATUS, Married Parents' Use of Time Summary.

137 **Children who are at school (or on the bus or playing sports) from 8:00 a.m. to 3:00 p.m.** Bianchi, Robinson, and Milkie, *Changing Rhythms of American Family Life*, p. 145. The 2002 Panel Study of Income Dynamics Child Development Supplement looked at children's time use; kids aged 5–11 spend 32.5 hours per week at school, 2.2 hours on sports, and 1.0 hour on "organizations."

137 **the same amount that the average mom with a full-time job works** Per the ATUS Married Parents' Use of Time Summary, moms who work full-time and who are married to men who work full-time work 5.12 hours per day, or 35.84 hours per week.

137 **Indeed, one 2002 calculation from a study of children's time use** Bianchi, Robinson, and Milkie, *Changing Rhythms of American Family Life*, p. 150.

137 **Married stay-at-home moms with kids under age six spend 22.5 hours per week** ATUS, Married Parents' Use of Time Summary.

138 **average child aged two to eleven watches nearly 4 hours of TV A2/ M2** Three Screen Report, 4th Quarter 2008, Nielsen, Feb. 23, 2009.

138 **Jeremy Adam Smith's 2009 book,** The Daddy Shift Smith, *The Daddy Shift*, p. 157.

139 **Moms who are not in the workforce currently spend about 26 hours per week on housework** ATUS, Married Parents' Use of Time Summary. This figure does not include grocery shopping, though it does include cooking.

147 **in 1975, married parents spent 12.4 hours with each other, solo** Bianchi, Robinson, and Milkie, *Changing Rhythms of American Family Life*, p. 104.

147 **the lesson I take from the story of Empress Maria Theresa** See Edward Crankshaw, *Maria Theresa* (London: Longmans, Green and Co., 1969).

150 **In 2008, according to the Families and Work Institute, young fathers** "Times Are Changing: Gender and Generation at Work and at Home," The Families and Work Institute, March 26, 2009, see Figure 14.

151 **Though they doubled the amount of time they spent on housework** Bianchi, Robinson, and Milkie, *Changing Rhythms of American Family Life*, p. 93.

151 **dads actually spend slightly *more* time playing with their kids** ATUS, Married Parents' Use of Time Summary. Per day, the figures for couples in which both parents work full-time are 0.19 hours for moms and 0.23 hours for dads, or roughly 1 hour and 20 minutes for moms per week, and 1 hour and 36 minutes for dads.

151 **In 2008, according to the Families and Work Institute, 49 percent of men** "Times Are Changing," p. 16.

152 **how to make a grout cleaner of fresh lemon and cream of tartar** Nicole Sforza, "Back-to-Basics Cleaning," *Real Simple,* April 2009, p. 136.

153 **spend just 1.3 hours per week doing dishes, as opposed to 5.1 hours** Bianchi, Robinson, and Milkie, *Changing Rhythms of American Family Life,* p. 93.

CHAPTER 7: Don't Do Your Own Laundry

157 **Around Mother's Day each year, Salary.com** "Salary.com's 9th Annual Mom Salary Survey Reveals Stay-at-Home Moms Would Earn $122,732 in the U.S. and $135,661 in Canada," Salary.com press release, May 5, 2009.

157 **the essayist Judy Syfers caused quite a stir** Judy Syfers, "I Want a Wife," originally in *Ms.,* Dec. 1971, see http://www.columbia.edu/~sss31/rainbow/wife.html.

160 **the 31 hours the American Time Use Study finds that dual-income couples with kids devote** ATUS, Married Parents' Use of Time Summary. When both spouses work full-time, moms spend 2.08 hours per day on household activities and 0.62 hours purchasing goods and services. Dads spend 1.39 hours on household activities, and 0.39 hours purchasing goods and services. For a 7-day week this totals 31.36 hours.

161 **with annual household expenditures of around $50,000** "Consumer Expenditures in 2007," Bureau of Labor Statistics news release, Nov. 25, 2008.

165 **couples spend a combined 9.24 hours per week** ATUS, Married Parents' Use of Time Summary. Married moms who work full-time spend 0.14 hours per day grocery shopping and 0.79 doing food prep and clean up; dads spend 0.07 hours per day grocery shopping and 0.32 doing food chores. For a 7-day week this totals 9.24 hours. They spend 0.42 hours per day, combined, playing with their kids; for 7 days this is 2.94 hours.

166 **Nu-Kitchen charges $7.95** As of Sept. 3, 2009; see http://www.nu-kitchen.com.

166 **Webvan lost something around $1 billion** Ray Delgado, "Webvan Goes Under: Online Grocer Shuts Down—$830 Million Lost, 2,000 Workers Fired," *San Francisco Chronicle,* July 9, 2001.

166 **Fresh Direct in New York having forecasted double-digit growth in 2009** Eliot Caroom, "Online Grocers Recession Proof? Cost-Cutting Consumers Eat In and Feed Double Digit Growth," *Inc.,* Feb. 17, 2009.

168 **Americans spend about half our food dollars in restaurants** 2009 Restaurant Industry Pocket Factbook, National Restaurant Association.

168 **As of 2009, we were spending about $35 per week for every man, woman, and child** Restaurant Industry Pocket Factbook, National Restaurant Association. Sales were forecast to hit $566 billion; with 300 million Americans, this comes out to $1,887 dollars per year per person, or a little over $36 per week.

169 **$876 per year for the convenience of cell phone service** "Feature-Rich Wireless Mobile Phones Increase Average Consumer Service Spending for Both Handset Manufacturers and Service Providers," J. D. Power and Associates press release, Nov. 15, 2007.

169 **average cable bill in the United States is now around $71** Todd Spangler, "Study: Average Cable TV Bill is $71 Per Month," *Multichannel News,* April 16, 2009.

169 **the average tax refund in the United States is now well over $2,000** "Tax Stats at a Glance," Internal Revenue Service, for tax year 2006. See http://www.irs.gov/taxstats/article/0,id=102886,00.html.

170 **married mothers spent 5.1 hours per week on cleaning chores, and married fathers spent 1.8** Bianchi, Robinson, and Milkie, *Changing Rhythms of American Family Life,* p. 93. This figure is just for housekeeping and does not include laundry or cooking and food chores.

175 **National Gardening Association found that 30 percent of all U.S. households** "Homeowners Spend a Record $45 Billion on Lawn and Landscape Services," National Gardening Association press release, Aug. 6, 2007.

176 **Merry Maids, the dominant player** "Fast Facts About Merry Maids," see http://www.merrymaids.com/company/.

CHAPTER 8: A Full Life

179 **For some reason a few years ago, the paper had dispatched a style reporter** Rachel Dodes, "Media-Mogul Fashion Dilemma," *The Wall Street Journal,* July 22, 2006.

180 **We feel like the businessmen-turned-hostages** Ann Patchett, *Bel Canto* (New York: Harper Perennial Modern Classics, 2008), p. 108 (first published by HarperCollins in 2001).

180 **a Japanese executive named Tetsuya Kato** Patchett, *Bel Canto*, pp. 126–28.

182 **One *Time Out New York Kids* article quoted Susan Linn** Lenore Skenazy, "The Power of Free Play," *Time Out New York Kids,* June 2009. See also Susan Linn, *The Case for Make-Believe: Saving Play in a Commercialized World* (New York: New Press, 2008).

183 **Americans have just 16.5 hours of self-reported leisure time** Schor, *The Overworked American,* p. 1.

183 **parents of young kids, have at least 30 hours of weekly free time** Robinson and Godbey, *Time for Life,* pp. 128–29, for 1985 figures; Bianchi, Robinson, and Milkie, *Changing Rhythms of American Family Life,* pp. 116–17, for these numbers.

184 **more than 30 hours per week watching television** A2/M2 Three Screen Report, 4th Quarter 2008, Nielsen.

184 **television as a primary activity closer to 20 hours per week** ATUS 2008 numbers (2.77 hours per day, or 19.39 per week).

185 **a 1–10 scale of enjoyment** Robinson and Godbey, *Time for Life,* p. 340.

187 **lowering the risks of the worst consequences of inactivity** "2008 Physical Activity Guidelines for Americans," CDC, see http://www.cdc.gov/physicalactivity/everyone/guidelines/adults.html.

189 **Joyce Carol Oates once wrote, "The structural problems . . ."** Joyce Carol Oates, "Writers: See How They Run," *The Writer,* Aug. 2000.

189 **Radcliffe, then 6 months pregnant with her daughter, Isla** "Pregnant Radcliffe Still Training," BBC Sport, Oct. 9, 2006. The *Vogue* profile was in the April 2007 issue.

195 **Women with breast cancer who lack close friends are more likely to die** Candyce H. Kroenke et al., "Social Networks, Social Support, and Survival After Breast Cancer Diagnosis," *Journal of Clinical Oncology* 24: 7 (March 1, 2006), pp. 1105–11.

195 **close friendships can help slow brain deterioration as we age** Tara Parker-Pope, "What Are Friends For? A Longer Life," *The New York Times,* April 20, 2009.

195 **People with strong friendships get fewer colds** Ibid.

195 **for a study published in 2008** Simone Schnall et al., "Social Support and the Perception of Geographical Slant," *Journal of Experimental Social Psychology* 44 (2008), 1246–55.

196 **One 2007 study of Microsoft workers found that** Shamsi T. Iqbal and Eric Horvitz, "Disruption and Recovery of Computing Tasks: Field Study, Analysis, and Directions," 2007, see http://research.microsoft.com/en-us/um/people/horvitz/chi_2007_iqbal_horvitz.pdf.

196 **As Lord Chesterfield** Famous Quotes and Authors, http://www.famousquotesandauthors.com/authors/lord_chesterfield_quotes.html.

202 **"I don't know what to do with myself when I'm not singing."** Patchett, *Bel Canto*, p. 123.

Index

Italic page numbers refer to charts and exercises.